Studies in Traditional Cornish

by

Nicholas Williams

MA PhD DipCeltStud FLS ITIA
Emeritus Professor in Celtic Languages
University College, Dublin

evertype
2016

Published by / *Dyllys gans* Evertype, 72 Woodgrove, Portlaoise, R32 ENP6, Ireland / *Wordhen*. *www.evertype.com*.

First edition 2016.
Kensa dyllans 2016.

Editor / *Penscrefer*: Michael Everson.

ISBN-10 1-78201-038-6
ISBN-13 978-1-78201-038-8

Typeset in Palatino by Michael Everson.
Olsettys yn Palatino gans Michael Everson.

Cover / *Cudhlen*: Michael Everson

Printed by / *Pryntys gans* LightningSource.

CONTENTS

INTRODUCTION

There are eight chapters below; seven deal with various aspects of the historical phonology, morphology and syntax of traditional Cornish. One article examines the Cornish form of the *englyn*, a three-lined stanza common to both Cornish and Welsh. The first five of the chapters originally appeared as articles in *Cornish Studies*. Two further chapters were first given as short papers at the *Skians* conferences of 2014 and 2015 respectively. The last chapter of the book discusses the auxiliary verbs of traditional Cornish and has not been published hitherto. Because the sections below were written at different times and for varying purposes, there is a certain degree of overlap in their subject-matter.

Cornish lacks native speakers, thus revivalists have no one whose pronun-ciation or idiom can serve as a model for their own speech. It is therefore of vital importance that we who attempt to use revived Cornish should be as familiar as is possible with the traditional language as it survives in the Middle and Late Cornish texts. Indeed reading those texts carefully can be both most instructive.

Here for example are a few random points that are apparent from a close examination of surviving Cornish literature and which are discussed below. The Cornish word for 'very' before adjectives and adverbs is not *pur* [py:r] but *pòr* [pɔr]. The duals **dywscovarn* 'ears' and **dywarr* 'legs' are unattested, since traditional Cornish said *scovornow* and *garrow*. The normal word in Cornish for 'hand' was *dorn* rather than *leuv*, although the plural was *dewla*. The English expression 'hands and feet' is rendered in Cornish as *treys ha dewla*. Although one can say *yn tâ* for 'well', **yn trog* is wholly unattested. For 'badly written' or 'badly hurt', for example, one must say *drog-screfys* and *drog-pystygys*. Revivalists have always assumed that to say 'when my father died' one would say *pàn verwys ow thas* or *pàn wrug merwel ow thas*. In fact traditional Cornish was more likely to say *pàn veu marow ow thas*, and thus employ a common Celtic idiom. Handbooks of revived Cornish have hitherto taught that to render the perfect in such expressions as 'it has happened' or 'he has fallen' one should use the particle *re* with the preterite of the relevant verb, and that for *mos* and *dos* the usual perfective forms are *gallas* and *dueva* or *re dheuva*. While all such expressions are attested, the default method for rendering the perfect of intransitive verbs in the traditional language is to use the verbal adjective with the verb *bos* 'to be': *wharvedhys yw, codhys yw, devedhys yw, gyllys yw*, etc. The circumlocutions **dos ha bos* and **mos ha bos* for 'to become' are without warrant in traditional Cornish. For 'he became a doctor', for example, traditional Cornish would have said *ev a veu gwrës medhek* or simply *ev a veu medhek*. Furthermore *me a vydn mos tre* does not mean 'I want to go home' but simply 'I will go home.' To express volition in such cases one says *Me a garsa mos tre*.

Slightly fuller discussions below attempt to describe the way in which reflexives in Cornish can be made with *honen* rather than the prefix *om-*; how *gallos* 'to be able' is used in final clauses and how *dos* 'to come' as an auxiliary verb can be useful in conditional sentences. The accepted view has always been that expressions like *yth esof ow prena* means 'I am buying', whereas a close reading of the texts shows that the sentence is more likely to mean 'I buy', e.g. *yth esof ow prena ow dyllas obma* 'I buy my clothes here.' In this respect traditional Cornish resembled Welsh and Scottish Gaelic.

All these points and many others are apparent from the Cornish texts themselves and are discussed below. I publish them here in the hope that they will perhaps be of use to Cornish learners. Quite possibly the observations made in the following pages will encourage some speakers to carry out their own examination of the texts and thus add to what is known of *agan yêth ny*.

Nicholas Williams
Dublin, 2016

ABBREVIATIONS AND REFERENCES

AB = Edward Lhuyd, *Archæologia Britannica* (London 1707 [reprinted Shannon 1971])

ACB = William Pryce, *Archæologia Cornu-Britannica* (Sherborne 1790)

BBCS = *Bulletin of the Board of Celtic Studies*

BF = O. J. Padel, *The Cornish Writings of the Boson Family* (Redruth 1975)

BG = Roparz Hemon, *Breton Grammar*, 3rd edition, translated, adapted and revised by Michael Everson, Cathair na Mart, 2011. ISBN 978-1-904808-71-8

Bilbao MS = Henry Jenner, 'The Cornish Manuscript in the provincial library at Bilbao, Spain', *Journal of the Royal Institution of Cornwall* 21 (192-25): 421-37

BK = Graham Thomas and Nicholas Williams (editors), *Bewnans Ke: The Life of St Kea* (Exeter 2007)

BM = Whitley Stokes (ed.), *Beunans Meriasek: the life of St Meriasek, Bishop and confessor, a Cornish drama* (London: Trübner and Co. 1872)

Borlase = Williams Borlase, *Antiquities of the County of Cornwall* (London 1754)

Carew = F. E. Halliday (ed.), *Richard Carew of Antony: the survey of Cornwall* (London 1953)

CF = *The Charter Fragment*, text from E. Campanile, "Un frammento scenico medio-cornico", *Studi e saggi linguistici* 60-80, supplement to *L'Italia Dialettale* 26

CfA = R. Morton Nance, *Cornish for All: A Guide to Unified Cornish* (revised edition), Federation of Old Cornwall Societies, St Ives (1949)

CT3 = Nicholas Williams, *Cornish Today: an examination of the revived language*, third edition (Westport: Evertype 2006, ISBN 978-1-904808-07-7)

CW = Whitley Stokes (ed.), *Gwreans an Bys: the Creation of the World*, (London: Williams & Norgate 1864 [reprinted Kessinger Publishing 1987, ISBN 0-7661-8009-3])

DC = Roparz Hemon, *Doctrin an Christenien*, Dublin, 1977.

DIL = Royal Irish Academy, *Dictionary of the Irish Language* (Dublin 1983)

ECa = J. EC (editor), 'Études Corniques V: Les dix commandements', *Revue Celtique* 24 (1903), 1-10

ÉCII = Joseph Loth, 'Études Corniques ii', *Revue Celtique* 23 (Paris 1902)," 173-200

EWGP = Kenneth Jackson, *Early Welsh Gnomic Poems* (Cardiff 1935)

Fleuriot = Leon Fleuriot, *Le Vieux Breton: elements d'une grammaire*, Paris, 1964.

GMW = D. Simon Evans, *A Grammar of Middle Welsh* (Dublin 1964)

Hardie = D.W.F. Hardie, *A Handbook of Modern Breton (Armorican)*, Cardiff, 1948.

HMSB = Roparz Hemon, *A Historical Morphology and Syntax of Breton* (Dublin 1984)

JCH = 'Jowan Chyanhor', text from BF: 14-23

Keigwin = John Keigwin's translation of *Genesis* 1, from Gwavas collection, British Library Add. MS 28554

KemK. = E. G. Retallack Hooper (editor), *Kemysk Kernewek: A Cornish Miscellany* (Redruth 1964)

Kervella = *Yezhadur Bras ar Brezhoneg*, La Baule, 1947.

LAM = Alan M. Kent and Tim Saunders (editors), *Looking at the Mermaid: a reader in Cornish literature 900-1900* (London 2000)

LC = Late Cornish.

ABBREVIATIONS AND REFERENCES

LHEB = Kenneth Hurlstone Jackson, *Language and History in Early Britain* (Edinburgh 1953)

LPK = *Lyver Pysadow Kemyn*, Diocese of Truro (1980)

MB = Middle Breton.

MC = Middle Cornish.

ModB = Modern Breton.

Nance 1938 = R. Morton Nance, *A New Cornish-English Dictionary* (St Ives [reprinted Redruth 1999])

Nance 1952 = R. Morton Nance, *An English-Cornish Dictionary* (Marazion 1952) [reprinted 1978]

NBoson = Nicholas Boson, *Nebbaz Gerriau dro tho Carnoack*, BF: 24-37

OB = Old Breton.

OCV = Eugene Van Tassel Graves, *The Old Cornish Vocabulary*, Columbia University, PhD 1962 Language and Literature, linguistics. University Microfilms, Inc., Ann Arbor, Michigan

OM = 'Origo Mundi' in Norris, *The Ancient Cornish Drama* i-ii (London 1859 [reprinted New York 1968]) i: 1-219

PA = *Pascon agan Arluth* "The Passion of our Lord", text from Harry Woodhouse, *The Cornish Passion Poem in facsimile* (Penryn 2002)

PC = 'Passio Christi Nostri Jhesu Christi' in Norris, *The Ancient Cornish Drama* i-ii (London 1859 [reprinted New York 1968])i: 221-479

RCEV = Andre Hawke, 'A Rediscovered Cornish-English Vocabulary', *Cornish Studies* (Second Series) *Nine* (Exeter 2001), 83-104

RD = 'Resurrexio Domini Nostri Jhesu Christi' in Norris (1859) in Norris, *The Ancient Comish Drama* i-ii (London 1859 [reprinted New York 1968]) ii: 1-199

SA = *Sacrament an Alter*, the last sermon in the Tregear manuscript, ff. 59-66a, pp. 38-43 in Bice's edition of TH.

TH = John Tregear, *Homelyes xiii in Cornysche* (British Library Additional MS 46, 397) [text from a cyclostyled text published by Christopher Bice ([s.l.] 1969)]

WG = J. Morris Jones, *A Welsh Grammar* (Oxford 1930)

Williams 2006a = "A problem in Cornish phonology" in Nicholas Williams, *Writings on Revived Cornish* (Westport: Evertype 2006, ISBN 978-1-904808-08-4), 1–25

I-AFFECTION IN BRETON AND CORNISH[1]

What is i-affection?

I-affection is a widespread phenomenon in the Brythonic languages. The term refers to the way in which a short or long *i* in a syllable fronts and raises the vowel in the preceding syllable. There are two kinds of *i*-affection. The first, known as final *i*-affection, involves instances where the affecting *i* was in a final syllable now lost, e.g. Cornish *tew* 'is silent' < Proto-British *tawit*, Breton *sent* 'saints' < Late Latin *santī*. The other kind is known as internal affection. Here the affecting vowel is in a medial syllable and in consequence remains, e.g. Cornish *melin*, *melyn* 'mill' < Latin *molina*, Cornish *Costentyn* < Latin *Constantīnus*, Breton *terriff*, *terriñ* 'to break' < Proto-British *torrīma*.[2] One sometimes finds final and internal *i*-affection together, so-called 'double *i*-affection'. Take, for example, the Breton word *ebestel* 'apostles' < Latin *apostoli*. Here the final long *i* (subsequently lost) has raised *o* > *e* and then the newly affected vowel has raised *a* to *e* in the preceding syllable.

There are occasions where expected *i*-affection does not occur. Some instances are peculiar to one language or dialect. Compare, for example, Welsh *defnydd* 'matter' with *i*-affection but MB *daffnez* 'matter' without it, though both derive from Proto-British *damnijo-*. Notice also that the contrary phenomenon of *a*-affection can also prevent *i*-affection. A good example is Welsh *Hafren* 'Severn' < Proto-British *Sabrina*. Here the final *a* had already lowered the short *i* in *Sabrina* to *e* before it could cause *i*-affection. Had the *i* in *Sabrina* been long, i-affection would have occurred, and the name would appear in Welsh as *Hefren* (LHEB: 576).

I-affection is phonetically similar to what in the Germanic languages is known as *i*-umlaut. *I*-umlaut is responsible for such alternations as German *Mann*, *Männer*, English *man*, *men*; German *Fuß*, *Füße*, English *foot*, *feet*, and in the verbal system, German *ich falle* 'I fall' but *er fällt* 'he falls'. *I*-umlaut is also the cause of less obvious oppositions, for example, English *fox* but *vixen*, *God* but *giddy*, originally 'possessed by a god', and *blood* but *bless*, originally 'to sprinkle with blood.' The fronting of vowels in anticipation of an *i* in the next syllable is very common in languages. In spoken French, for example, the word *joli* 'pretty' is

---

1 First published in *Cornish Studies*. Second series: Fourteen. 2006. Exeter: University of Exeter Press. Pp. 24–43. ISBN 0-85989-799-0.

2 The Welsh personal name *Tegid* is from Latin *Tacitus* by internal *i*-affection. Many years ago I suggested (BBCS 22 (1967), 236-8) that the name of the British king *Pygys* at BM 2463 might be a misreading for *Tygys* 'Tegid, Tacitus'. In view, however, of the sixth-century Cornish inscription containing the name RICATI < ?*Rigocati* (LHEB 456-7), *Pygys* might be better understood as a misreading for *Rygys*, the expected MC development of *Rigocatus*.

1

not [ʒoli] but [ʒœli], where the first vowel is fronted to [œ] in anticipation of the following *i*.

I-AFFECTION IN THE MIDDLE BRETON VERB

In Breton *a* and *o* are changed to *e* by *i*-affection, *ou* becomes *eu* and *e* may also become *i*. The unaffected vowel is usually seen in the second person singular imperative, e.g. *car* 'love', *caf*, *kaf* 'find' and *lavar* 'say'. *I*-affection occurs in a variety of places in the verbal system. I will discuss briefly some parts of the Breton verb, where *i*-affection tends also to occur in the corresponding positions in Cornish.

The third person singular present indicative

In MB one finds such forms as *seu* 'stands' (stem *sav*), *queff* 'gets' (stem *kaf-*)," *re* 'gives' (stem *ro-*). *I*-affection is very common in the third singular present-future in Welsh also, e.g. MW *seif* 'stands' (cf. MB *seu*), *keiff* (cf. MB *queff*), *eirch* 'asks' (stem *arch*), *keidw* 'keeps' (stem *cadw*), *pyrth* 'bears' (stem *porth*).[3]

I-affection in the third singular of the present can probably to be derived from an original conjunct desinence in *-īt*. Thus MB *seu* 'stands, rises' and Middle Welsh *seif* 'stands' are both reflexes of Proto-British **stam-īt*. *I*-affection is also normal in MB in the second person singular, and the first, second and third person plural of the present. Since, however, I am interested in the comparison with Cornish and these latter forms of the verb are poorly attested in MC and LC, I will not discuss them in either Breton or Cornish.

The third person singular of the *i*-preterite

In OB, but not in MB, one finds forms of the third singular of the preterite in *-is* with *i*-affection of the preceeding vowel, e.g. *guoteguis* 'silenced', *dichreuis* 'began' and *ecdiecncis* 'escaped', in which i-affection occurs (Fleuriot 1964: 308). Such forms are exactly comparable with similar MW preterites in *-is*, e.g. *trenghis* 'perished', *kedwis* 'kept', *delis* 'caught', *gelwis* 'called', *diengis* 'escaped', *enwis* 'named', *erchis* 'asked' and *seuis* 'stood', all with *i*-affection. Similar preterites are also common in MC, e.g. *leverys* 'said,' *yrhys* 'asked,' *sevys* 'stood', etc.

The ending *-is* (*-ys*) of the Breton, Welsh and Cornish third person singular derives from an earlier desinence **-iss < *-īsti*. Alongside this ending, Brythonic also had an ending **-ass < *asti*, which becomes *-as* in Welsh and Breton, giving such third person singular preterites as MB *credas* 'believed' and *clevas* 'heard'; MW *gwelas* 'saw' and *twyllas* 'deceived.' Preterites in *-as*, as we shall see, are common in MC and LC also. The preterite ending in *-as*, lacking as it did a high front vowel, could not cause *i*-affection in any of the three Brythonic languages. We thus find MW *cafas*, MC *cafas* and MB *caffas*, all meaning 'got, found' and all with unaffected *a* in the root.

---

3 My MB examples are taken from HMSB and my MW examples from GMW.

The verbal noun in -*el*

This regularly shows *i*-affection in MB: *meruel, mervell, mervel* 'to die' (stem *maru-*); *seuell, sevel* (stem *sau, sav;* cf. Welsh *sefyll*), *teuell, tevel, teuel* 'to be silent' (stem *tau, tav*), *feliel* 'to fail' (stem *fall*), and with dissimilation of the final consonant, *teurell* 'to throw' (stem *taul*) and *gueruel* 'to call' (stem *galu*). The suffix -*el* is believed to derive from Proto-British **-ilis* (WG: 393).

THE LOSS OF *I*-AFFECTION FROM MODERN BRETON

Modern Breton has largely dispensed with *i*-affection in the verbal system. As we have noted above, the present tense in MB commonly shows *i*-affection in the third person singular. *I*-affection also occurs in the other persons of the present, except the first person singular, which invariably exhibits the root vowel. Thus in MB one finds, for example, *leverez* 'thou sayest', *leveret* 'you say', *leveront* 'they say', all with double *i*-affection, but *lavaraff* 'I say', without it. The first person singular of the present without *i*-affection together with the second singular imperative (e.g. *lavar*) and the imperfect (e.g. *lavaren, -es, -e,* etc.) provided a basis for the analogical deletion of *i*-affection from much of the verbal system in ModB. *I*-affected forms do occur in the verbal system of ModB but they are the exception rather than the rule.[4]

In MB *i*-affection is regular in the third person singular of the present, but tends to be lost in ModB in this position. A striking example of such loss in ModB can be seen in the two versions of *Doctrin an Christenien*. The first text was published in 1622 and is written in MB; the second is in ModB and was published in 1677. The first sentence of the 18th lesson reads as follows in the two texts:

1622

M. Petra a dle vn guir Christen da ober bemdez pan seu e guele? 'M. What should a true Christian do each day when he rises from his bed?'

1677

Petra a dle ur guir Christen da ober dious ar mintin pa sao? 'What should a true Christian do when he rises in the morning?' (DC: 50, 51).

The MB has *pan seu* 'when he rises' (cf. Cornish *pan sef*) with *i*-affection, while the ModB text has *pa sao* without it.

As has been noted above, in MB -*as* has already replaced -*is* as the regular third person singular ending of the preterite. Because the desinence -*as* does not cause *i*-affection, í-affection is already absent from the most frequently used person of the MB preterite, though it is usual in the first and second persons.

---

4 'Vowel affection tends to disappear in Modern Breton, or becomes irregular' HMSB: 177.

By the ModB period *i*-affection has in many verbs disappeared from the preterite entirely.

In ModB *i*-affection is still usual with verbal nouns ending in -*iñ* and -*el*, for example, *terriñ* 'to break' (stem *torr*), *pibiñ* 'to bake' (stem *pob*), *sevel* 'to stand' (stem *sav*), *mervel* 'to die' (stem *marv*) *envel* 'to name' (stem *anv*). Elsewhere *i*-affection has largely disappeared. Hemon, for example, says:

> The root of certain verbs sometimes changes under the influence of an ending. In this case, both regular and irregular forms coexist: **lavarout** 'say' gives **lavarit** and **livirit, lavarot** and **leverot. Karout** 'love' gives **karit** and **kirit, karot** and **kerot** (BG: 61).

Kervella (124-25, § 206) is more radical still. He prints the entire paradigm of the verb *karout* 'to love' and the stem in every person of nine separate tenses is *kar-* throughout, affected forms *ker-* and *kir-* being wholly absent.

I-AFFECTION IN MIDDLE AND LATE CORNISH

In MC *a* becomes *e* by *i*-affection, *o* becomes *e* and *ow* becomes *ew*. It is not possible to say with any certainty that *e* becomes *y* in MC by *i*-affection, since it is by no means clear that the short vowels represented by ‹e› and ‹y› are distinct and separate phonemes. There are, moreover, other factors involved in some vowel alternations in Cornish. Historically *e* alternates with *o* in some verbs quite independently of *i*-affection: for example, the monosyllabic singular imperative *dog* 'carry' (W *dwg*) alternates with disyllabic forms, such as the first person singular of the present, *degaf* (W *dygaf*). It is theoretically possible that the alternation between *o* in the monosyllables *colm* 'bind!' and *tor* 'break!' on the one hand, and *e* in the dissyllables *kelmys* 'bound' and *terrys* 'broken' on the other, are in Cornish of the same origin as the *o* ~ *e* alternation in *dog* ~ *degaf*. In other past participles, such as *lethys* 'killed' and *gwenys* 'pierced,' the vowel is the result of *i*-affection of *a*. It is reasonable," therefore, to assume that in *kelmys* and *terrys* the *e* is the result of *i*-affection of *o*.

From the sixteenth century onwards original *ew* in Cornish disyllables and polysyllables has a marked tendency to become *ow*. Thus *clewes* 'to hear' becomes *clowas* and *tewlel* 'to throw' becomes *towlel*. Tregear, for example, writes the past participle of *kewsel* 'to speak' as *kowses* and *kewses* within a few lines of each other (TH 1). In earlier MC the past participle of *tewlel* 'to throw, to intend' is *tewlys, teulys*:

> *y doull ganso o* **tewlys** 'his plan was plotted by him' PA 7c
> *yn trok horn y fyth* **teulys** 'into a coffin of iron he will be thrown' RD 2166
> *the vn carn y fue* **teulys** 'onto a pile he was thrown' RD 2333.

In LC -*ys* of the past participle is often written with *e* or *a*, suggesting that the unstressed vowel has become schwa. The result of the two phonetic developments of stressed *ew* > *ow*, and the weakening of unstressed -*yz*, would lead us to expect to find *tewlys* written ‹towles› or ‹towlaz› in the later language. This is exactly what we do find:

> *mabe cothe adam **towles** why a weall tha vysshew bras* 'Adam's elder son you see cast to great mischief' CW 1501-02
> *Leben pe reg Jesus clowaz tero Jowan **towlaz** tha bressen* 'Now when Jesus heard that John had been thrown into prison' ÉCII: 189.

These forms are the result of spontaneous phonetic developments and have nothing to do with the analogical loss of *i*-affection. One could, nonetheless, argue that the regular development of *tewlys* > *towles, towlaz* assisted the analogical loss of *i*-affection elsewhere. The development *tewlys* > *towlaz* must incidentally also be borne in mind when discussing the two attested forms of the preterit, *kewsys* 'he spoke' and *cowsas* 'he spoke' (see below).

THE PRESENT-FUTURE

Lever 'says' > *laver*

I-affection is frequent in MC, though not universal, in the third person singular of the present-future. A good example of *i*-affection is provided by the form *lever*, the third person singular present-future of the verb *leverel* 'to say'. As can be seen from the following examples, *i*-affection is the rule in MC in this part of the verb:

> *del **lever** зyn an levar* 'as the Book tells us' PA 135d
> *A el me a **leuer** thy's* 'O angel, I tell thee' OM 736
> *a **leuer** y vos map dv* 'who says he is the son of God' PC 326
> *me a **leuer** an guyr thy's* 'I tell thee the truth' RD 64
> *Me a **lever** зyvgh mester* 'I tell you, master' BM 118
> *So me a **levar** thewgh why* 'But I tell you' TH 27
> *enoch me a **levar** thyes* 'Enoch, I tell thee' CW 2110.

The first person singular is *lavaraf* and the singular imperative is *lavar* 'speak!' Forms like these began to influence the third person singular of the present-future so that it was analogically reshaped from *lever* to *lavar, laver*. The variant *lavar, laver* 'says' is first to be noted in Tregear's Homilies (c. 1555). It is not uncommon thereafter:

> *kepar dell **lavar** an Abostyll pedyr* 'as the apostle Peter says' TH 3a
> *den veith ny **lavar*** 'no man says' SA 59
> *Pew a **laver*** 'Who will say?' SA 59
> *me a **laver** the gee* 'I tell thee' SA 62
> *Martesyn te a **lavar*** 'Perhaps thou wilt say' SA 62a

*me a **laver** e bask e honyn* 'I say "his own passover"' SA 64a
*why a **lavar** gwyre dremas* 'you speak true, good man' CW 588
*eva me a **lavar** theis* 'Eve, I tell thee' CW 792
*me a **lavar** theis an case* 'I will tell the the case' CW 903
*me a **lavar** theis dibblance* 'I tell the plainly' CW 1839
*ha me a **lavar** dhîz:* 'and I will tell thee' BF: 17.

This is a well-attested and incontrovertible example of the analogical loss of *i*-affection.

kef, kyf 'finds, gets' > caf

We have already noted MB *queff* 'gets', MW *keiff*, ModW *caiff* 'gets'. The equivalent in MC is *kyf, kef*, which is widely attested:

*a **gef** bos lour* 'that will get enough fodder' OM 1060
*ef a **gyf** yn araby* 'he will find in Arabia' OM 1930
*ena why a **gyf** asen* 'there you will find an ass' PC 176
*me a'n **kyf** by god ys blod* 'I will find him by God's blood' RD
*ny **gyf** methek a'n sawya* 'he will not find a doctor who will heal him' RD
   1648
*me an **kyff** lel* 'I find it truly' BM 392
*ena wy a **gyff** yn lel* 'there you will find truly' BM 967
*me as **kyef** pan vydnaf ve* 'I get them when I want' CW 1457
*ty a **gyef** in yet vdn eall* 'thou wilt find an angel in the gate' W 1753.

By the LC period this has apparently given way to a form *caf*. I know of only one example, from the folk-tale 'Jowan Chy an Horth' recorded by Lhuyd from Nicholas Boson at the end of the seventeenth century:

*ha enna ti an **kâv*** 'and there thou wilt find him' AB: 257a.

If we had more LC, we would no doubt have more examples of *caf* 'gets, finds' without *i*-affection.

THE CORNISH PRETERITE IN -YS

Kewsys 'spoke' > cowsas

The *-ys* preterite *keusys, kewsys* with *i*-affection is common in MC. Nonetheless from the earliest texts there is a slight tendency to replace it with the *-as* preterite without *i*-affection. In *Pascon agan Arluth*, for example, one finds both A. *kewsys* and B. *cowsas*, both meaning 'spoke':

A)

an ioull ʒe adam **kewsys** 'the devil spoke to Adam' PA 6c
An ioul ʒe grist a **gewsys** 'The devil spoke to Christ' P A 14a
ihesus a **gewsys** *arta* 'Christ spoke again' PA 34c
Ihesus a **gewsys** *arte* 'Jesus spoke again' PA 74a
Kayphas arta a **gewsys** 'Again Caiaphas spoke' PA 93a
pylat a **gewsys** *yn scon* 'Pilate spoke at once' PA 101c
Iudas scaryoth a **gewsys** 'Judas Iscariot spoke' PA 104a
Han eʒewon a **gewsys** 'And the Jews spoke' PA 105a
hy a **gewsys** *del ylly* 'she spoke as she was able' PA 166a.

B)

an lauar crist pan **gowsas** 'when Christ spoke the word' PA 68a
orto Ihesus a **gowsas** 'to him Jesus spoke' PA 80d
pedyr arta a **gowsas** 'Peter spoke again' PA 84d
gurris ve yn y golon yn delma gul may **cowsas** 'it was put in his heart so to
  do, so that he spoke' PA 89bc
worth ihesus ef a **gowsas** 'to Jesus he spoke' PA 92a
pan **gowsas** *crist yn della* 'when Christ spoke thus' PA 94b
Pylat arte a **gowsas** 'Pilate spoke again' PA 126c
awatta ef a **gowsas** *agis mygtern* 'behold, he said, your king' PA 147c
ʒe stirya yw a **gowsas** *arluth prag y hysta vy* 'what he said is to be
  interpreted, Lord, why didst thou forsake me? PA 201c
Marrak arall a **gowsas** 'Another soldier spoke' PA 246a.

The unaffected form *cowsas* is the normal one in later Cornish:

Dew a **cowsas** *an ger* 'God spoke the word' SA 61a
y **cowses** *gans chardge pur greyf* 'he declared with a strong injunction'
  CW 1538
kyns lemyn sure a **gowzas** 'who spoke before now' CW 2422
Ha e **gowzas** 'And he spoke' ÉCII: 179
Ha an dean a **gowzas** 'And the man spoke' ÉCII: 179
Ha an arleth Deew a **gowzas** *tha an venen* 'And the Lord God spoke to the
  woman' ÉCII: 179
Tha an venen e cowzaz 'To the woman he spoke' ÉCII: 181
Ha tha Adam e a **gowzas** 'And to Adam he spoke' ÉCII: 181
Deu a **Couzas** *an geryou ma* 'God spoke these words' BF: 41
Deiu **Cowsas** *Gerria ma* 'God spoke these words' BF: 55.

We have seen above that MC past participle *tewlys* appears as *towlaz* in LC.
LC *cowsaz* 'spoke' might therefore be the regular phonetic development of MC
keusys, kewsys with erstwhile *i*-affection, rather than a variant in *-as* without it.
The change of *ew > ow* was still in progress by the time of the manuscript of PA,

7

i.e. by the early fifteenth century at the latest. *Cowsas* in PA, therefore, is perhaps unlikely to be development of *kewsys*. It is more probably a different form of the preterite. If *cowsas* and *kewsys* 'spoke' co-existed in Middle Cornish, LC *cowsas, cowzas* can either be understood as continuing MC *cowsas* or, as is perhaps more likely, as representing the LC reflexes of both MC *kewsys* and *cowsas*. This latter view gets some corroboration from Tregear's spellings, *eff a gowses* TH 43, *eff a gowsys* TH 43, which are halfway between *kewsys* and *cowsas*. At all events, it seems likely that the prevalence of *cowsas* in the later language may have assisted the loss of *i*-affection in other preterites.

Tewlys 'threw' > towlas

The past participle of the MC verb *tewlel* 'to throw, to intend' has been mentioned above. The verb in MC has a preterite in *-ys*:

> *ef as **tewlys** dre sor bras ʒen eʒewon yn treʒe* 'he threw them in great anger
> in among the Jews' PA 103c
> *me re **teulys** dew grabel* 'I have thrown two grappling-hooks' RD 2271.

By the later sixteenth century this has been replaced by a preterite in *-as*:

> *rag an wethvas a ruke offrennia ii mittes, hy a **dowlas** in offering a Dew moy
> agis y oll* 'for the widow offered two mites, she cast into the offering-box
> of God more than them all' SA 64.

The third person singular ending of the *-ys* preterite is always written ‹is› in SA, e.g. *ha'n hynwis e gois* 'and he called it his blood' SA 61a; *Ef a causis an geir* 'He spoke the word' SA 62; *me a leveris thees* 'I told thee' SA 62a; *Peder a leveris* 'Peter said' SA 63; *ef a ruk e corf ha leveris* 'he made his body and said' SA 64a and *An keth Austen ma a leveris* 'This same Augustine said' SA 66. The form **towlas* seen in *hy a dowlas* at SA 64 cannot, therefore, be a phonetic development of the preterite *tewlys* 'threw.' In this respect it differs from the LC past participle *towlaz* 'thrown' (see above), which could quite easily represent MC *tewlys*. The preterite **towlas* in SA must be an analogical replacement of an *-ys* preterite by an *-as* preterite, in which there is no trace of *i*-affection.

Sevys 'stood up, arose' > savas

In other verbs the loss of *i*-affection is more certain, for example in the preterite of *sevel* 'to stand'. The MC *-ys* preterite of the verb is *sevys*, which is well attested:

> *onan yn ban a **sevys*** 'one stood up' PA 81a
> *Ena pan **sevys** yn ban* 'Then when he stood up' PA 166a
> *En marrek na a **sevys** oll yn ban y goweʒe* 'That soldier roused his
> companions completely' PA 245a

*Ihesu crist … **sevys** gallas 3e gen le* 'Jesus Christ has risen, he has gone to
　　another place' PA 255b-c
*Del **sevys** mab du ay veth* 'As the son of God rose from his grave' PA 259a
*kepar del **sevys** a'n beth* 'just as he rose from the grave' RD 666
*ny **seuys** nes* 'he did not rise at all' RD 1021.

In LC, however, one finds several examples of *savas* for *sevys:*

*Ha e **savaz** am'àn amez e uili* 'And he got up out his bed' BF: 18
*ha mi a **savaz** am'àn* 'and I got up' BF: 18
*ne rege hi doaze ha **zavaz** derez leba era an flô* 'until it came and stood over
　　the place where the child was' ÉCII: 196.

This is a clear instance of the loss of *i*-affection in the preterite.
　　Closely related to the verb *sevel* is the verb *drehevel* 'to raise, to rise.'.This has
a preterite in *-ys* with *i*-affection in MC, of which only one example is known to
me:

Y *ij luff y **trehevys*** 'he raised his two hands' BM 4431.

John Boson, however, in his version of the Apostles' Creed uses a form with *a*
rather than *e* in the stressed syllable:

*ha an trugga deth Eau **derauas** arta durt an Marrow* 'and the third day he
　　rose again from the dead' BF: 41.

Here also *i*-affection has been lost.

Leverys 'said' > *lavaras*
The third person singular of the preterite of the verb *leverel* 'to say' is *leverys* in
MC. The form is very frequent and I cite here only a handful of examples:

*Iudas fals a **leuerys*** 'false Judas said' PA 36a
*ha'n el thy'm a **leuerys*** 'and the angel said to me' OM 844
*ty re'n **leuerys** iudas* 'thou hast said it, Judas' PC 759
*an el thy'n a **leuerys*** 'the angel told us' RD 1062
***leferys** offeren* 'he said mass' BM 4419
*an tas a **leverys*** 'the Father said' TH 1
*ha ef a ruk e corf ha **leveris*** 'and he made his body and said' SA64a
*ha in delma y **leverys** an gyrryow ma* 'and thus he said these words' CW
　　1374-75.

By the LC period the unstressed syllables have been reduced to schwa but the
stressed *e* < *a* by *i*-affection remains. We thus find such forms as *laveraz* BF: 19,

laveraz BF: 51, 52 x 6, and *laveras* BF: 52. These are examples of a purely phonetic development. Since the stressed vowel is still *e*, *i*-affection is still apparent. Not infrequently in LC, however, the stressed vowel *e* has been analogically replaced by *a*, in the following instances for example:

> *eue* **levarraz** *droua* 'he said that it was' BF: 25
> *Deu a Couzas an geryou ma ha* **lavaras** 'God spoke these words, and said' BF: 41
> *ha Deu* **lavaras** *dothans* 'and God said to them' BF: 53
> *Ha Deu* **lavaras**, *Mero* 'And God said, Behold' BF: 53
> *Deiu Cowsas Gerria ma-ha* **lavaraz** 'God spoke these words-and said' BF: 55
> *Ha e a* **lavarraze** 'And he said' ÉCII: 174
> *Ha an vennen a* **lavarraz** *tha an hagar-breeve* 'And the woman said to the evil serpent' ÉCII: 175
> *Deew a* **lavarraz** 'God said' ÉCII: 175
> *Ha an hagar-breeve a* **lavarraz** *tha'n vennen* 'And the evil serpent said to the woman' ÉCII: 175
> *Ha an arleth Deew a gerias tha Adam ha* **lavarraz** *thotha* 'And the Lord God called to Adam and said to him' ÉCII: 178
> *Ha e* **lavarraz** 'And he said' ÉCII: 178
> *Ha an arleth Diew a* **lavarras** *tha an hagar-breeve* 'And the Lord God said to the evil serpent' ÉCII: 180
> *Ha an tempter theath thotha ha* **lavarraz** 'And the tempter came to him and said' ÉCII: 186
> *Buz e gwerebas ha* **lavarraz** 'But he answered and said' ÉCII: 186
> *Ha* **lavarraz** *thotha: mo thosta maab Deew* 'And said to him: if thou art the son of God' ÉCII: 187
> *Chreest a* **lavarraz** *thotha* 'Christ said to him' ÉCII: 187
> *Ha* **lavarraz** *thotha: oll a rimah ve vedn ry theeze* 'And said to him: all these I will give' ÉCII: 188
> *Ha en gye* **lavarraz** *thotha* 'And they said to him' ÉCII: 195.

In these cases all trace of *e* by *i*-affection has been lost. *I*-affection has been analogically removed.

debrys 'ate' > *debras* > *dabras*

In the MC texts the verb *dybry, debry* 'to eat' has a preterite in *-ys* in the third person singular:

> *kemer tyyr spus a'n aval a* **dybrys** *adam the das* 'take three pips of the apple which thy father Adam ate' OM 823-24.

By the sixteenth century *dybrys* has been replaced by a preterite in *-as*:

> *hy a gemeras ran an frut hag an **debbras*** 'she took part of the fruit and ate
> it' TH 3a
> *hag eff a **thebbras*** 'and he ate' TH 3a
> *agan Savyour a **thebbras** an pascall one* 'our Saviour ate the paschal lamb'
> TH 52.

Nicholas Boson, recorded by Lhuyd, has *ha'n bara dzhei a dhabraz* 'and the bread they ate' BF: 19; cf. AB: 253a. Here **dabraz* is unmotivated, given that the unaffected stem is *deber* rather than **daber*. It seems that analogy with other verbs which demonstrate *e-a* alternation has produced the unwarranted form *dhabraz*, This can, nonetheless, be regarded as a further analogical loss of *i*-affection.

THE CORNISH VERBAL NOUN IN *-EL*

Sevel 'to arise' > saval
As has been noted above, the verbal noun suffix *-el* < **ilis)* causes *i*-affection of the preceding vowel. A good example is the verbal noun *sevel* 'to stand' (cf. *sevys* 'arose' discussed above). This is common in the MC texts, e.g. *sevel* OM 2575; *sevell* PA 240d; *seuel* OM 1348, 1407, *1690*; *seuell* PA 22c, 22d. In the later MC texts the final syllable is often reduced to *-al, -all*, e.g. *sevall* CW 93, 1210, 1774. Nonetheless the root vowel here is still *e*, the reflex of *a* by *i*-affection. There is some evidence that in LC the root vowel was altered to *a* by analogy with the stem form *saf*. There are only two examples known to me:

> *Pe reg e saval, e comeraz an flô* 'When he got up, he took the child' ÉCII: 198
> *îz **saval*** glossing *Seges, Standing corn* AB: 147c.

Though poorly attested, *saval* for *sevel* is a further example of the analogical loss of *i*-affection.

Leverel 'to say, to tell' > lavaral
The verbal noun *leverel, leferel* (cf. *lever* and *leverys* discussed above) is common in MC. By the sixteenth century the unstressed final syllable has weakened to the neutral vowel schwa and is written in a variety of ways: *leverall* SA 59 x 4, CW 1175; *leverol* BF: 31 x 3 and *laveral* BF: 15, 16. In all these cases the stressed syllable remains *e* < *a* by *i*-affection. On occasion in LC, however, one finds forms where the stressed syllable has been analogically changed from *e* > *a* (cf. *lavaras, lavaraz;* etc., of the preterite):

ha mee ved'n. lavarel deese 'and I will tell thee' BF: 16
ha me vedn lavarel dhîz 'and I will tell thee' BF: 17
a reeg doaze teeze veer thor an Est tha Jerusalem, Lavaral 'wise men came from the East to Jerusalem, saying' ÉCII: 194.

There is also a reduced form of the verbal noun, written *lawl, laule* or *laol*. This I take to be a reduction of *lavarel, lavaral*, possibly via the stages: *l'var'l* with loss of unstressed syllables, > *larl* with simplification of the impossible cluster *lv*, > *laul* by vocalization of the cluster *rl* > *ul*. The reduced form of the verbal noun is well attested:

pu reg laule theese? 'who told thee?' ÉCII: 179
a restah debre thort an gwethan a reege a vee laule theeze a na rosesta debre? 'didst thou eat from the tree from which I told thee: thou shouldst not eat?' ÉCII: 179
thor an wethan a reege a vee lawle theeze chee na raage debre anothe 'from the tree I told thee, thou shalt not eat from it' ÉCII: 182
Ha an arleth Doew reg lawle 'And the Lord God said' ÉCII: 183
Thort an termin notha Jesus reg dalla a boroga ha tha laale 'From the time from which Jesus began to preach, and to say' ÉCII: 190
Ha e ez devannaz tha Bethalem, ha reg laule thonz 'And he sent them to Bethlehem and said to them' ÉCII: 196
cowsez gen Arleth neve der an prophet o laule 'spoken by the Lord of heaven by the prophet, saying' ÉCII: 198-99
a ve cowzez gen Jerman an prophet, laule 'that was spoken by the prophet Jeremiah, saying' ÉCII: 199
Kouza, lâol glossing *Dico … To say, to speak, to tell* AB: 54c
Dho dissembla, dha lâol gou glossing *Simulo … To feign, to counterfeit,* &c. AB: 150b-c
an peath eggee e Lal tha ni da zeel 'that which he tells us on Sunday' LAM: 228.

Although reduced in form, *lawle* should be considered a variant of *lavaral* and thus further evidence for the loss of *i*-affection in LC.

THE REPLACEMENT OF -*EL* AND -*Y* OF THE VERBAL NOUN

In ModB, as we have seen, the suffix -*el* of the verbal noun, which causes *i*-affection, is frequently replaced by a suffix which does not. Thus, for example, MB *leverel* becomes ModB *lavarout*. Something similar appears to occur in LC, where the two endings -*el* and -*y* of the verbal noun are on occasion replaced by -*a*. I have only a handful of examples:

dho **honụa** glossing *Appello … To Name or Call* AB [4]3a (MC *henwel*)
dho **tụlla** glossing *Perforo, To bore through* AB: 117c; *Tolla, Bore; Tellyz;
Bored, perforated,* &c. AB: 248a (MC *telly*)
a **towlah** *rooze en mor* 'throwing a net into the sea' ÉCII: 191
ha lebben thera Ma **toula** *tho gwellaz mar pel itna* 'and now I am intending
to see as far it it BF: 29 (MC *tewlel*).

Lhuyd's *Dho honua* 'to name' is curious, given that the expected unaffected stem
would be *hanow*, rather than **honow*. I assume that *honua* derives from **hanwa*,
where the labialized consonant cluster *nw* has lowered *a > o*. In this context one
should note that Thomas Boson writes:

Naras **hanwall** *de Arlith Deu heb oatham, rag na vedn an Arlith gave do Neb
ra E* **hanwelle** *heb oatham* 'Thou shalt not name thy Lord God in vain,
for the Lord will not forgive anyone who names him in vain' BF: 41.

One might take the forms *hanwall, hanwelle* to be comparable with *saval*
discussed above, i.e. with loss of *i*-affection even before *-el*. There is evidence,
however, that MC internal *e* is on occasion lowered to *a* before *n*, e.g. *hana* x 2
(MC *henna*) 'that, this, he' glossing *Is* and *Iste* AB: 73b.[5] *Hanwall, hanwelle* may
conceivably be examples of the analogical loss of *i*-affection. They may also be
phonetic developments of *i*-affected *henwel* itself.

The replacement of *-el* by *-a* in *towla < tewlel* is mentioned above for the sake
of completeness. It must be admitted that the stem would have been *towl-* even
without the change of suffix from *-el > -a* (*cf. cowsys < kewsys* above).

Notice incidentally that Lhuyd cites *dho golli* (alongside *Kelli*) glossing *Perdo,
… To lose, to destroy* AB: 117b and *Dho losʒi* glossing *Uro … To burn, to parch* AB:
177c. In both cases the final *-i/-y* remains, but *i*-affection has been lost in the
stem.

A further loss of *i*-affection occurs when instead of a form in *-el* with *i*-affection
the bare stem without *i*-affection is used as the verbal noun. The most obvious
example is the common variant of the verbal noun *cows* 'to speak', which occurs
alongside *kewsel, cowsel:*

heb **cows** *ger y clamderis* 'without speaking a word she fainted' PA 165d
rag **cous** *orthyf ha talkye* 'to converse with me and to talk' OM 150
rak ef the **cous** *whetlow gow* 'because he utters false stories' PC 1392
pan eses ganso ov **covs** 'when thou wast talking to him' BM 1051
hag inweth ow **cows** *dre y apostylls* 'and also talking through his apostles'
TH 7a.

---

5 I have discussed this lowering of *e* before *n* in *Studia Celtica* 32 (1998), 143-6, reprinted
in Williams 2006a.

Cows 'to speak' also has a LC form in *-a*, seen for example in *Mêz cowsa nebaz an gwella* 'But to speak little is best' LAM: 246; *Kouza* glossing *Dico* ... *To say, to speak* (AB: 54c) and in the famous sentence quoted by Carew, *Meea na vidna cowza sawzneck* 'I can speak no Saxonage' LAM: 272.

The only other example known to me of a verbal noun in *-el* replaced by the unaffected stem-form is cited by Lhuyd: *Dho maru* glossing *Intereo* ... *To die, to fail or come to naught* AB: 72a. The more usual form is *merwel* with *i*-affection (cf. MB *meruel, mervell, mervel* cited above).

THE PAST PARTICIPLE

The past participle in MB and ModB ends in *-et*, and this does not cause *i*-affection. It is apparent from the OB personal names *Matganet, Matgganet, Daganed*, all containing the element *-ganet* 'born' (Fleuriot: 314) that *-et* without *i*-affection was already in place in the earliest recorded stages of the language.

In MC on the other hand the ending of the past participle is *-ys < *īto)* and this has always caused *i*-affection:

> ***ervys*** 'armed' (stem *arf*) PC 939, RD 351; *yrvys* PA 241d, 242b, 250c, OM 2141, 2170, 2204
>
> ***gesys*** 'left' (stem *gas*) PA 182d, 184c, 233d, OM 1492, 1589, 1606, BM 1254, TH 40a x 4; *geses* TH 1; *gesis* SA 61; *gerys* TH 25a
>
> ***gevys*** 'forgiven' (stem *gaf*) PA 185c, TH 38a, 44; *gyfys* PC 529; *gefys* RD 1102
>
> ***gylwys*** 'called' (stem *galow*) PA 124a, OM 676, 952, BM 1, TH 1a, 2a, 6, 7a; *gilwis* SA 64; *gelwys* BM 168, 512, 645
>
> ***guenys*** 'pierced' (stem *gwan*) PC 2376, RD 2603; *gwenys* TH 15a, CW 1572
>
> ***hynwys*** 'named' (stem *hanow)*) PA 214a, 217a, 217d, TH 29; *henwys* OM 1771, BM 2550, CW 375, TH 31a; *henwis* SA 66a x 2, CW 12; *henways* BM 2455
>
> ***kechys*** 'caught' (stem *cach*) PC 2293; *kychys* RD 2596; *chechys* PA 48d
>
> ***kefys*** 'got' (stem *caf*) PA 98c, 246d, TH 6, CW 743; *keffys* PA 119c, 128d, RD 1901, TH 10a; *kyfys* PA 141b, TH 37; *kyffys* TH 11; *kyffes* TH 1; *kevys* CW 1496, 1745, 1896, 2205
>
> ***kenys*** 'sung' (stem *can)*) PC 903[6]
>
> ***kerys*** 'loved' (stem *car*) RD 1221, BM 187,675, TH 26 x 2,31, 31a; *keris* PA 214d, BM 288, 570; *kerrys* CW 1327
>
> ***leddrys*** 'stolen' (stem *lader*) RD 354
>
> ***leȝys*** 'killed' (stem *lath*) PA 17d, 49d, 95b, 98b, 118a, 119b, 128c, 141c, 210d; *lethys* OM 596, RD 340, 428, 593, BM 881, 976,1517; *lethis* TH 23

---

6 PC 902-4 reads as follows: *peder me a leuer thy's/ kyns ys bos kullyek kenys/ terguyth y wregh ov naghe*. Previous commentators have taken *kullyek-kenys* to be a noun meaning 'cock-crow'. This cannot be correct. I take *kenys* to be a past participle used actively: 'Peter, I tell thee/ before the cock shall have crowed/ thou shalt deny me thrice.'

megys 'nourished' (stem *mag*) BM 3872, 3886, 3893, TH 41, 49; *megis* SA 63a.

Lhuyd makes clear that -*ys* is usually pronounced -*ez* or -*az* in LC. Speaking of the past participle he says:

I am sensible that the Modern Pronunciation of the Cornish, does not confirm the Termination of this Participle's being always in -*yz*: For they generally end it in *ez*, Saying *Kreiez*, Called; *Trehez*; Cut; *Miskemerez*; Mistaken; *Dyliez*, Revenged; *Guerhez*; Sold, &c. and sometimes in *az*: As *Ledhaz*, Slain; *Kyrtaz*, Delayed; *Guesgaz*, Worn; tho' not seldom, also in *yz*: As *Devydhyz*; Quenched; *Devedhyz*; Come; *Bidhyz*; Drowned; *Kelmyz*; Bound; *Huedhyz*, Swoln (AB: 248b).

We must assume that the vowel of the suffix -*ys* in LC was actually the neutral vowel schwa, which Lhuyd heard differently in different environments. It should be noted that in the LC past participle *i*-affection is usually present in those verbs that can have it. Here are a few examples:

engrez 'angered' (stem *anger*) ÉCII: 199
gerres 'left' (< *gesys*; stem *gas*) LAM: 230
humbregez 'led' (stem *humbrank, humbrag*) ÉCII: 185
kevez 'found' (stem *caf*) BF: 25, 27; *keevez* BF: 25
kellez, kelles 'lost' (stem *coll*) BF: 46, 48; *Kellyz* glossing *Perditus ... lost, destroy'd, undone* AB: 117b
ketchys 'taken' (stem *cach*) Borlase 395
Kelmyz 'bound' (stem *colm*) AB: 248b
Ledhaz 'killed, slain' (stem *lath*) AB: 104c, 248b
Selliz 'salted' (stem *sall*) AB: 143c
Teʒez 'choked' (stem *tag*) AB: 157c.

The two forms *ledhaz* and *Teʒez* cited by Lhuyd are clearly LC, as can be seen from the reduced final syllable. Lhuyd in his Cornish grammar also also cites the following past participles with *i*-affection: *ervyz, yrvyz* 'armed' (stem *arf*); *gevyz; givyz;* 'forgiven' (stem *gaf*); *guenyz; guinyz* 'pierced' (stem *gwan*); *meʒyz* 'bred' (stem *mag*) AB: 248a. It is not clear whether these are LC forms which he had actually heard or MC forms he had merely read in manuscript. Lhuyd's *Po marh ledryz* 'When a horse is stolen' AB: 249a, on the other hand, is clearly a contemporary phrase which Lhuyd heard in Cornwall. This patently contains the past participle *ledryz* 'stolen' (stem *Lader*) with *i*-affection.

Although the past participle is the most favourable environment in LC for the persistence of *i*-affection, there are a number of LC examples of the past participle without *i*-affection, where it would be expected:

*pan glowa an nowethys y vos **lathys** '*when he hears the news that he is killed' CW 1137

*rag tho angye **lathez** '*for they are killed' ÉCII: 200

*Po the'ns **Salles** da '*when they are well salted' BF: 43

*Path' ens **salles** dah '*when they are well salted' BF: 44

*na vedn an Tavaz ma beska boz **kavas** arta en us ni '*that this language will never be found again in our age' BF: 46

*garres ew ni '*left are we' BF: 59 (for **gasys*)

But Kòlhyz, Lost AB: 248a.

In the LC past participle too, then, analogy has been at work and *i*-affection is beginning to be lost.

CONCLUSION

In ModB *i*-affection in the verbal system has been largely removed by analogy. Although the sources are fragmentary, there is good evidence that *i*-affection was similarly being deleted from the verbal system of LC. The analogical loss of *i*-affection in the Breton verb is one of the features which distinguish ModB from MB. ModB as a written language is generally held to have begun in 1659 with the publication of Julien Maunoir's grammar (Hardie 1948: 9). At this same period Cornish was confined to the far west of Cornwall and was rapidly disappearing. Although Cornish lingered on in Mount's Bay until c. 1785, it had ceased to be a community language by the early eighteenth century. By the LC period, analogy had already begun to delete *i*-affection from the verbal system. If Cornish, like Breton, had survived into the nineteenth and twentieth centuries, we can be sure that *i*-affection would largely have disappeared from the Cornish verb.

THE CORNISH *ENGLYN*[7]

Lhuyd's Cornish *englyn*

Towards the end of his Cornish grammar Edward Lhuyd alludes to some Welsh *englynion,* for example, *Englynion y Clyweit* 'the Stanzas of Hearing,' *Englynion y Beddau* 'the Stanzas of the Graves' and the *Bidiau* [These are gnomic stanzas containing many examples of *Bid* 'Is wont to be']. He then tells us that he heard one *englyn* in Cornwall:

> *An lavar kôth yu lavar guîr,*
> *Bedh dvrn rê ver, dhvn tavaz rê hîr;*
> *Mez dên heb davaz a gvllaz i dîr.*

> 'What's said of old, will always stand:
> Too long a tongue, too short a hand;
> But he that had no tongue, lost his land' (AB: 251c).

It is noteworthy that the word for 'short' in this *englyn* is *ber*. This word elsewhere in Middle Cornish occurs only in the fossilized phrases 1) *a ver spys* and 2) *a ver dermyn,* both of which mean 'in a short while, soon'. Here are some examples of the two expressions from the Middle Cornish texts:

1)
*hep gul dyel **a ver speys** OM 947*
*yn certan hag **a ver spys** OM 1540*
*lauar thy'mmo **a ver spys** PC 509*
*the volungeth **a ver spys** PC 2053*
*ha crousyough ef **a ver spys** PC 2166*
*gura gueres thy'm **a ver spys** RD 1 721*
*rnyr worto hag **a ver spys** RD 1729*
*arluth ker hag **a ver spys** RD 1785*
*ihesu gront dovyr **a wur speys** BM 668*
*the covs gena **a fur spas** BM 3979.*

2)
*me a'th kelm fast **a ver termyn** OM 1361-62*
*cous er the fyth **a ver termyn** OM 1441*
*rag the throg **a ver dermyn** OM 1601*

---

7 First published in *Cornish Studies.* Second series: Fifteen. 2007. Exeter: University of Exeter Press. Pp. 11–26. ISBN 0-85989-808-9

*ha kerenys **a ver dermyn*** OM 2381
*ny a thy **a ver termyn*** PC 1654
*leuereugh **a ver termyn*** PC 1690
*man gueller **a ver termyn*** PC 1963
*genevy **a fur termyn*** BM 1741.

In Middle Cornish the ordinary word for 'short' is *cot*, as can be seen from the following examples:

*na vo hyrre es am syn na byth **cotta** war nep cor* 'that it be no longer than my mark nor any shorter in any way' OM 2511-12

*re **got** o a gevelyn* 'it was too short by a cubit' OM 2520

*lemyn re **got** ev a gevelyn da yn guyr* 'now it is too short by a good cubit truly' OM 2540-41

*tres aral re **got** in guyr* 'another time too short truly' OM 2549

cot yv the thythyow thegy 'short are your days' RD 2037

me a ra pur pur cot y guyns 'I will render his wind very short' BM 2253

*an lesson **cut** ma* 'this short lesson' TH 26

*ha wosa an tyrmyn **cut** a vethyn ny omma* 'and after the short time we will be here' TH 26

*in kyth same lesson bean **cut** ma* 'in this very same short lesson' TH 28a

*an moar brase yn **cutt** termyn adro thom tyre a vyth dreys* 'the great sea will be brought round my land in a short time' CW 88-9

*in **cutt** termyn ages negys cowsow y praya* 'in a short time tell your business, I pray' CW 592.

In the englyn, however, *ber* is used in the phrase *re ver* 'too short', and was apparently at the time of composition the ordinary word for 'short'. This would perhaps suggest that the *englyn* dates from the early Middle Cornish period, when *ber* (Welsh *byr*) was still the usual word for 'short.'

Lhuyd cites his Cornish *englyn* in *Archæologia Britannica* of 1707. Two variant versions of it also occur in Pryce's *Archæologia Cornu-Britannica* of 1790. The first reads as follows:

> *An Lavor gôth ewe lavar gwîr*
> *Ne vedn nevera doas vas a tavas re hîr*
> *Bes den heb tavaz a gollas e dîr* (ACB: F f).

The second version cited by Pryce is from a letter written by Edward Lhuyd. In the letter, which was written to T. Tonkin on March 16th, 1702/03, Lhuyd says he heard the stanza from the clerk of St Just. This version reads as follows:

> *An lavar koth yw lavar gwîr*
> *Na boz nevra dôz vâz an tavas re hîr*
> *Bez dên heb davaz a gollaz i dîr.*

THE CORNISH *ENGLYN*

This last version is from a letter of Lhuyd's and Pryce's first version with its ô and î circumflex also looks as though it has originally come from Lhuyd. It would seem then that all three variants come directly or indirectly from Lhuyd.

Lhuyd himself tells us that he heard the *englyn*, rather than read it in manuscript. It existed, moreover, in three slightly different versions. This would suggest that the *englyn* formed part of the Cornish oral tradition. Since, however, the language of the *englyn* is probably much older in origin than the eighteenth century, we should not be astonished to see that the original stanza has been reshaped by centuries of oral transmission. Even so the underlying form is clear enough. We are dealing with a stanza of three lines of between eight and eleven syllables rhyming *aaa*. This is immediately reminiscent of the *englyn milwr* of Welsh, a form of *englyn* common in *Canu Llywarch Hen* and elsewhere. In the *englyn milwr* the syllable count is usually either seven syllables or more rarely eight syllables. There are sequences of *englynion milwr* in existence, however, in which the syllabic count is much less regular. Here are some examples:

A)
Bid wlyb rhych; bid fynych mach;
bid chwyrn colwyn, bid wenwyn gwrach;
bid cwynfan claf, bid lawen iach.

Bid chwyrniad colwyn, bid wenwyn neidr;
bid nofiaw rhyd wrth beleidr;
nid gwell yr odwr no'r lleidr.

The furrow is usually wet; surety is often required;
a puppy is quick, a hag is venom,
the sick man is lamentation, happy is the healthy man.

The puppy snores, the snake is venom,
the ford rushes across sunbeams,
no better is the accomplice than the thief (EWGP: 36).

B)
A glyweist di a gant y vronvreith
pan dramwych dros diffeith
na vit dy elin dy gedymdeith

Did you hear what the thrush sang?
When you travel through wild country,
let not your enemy be your companion (BBCS iii (1927) 10).

In the first of the two *englynion* at A) above the syllabic count is 7, 8, 8 and in the second it is 9, 7, 7. In stanza B) above the syllable count is 8, 6, 9.

Whatever the original length of the line in the Cornish *englyn,* I assume that the metrical form of three lines rhyming *aaa* is a common inheritance of Welsh and Cornish. It is probable also that in the early *englyn* from which both the Welsh and the Cornish *englyn* derives, the syllable count was considerably less regular than it later became in Welsh.

Until now the term *englyn* was exclusively known from Welsh but was unattested in Cornish. The word now, however, appears in the recently-discovered Cornish play *Bewnans Ke.* In the second part of the drama King Arthur and his court are at Caerleon upon Usk, where the king has just received twelve legates from Lucius, emperor of Rome. Arthur says:

> *Dun ow amors ha'm cuvyon,*
> *gans solas hag **eglynnyon***
> > *ha merth ha melody whek.*
> > > *Th'agan palas gwel ew thyn*
> > > *revertya gans cannow tek*
> > > *ha predery, ren Austyn!*
> > > > *a'gen gwayow.*

Come, my friends and my dear ones,
with entertainment and *englynion*
and mirth and sweet melody.
It is better for us
to return to our palace with sweet songs
and to consider, by St Augustine!
our moves (BK 2058-64).

The term *eglynnyon* in the second line of that passage is clearly the Cornish plural of **eglyn, *englyn,* verse'. All our surviving Middle Cornish poetry has a religious background. It is perhaps interesting, therefore, that the metrical form **eglyn* in this passage in *Bewnans Ke* is associated with a courtly or royal *milieu* and is thus not expressly religious in context.

The term **eglyn* is only one of the correspondencies between Welsh and Cornish in metrical matters. There are others. It is noteworthy, for example, that the line in the Welsh *englyn milwr* is heptasyllabic as is the line of the common Welsh verse-form known as *cywydd.* This basic seven-syllable line is reminiscent of the seven syllables of the Cornish line of verse, seen, for example in *Pascon agan Arluth* and in the *Ordinalia.* The seven syllable line of Welsh and Cornish contrasts remarkably with the dominant line in Breton metrics, which has eight syllables.

In Welsh there are two words for 'poet', *prydydd* and *bardd. Prydydd* is the more elevated term of the two, deriving as it does from a Proto-Celtic form **k^{w}rutiyo-* 'maker, shaper'. *Bardd* on the other hand is identical with *barth* 'mime or jester' in OCV. Breton uses *barzh* exclusively for 'poet.' The Welsh term *prydydd* has its exact congener in Old Cornish *pridit* 'poeta' [poet]. It seems, moreover, that the word survived into the Middle Cornish period, since in *Bewnans Ke* a messenger addresses a Roman senator thus:

> *Beal syr du don vous bon ior,*
> *movn senior an **prydyth** mort* (BK 2496-97).

I take *an prydyth mort* here to be for *re'n prydyth mort* 'by the dead poet', a reference to Virgil, who was greatly revered in the Middle Ages. I would translate the whole: 'Fair sir, God give you good day, my lord, by the dead poet.' It would seem, then, that *prydyth* 'poet' was still known by the author of *Bewnans Ke* in the middle of the fifteenth century. I take it that *prydydd ~ prydyth* 'poet' was again part of the common inheritance of Welsh and Cornish.

The original form of Lhuyd's *englyn*

It seems that the version cited by Lhuyd in *Archæologia Britannica* is the most archaic and probably therefore the most authentic of the three variants of the *englyn*. Since I believe that the *englyn* is in origin early Middle Cornish, I will respell it in a more traditional orthography:

> *An lavar coth yw lavar gwyr,*
> *byth dorn re ver the'n tavas re hyr;*
> *mes den hep davas a gollas y dyr.*

It is unmistakable that in the second line here the verb *byth* (Lhuyd's *Bedh*) is without preverbal particle. The absence of particle is a distinctive feature of Welsh gnomic poetry of this kind. Compare, for example, from the *Bidiau:*

> *Bit wenn gwylan, bit vann tonn;*
> *bit hyuagyl gwyar ar onn;*
> *bit lwyt rew; bit lew callonn*

> 'A gull is wont to be white, a wave is wont to be weak,
> blood is easily spattered upon a spear-shaft;
> frost is wont to be hoar; a heart is often broken' (EWGP: 34).

I would therefore suggest that the middle line of the Cornish may originally have read: **byth dorn re ver, byth tavas re hyr* 'a hand is wont to be too long; a tongue is wont to be too short'. I would tentatively reconstitute the whole *englyn* as follows:

> *An lavar coth yw lavar gwyr:*
> *byth dorn re ver, byth tavas re hyr;*
> *mes den hep davas a gollas y dyr.*

Here the syllabic count is 8, 8 and 10.

In two of our three examples of the stanza *hep* 'without' in the third line lenites the initial consonant of *tavas* 'tongue'. In the Middle Cornish texts *hep* lenites only *d* and *g* and even then only sporadically, for example, *hep thout* 'without doubt' OM 2668, *hep thanger* 'without hesitation' OM 1615, *hep wow* 'without a lie' OM 659, 2496, *hep worfen* 'without end' PC 1562. If the lenition in *hep davas* is authentic, the *englyn* quite possibly dates from a period when *hep* also lenited initial *t*. The phrase *hep davas* may thus be a further indication of the early date of the stanza.

The *englyn* must date from the Middle Cornish period, however, as can be seen from the internal rhyme between *davas* and *gollas*. The word for 'tongue' in Old Cornish was *tauot*, a form which would not have given rhyme with *collas* 'he lost'.

It is just possible, I think, that the final line represents a reshaping of the original syntax. Just as *byth* (Lhuyd's *bedh*) survives without preverbal particle in the second line, it may be that the verb in the last line stood originally at the head of its clause without particle. In which case the *englyn* may originally have been something like the following:

> *An lavar coth yw lavar gwyr:*
> *byth dorn re ver, byth tavas re hyr;*
> *mes collas den hep davas y dyr.*

If this version is correct, we have repetition in the first two lines: *lavar* x 2, *dorn* x 2; internal rhyme *collas* ~ *davas* and alliteration in *den : davas : dyr*.

The expression *kelly tyr* or *kelly y dyr* does not mean 'lose one's territory', but rather 'lose ground', 'fall back' or 'lose one's opportunity'. The poet is contrasting the disadvantage of too long a tongue when work is to be done with the advantage of being able to speak up for one's rights. I should translate the whole as follows: 'The old saying is a true saying: the hand is too short, the tongue is too long—but a man without speech lost his chance.'

A second Cornish *englyn*

Pryce prints what is probably a second *englyn* of the same kind as follows:

> *Po rez deberra an bez, vidn heerath a seu; po res dal an vor, na oren pan a tu,*
> *Thuryan, houl Zethas, go Gleth, po Dihow*

This he translates:

> 'When thou comest into the world, length of sorrow follows; when thou beginnest the way, 'tis not known which side, East, West, to the North or South' (ACB: E e 4 *verso*).

Notice also that Pryce prints the whole as continuous text, apparently not realizing that it was a three-line stanza. This in itself is no bad thing, because it is clear that Pryce has printed the item as he heard it, and has in consequence not edited it to any great degree. I would divide Pryce's text into lines as follows:

> *Po rez deberra an bez, vidn heerath a seu;*
> *po res dal an vor, na oren pan a tu,*
> *Thuryan, houl Zethas, go Gleth, po Dihow.*

The original language of this *englyn* is unmistakably archaic. It is noteworthy, for example, that the word *houlzethas* is known otherwise only from Lhuyd, who gives C[ornish] *Houlzedhas* s.v *Occasus* 'Sunsetting; the West' (AB: 104c). Usually in Cornish, however, the word for 'west' is *west:*

> *Yma oma yn penwyth nebes a **weyst** the carnebre vn pronter ov cuthel guyth* 'There is here in Penwith a little to the west of Carnbrea a priest doing work' BM 783-85
> *Eugh thymo bys yn cambron a **west** the carnbre dyson* 'Go for me to Camborne west of Carnbrea indeed' BM 965-66
> *Pan nowothou, pan guestlow us genough why a'n cost **west**?* 'What news, what pledges have you from the west coast?' BK 2222-23
> *en pedden **West** pow Densher* 'in the western part of Devonshire' BF: 27.

Here, however, it is certainly used to mean 'west' rather than 'sunset'. The usual word for 'north' in Cornish is *north:*

> ***North** yst then chapel omma me a vyn mos the guandra* 'North-east of the chapel here I will go and wander' BM 664-65
> *golsowugh orth iubyter agis tassens a'n berth **north*** 'hearken unto Jupiter, your patron saint from the north' BM 2327-28
> *agen tassens an barth **north** re roys thynny pur guir y venedycconn* 'our patron saint from the north has given us his blessing' BM 3427-29
> *Ke souyth ha **north*** 'Go south and north' BK 2350.

Gogleth 'north' is otherwise unknown, though it may occur in the toponym *Vounder Gogglas* (CPNE: 106). Its use here is unusual and probably archaic.

Dihow, dyhow in Middle Cornish invariably means 'right hand, right side' rather than 'south', for example in the following:

> *yn nef y fe3aff tregis an barth **dyghow** gans am car* 'in heaven I shall dwell on the right hand of my Father' PA 93c
> *An lader an barth **dyghow*** 'The robber on the right hand' PA 193a

gvlan ef re gollas an plas a'm lef **thyghyow** *a wrussen th'y wythe a'n geffo graas* 'he has quite lost the place I should have made on my right side to keep him had he had grace' OM 420-22

theragoff sur disquethys ys guelys cleth ha **dyov** 'displayed before me indeed I saw them left and right' BM 1849-50

A rag oll an golyov a thuk crist cleth ha **dyov** *the vap den rag saluasconn* 'Ah, for all the wounds which Christ bore left and right for the salvation of mankind' BM 3049-51.

The only place known to me in which the word *dyhow* means 'south' is in the Old Cornish compound *dehoules* 'abrotanum' [southernwood].

The Cornish word *Thuryan* 'east' (cf. Welsh *dwyrain)* is otherwise unknown, since the usual word for' east' is *yst, est:*

gwyth yn hans compas tha **yest** 'keep yonder straight to the east' CW 1743

a reege doaze teeze veer thor an **Est** *tha Jerusalem* 'there came wise men from the east to Jerusalem' ÉCII: 194

ha pel da **East** *ev a Travaliaz* 'and far to the east he journeyed' BF: 15

Wor duath Gra Guenz Noor **East** *wetha pell* 'At last let the north-east wind blow afar' BF: 43.

From the point of view of vocabulary at least this *englyn* would thus seem to be very archaic.

It is also apparent that the stanza as it stands is corrupt. Pryce takes *vidn heerath a seu* to mean 'length of sorrow follows'. *Vidn* is a pre-occluded form of *vin, vyn* 'will' used to express the future, but *vyn* is so used with a verbal noun. Here the verb is *a seu* 'which follows' and is finite. I understand the phrase *vidn heerath a seu* to be a corruption of an earlier **pyn hyr a'th sew* 'long sorrow will follow thee'. The beginning of both the first and the second line is *po res < pan wres* 'when thou wilt'. *Gwres* 'thou dost' for *gwreth* is a late form, being first attested in the *Creation qf the World* (1611):

ganso pan **wres** *comparya* 'when thou dost compare with him' CW 160

pan **wres** *ortha vy settya* 'when thou dost attack me' CW 214

na **wres** *na* **wres**, *na barth dowte* 'thou shalt not, thou shalt not, fear not' CW 218-19

orthaf vy pan **wres** *settya* 'since thou dost attack me' CW 232

mara **gwrees** *ow dyskevera* 'if thou dost expose me' CW 577.

It is, I think, unlikely that *gwres* stood in the orignal *englyn*. It is also highly improbable that in such a terse verse form two lines would have begun in the same way. It is more likely, I think, that in one case at least *po res/po rez* is for **pan vo res* 'when it may be necessary'.

Pryce translates *pan rez dal an vor* as 'when thou beginnest the way', but it seems possible that this is a mistranslation, where *dal* has been understood as though for **dalleth*. I suggest that *dal* may be the verb < **dalgh* 'keep, hold to', not otherwise attested. **Dal* < **dalgh* would be exactly parallel with Welsh *dal*, *dala* 'keep, hold' < **dalg*. Compare also the Breton verb *derc'hel* 'to hold, resist', verbal adjective *dalc'het;* and also the lexicalized imperative *dal* 'tiens!, prends!' Although the verb **dal(gh)* is not otherwise attested in Cornish, the noun *dalhen* 'grasp' occurs in *syttyough dalhen scon ynno* 'seize (*literally* set a grasp in) him straightway' PC 976; and the verb *dalhenna* 'to grasp' occurs in *me a'n dalhen fest yn tyn* 'I will hold him very firmly' PC 1131. A Cornish verb **dalgh* would quite regularly have given **dal* in the same way that **calgh* 'penis' (cf. Breton *kalc'h* 'penis') has given *kal*, for example in *Komero 'vyth goz Kal* 'Take care of your cock' (BF: 58).

Pryce translates *Na oren pana tu* as 'tis not known' which side'. This is not strictly accurate; *na oren* must be for **na woryn* < *ny woryn* 'we know not', a late analogical form of *ny wothyn* 'we know not'; cf. *ny woryn pyscotter* 'we do not know how soon' TH 6a. Given that *na woryn* for *na wothyn* is late, the original verb here was probably not *oren* (*woryn* < *wothyn*), but perhaps a phrase that looked and sounded superficially similar. I should suggest that instead of *na oren*, the *englyn* may have read *na fors* 'it matters not', which would originally have alliterated with *forth* 'road'. I would also suggest that *pan a tu* < *py ehen a tu* is a later corruption of an earlier *py du* 'which side'. I would tentatively reconstruct the original *englyn* as something like the following:

Pub dybarth y'n bys pyn hyr a'th sew
pan vo res dal forth na fors py du,
duryan, howlsethas, gogleth po dyhow.

If we rearrange the four points of the compass in the third line we get:

Pub dybarth y'n bys pyn hyr a'th sew
pan vo res dal forth na fors py du,
howlsethas, gogleth, duryan po dyhow.

Here there is internal rhyme with *howlsethas* ~ *gogleth* and alliteration with *duryan : dyhow*. The rhyme *sew* 'follows' ~ *du* 'side' is reminiscent of such rhymes as *a's pew* 'owns' ~ *a'y tu* 'on his side' PC 2858 & 2859 or *dew* 'God' ~ *tew* 'side' CW 138 & 139 and *tew* 'side' ~ *bew* 'alive' CW 1256 & 1258. The rhyme of *dyhow* with *sew* and *du* has no parallel elsewhere. It is certain that *sew* and *du* have the same diphthong, i.e. [iʊ]. It may be that *dyhow* is to be pronounced with a triphthong [dioʊ], which was considered close enough to rhyme with *sew* and *du*. If so, we get three lines each with nine syllables. The simplest method for dealing with the awkward third line, however, is probably to omit *po* 'or' before *dyhow* 'south.' That would give us:

Pub dybarth y'n bys pyn hyr a'th sew
pan vo res dal forth na fors py du,
howlsethas, gogleth, duryan, dyhow.

Here each line has nine syllables, and the final segment of *dyhow* [oʊ] may be considered an adequate rhyme for *sew* [siʊ] and *du* [diʊ]. I should translate:

'In every quarter of the world long tribulation will follow thee,
when thou must hold to the road no matter which way,
west, north, east, south.'

This *englyn*, like the first one we have discussed, is gnomic. It deals with the necessity of suffering in the world, whichever way one is compelled to travel. Its subject matter is similar to that of Lhuyd's *englyn* and it is equally archaic. Indeed it is even possible that both *englynion* come from the same collection of stanzas.

A second Cornish *englyn*
Pryce cites a third stanza as follows:

Hithow gwra gen skîans da:
An gwîranath ew an gwella,
En pob tra, trea, po pella (ACB: F f 4).

This he translates:

Act to-day with prudence good:
The truth is the best,
In every thing, at home, or far off.

Pryce implies that the *englyn* derives from William Gwavas. It is noteworthy, moreover, that a version of the second and third lines occurs in a stanza also by Gwavas, also quoted by Pryce, which deals with the verdict given by the jury in the case of Gwavas *v.* Kelynack (1728):

Pengelly Broaz, ha dowthack tîz,
Rag pusgaz dêk angy roz brez:
Fraga? Gwiranath yw an gwella
En pob tra trea po pella.
Ha nessa, Hale têg gen lavar fyr,
Ol poble gwrêz dho adzhan gwîr;
Hellier tubm e helfias reb pul:
Comyns skîentek vye glan ol (ACB: F f 3 *verso*).

Kent and Saunders translate as follows:

> Great Pengelly and twelve men
> for fish tithe gave the word;
> Why? Truth is best
> in everything at home and far away.
> And next, fair Hale with a wise saying
> Help all people to know the truth,
> A warm hunter chased by a pool:
> Learned Comyns was all clean (LAM: 245)

That Gwavas uses two lines from the *englyn* in a second stanza seems to indicate that the *englyn* itself was proverbial, rather than an original composition of his own. Moreover the syntax of the two lines is rather better than in much of the verse ascribed to Gwavas. I suspect, therefore, that he was not the author of the *englyn* nor of the two lines quoted from it in the stanza about the verdict. It is more likely, I think, that Gwavas had heard or read the *englyn* somewhere and not only wrote it out but also quoted part of it in one of his own compositions. If so, the original *englyn* was almost certainly in existence before the eighteenth century.

If we look at the 'Gwavas *englyn*' a little more closely, we notice that there are only six syllables in the first line. I suspect that the word *skians* was originally *conscyans* 'conscience'. If we assume that the *englyn* was older than the early eighteenth century and was in proverbial use, it is likely that it dates ultimately from the Middle Cornish period. I would therefore respell it in a more traditional orthography as follows:

> *Hethyw gwra gans conscyans da;*
> *an gwyryoneth yw an gwella*
> *yn pup tra tre bo pella.*

I would translate:

> Act today with a good conscience;
> the truth is the best
> in all things at home or abroad.

Although it may well have been medieval in origin, there is nothing in the *englyn* to suggest unequivocally that it is from early Middle Cornish period. It should be noted, however, that there is alliteration between *gwyryoneth* and *gwella* in the second line and between *tra* and *tre* in the third. This relatively high degree of metrical ornament may mean that this third, rather unproblematic *englyn*, is from the same period as the other two we have been discussing.

Englynion composed by Lhuyd and John Boson

Although Lhuyd himself tells us that the *englyn* beginning *An lavar coth yw lavar gwyr* was the only one he heard in Cornwall, it is possible, though perhaps unlikely, that Lhuyd had seen or read others in manuscript while he was there. It appears that he believed a series of *englynion* to be a natural enough metrical form in Cornish, since his lament for William III in 1703 was written in *englyn* metre and contained nineteen three-line *englynion* preceded by a stanza of five lines. Lhuyd prefaces his lament with the words:

> *In Obitum Regis Wilhelmi 3tii Carmen Britannicum Dialectu Cornubiensis:*
> *Ad Normam Poetarum Seculi Sexti*

> On the Death of King William III, a British poem in the Cornish dialect:
> in the manner of the the poets of the sixth century (LAM: 232).

By his allusion to the poets of the sixth century, Lhuyd is perhaps implying that he is imitating the Welsh *cynfeirdd* rather than following any tradition existing in Cornwall.

His lament is interesting in that the syllabic count of the lines is irregular. In the second stanza, for example, the lines have seven, seven and nine syllables:

> *Lavar lemmyn, genz ewhal lêv*
> *Hannadzian down, ha garm krêv;*
> *Golsowez d'ola pen perhen trêv*

> Speak now, with loud voice
> Deep sighs, and strong cry;
> Let the head of every household hear your weeping (LAM: 232).

The tenth stanza, however, has ten, eleven and ten syllables in the line:

> *Sevowh a mann, ha sqwattyow goz dillaz;*
> *Ha gwllow goz bolow genz dowr an lagaz;*
> *Ha gwarrow goz pennow genz lidziw glâz*

> Arise, and scat your clothes,
> And wash your cheeks with the water of the eye;
> And cover your heads with grey ash (LAM: 232).

John Boson seems to have imitated Lhuyd's lament for William III. In a letter to William Gwavas dated 17th February 1712 Boson includes with translation his lament of four stanzas for James Jenkins of Alverton. It is in the same *englyn* metre as Lhuyd's lament. Most of the lines have ten syllables. The first stanza runs as follows:

THE CORNISH *ENGLYN*

En levra coth po vo Tour Babel gwres
Scriffas, Gomar mab Japhet vo en Beas
Ha Dotha Tavas Kornooack vo Res

Att building Babels Tower as Books doe tell
Did Gomer Grandson vnto Noah dwell
To whom the Ancient Cornish Language ffell (BF: 48).

It is noteworthy that the syntax of the whole is less than perfect. The English version would more naturally be rendered in Cornish as follows: *En levra coth po vo Tour Babel gwres/ Dell ew scriffas, yth era Gomer mab Japhet en Beas/ Ha dotha an Tavas Kornooack a vo Res*. The poor standard of John Boson's Cornish has been noted before now (see CT § 14.23). John Boson himself was almost certainly the author of this series of *englynion*.

Concluding remarks

Englynion, similar in form to the Welsh *englyn milwr*, were composed in Middle Cornish and three such *englynion* have survived. Unlike the stricter Welsh *englyn milwr* the Cornish *englyn* could have a varied number of syllables in each line, from seven to ten, or perhaps even eleven. The Cornish *englyn* is certainly related to the Welsh *englyn* and it seems likely that the two are developments of the same British metrical form. The term *englyn* is now attested (in the plural *eglynnyon*) and it is likely that the Cornish word **eglyn* or **englyn* was used for the three-lined stanza we have been discussing.

The metres of the Cornish plays are very strict, where lines of seven and sometimes four syllables are the norm. The variable syllable count of the Cornish *englyn* might suggest one of two things: 1) that the inherited stanza tolerated a variable syllable-count or 2) that the Cornish *englyn* was a popular form, where the exact syllable count was less important than the number of stresses. Given that the two *englynion* beginning *An lavar koth* and *Po rez deberra* are archaic in language, it seems likely that the traditional Cornish *englyn* was not a popular form at all, but a learned and ornate one. We must assume, then, that it could have a variable number of syllables in each line.

The relatively high degree of internal rhyme and alliteration in these two traditional *englynion* suggests that they were the work of specialist poets. The question then arises, who could have composed them? It is fairly certain that *Pascon agan Arluth* and the Cornish mystery plays were composed by educated clerics, many of whom learnt their craft in the college at Glasney. The Cornish *englyn* was probably in origin an aristocratic verse form, practised in the Cornish court before the loss of Cornish independence to the West Saxons in the tenth century. The term *prydyth* 'poet' now attested in *Bewnans Ke*, suggests that the speakers of Middle Cornish were familiar with the notion of professional poets and their poetry. Whether there were any poets in medieval Cornwall who were not also educated clerics is impossible to say with certainty. The absence of an independent royal court and native aristocracy makes it unlikely, in my view, that there were any wholly secular poets in Cornwall in the medieval period. In which case, it seems probable that the *englynion* beginning *An lavar kôth, Po rez deberra* and *Hithow gwrâ* were composed by educated clerics in the early Middle Cornish period.

THE PRETERITE IN CORNISH[8]

The Cornish imperfect

Like the other Celtic languages, Cornish distinguishes an imperfect, or past habitual, tense from a simple past or preterite tense. This distinction in the Celtic languages is sometimes a cause of difficulty for English-speaking learners, because English has only one past tense. Learners sometimes use the less correct tense. The problem is compounded in the case of Cornish by the absence of native speakers and also by the very limited amount of traditional Cornish that survives. It is possible nonetheless by reading the remains of Cornish literature to establish the preferred usage in the language of the two tenses, imperfect and preterite; and thus to decide when and where either of the two tenses is to be used in the revived language.

By far the commonest person in all verbs in all texts in Cornish is the third person singular. In the texts the third person singular of the imperfect in most verbs ends in *-e/-a* or *-y*. The preterite, on the other hand, in most cases ends in either *-as* or *-ys/-is*.

The distinction made in the Cornish texts between the imperfect on the one hand and the preterite on the other is often very revealing. Look at the following lines from *Pascon agan Arluth* for example:

> *I a **wyskis** cryst gans gwyn*
> *avel fol y an **scornye***
> *hag an **gweska** fest yn tyn*
> *betegyns ger ny **gewsy***
> *hag an **hombronkyas** bys yn*
> *pylat o Iustis ʒeʒe*

> [They dressed Christ in white;
> as a fool they mocked him
> and struck him very painfully;
> nonetheless he spoke not a word
> and they led him to
> Pilate, who was their magistrate] PA 114a-c.

It would seem that the simple narrative is rendered by the two preterites *wyskis* 'struck' and *hombronkyas* 'led'. The other three verbs *scornye*, *gweska* and *gewsy* are in the imperfect. We are not dealing here with repeated action, since

8   First published in *Cornish Studies*. Second series: Eighteen. 2010. Exeter: University of Exeter Press. Pp. 179-202. ISBN 0-85989-860-7.

Christ's silence was inaction, but rather with a continuous sense. One might translate the three imperfects loosely as 'they kept on mocking him', 'they kept on striking him' and 'he continued to say not a word.'

Another striking example of the distinction between imperfect and preterite can be seen in the following short passage from Tregear's homilies:

> *Yma S paule ow rebukya in y epistill thyn Corinthians, neb a ve in kythsam case na, ha y a re bostya hag a leuery, EGO PAULI, EGO APOLLO, y thesave ow syngy a Paule, y thesa ve ow singy a Apollo* 'St Paul in his epistle to the Corinthians rebukes them, who were in that very same position, and were boasting and saying, *Ego Pauli, Ego Apollo,* I side with Paul, I side with Apollos' TH 33.

The boasting and declaration of the two factions of the Corinthians were continuous, and appear therefore in the imperfect *y a re bostya* (for *y a wre bostya* 'they did [imperfect] boast'), *a leuery* 'they said'. The Corinthians were in disagreement among themselves when St Paul wrote to them. By Tregear's time, however, the dissension among the Corinthians was well in the past. Tregear therefore says of them *neb a ve in kythsam case na* and puts the verb (*ve*) in the preterite, to indicate that this state of affairs is now finished.

The preterite of *bos* 'to be'

The difference between the imperfect and the preterite is in particular noticeable in the forms of the verb *bos* 'to be'. The third person singular appears in Cornish as *o* (cf. Breton *oa*, Welsh *oedd*) while the third singular of the preterite is *bue, be* (Middle Breton *boe*, Welsh *bu*). An instructive contrast between the use of the two tenses of *bos* can be seen in two separate lines in *Beunans Meriasek*. When Meriasek dies, the archangel Michael in heaven speaking to Christ of St Meriasek says, *ʒiso y fue servont lel* 'to thee he was (preterite) a loyal servant' BM 4339. A little later in the play the bishop of Cornouaille on earth says of Meriasek, *eff o lel servont ihesu* 'he was (imperfect) a loyal servant of Jesus' BM 4379. St Michael's remark implies that Meriasek's earthly task is now finished, he therefore uses the preterite. On earth, however, the bishop's comment is the prelude to a section of the play in which Meriasek's many saintly deeds are recounted. The bishop is referring to the continuous period of Meriasek's earthly life and the saint's many acts of piety. He therefore uses the imperfect. St Michael on the other hand by using the preterite emphasizes that Meriasek's earthly life is complete and that he deserves the bliss of heaven immediately.

The verbal adjective is frequently used together with the verb *bos* 'to be' to render the passive. Here the distinction between the use of the imperfect and the preterite is instructive. The imperfect with the verbal adjective indicates that the action is understood as a continuing state during which something else occurred. The preterite, on the other hand, indicates that the action is thought of as a single event. The imperfect of *bos* followed by the verbal adjective can often, therefore be translated as pluperfect. The preterite with the verbal adjective is a past passive. The imperfect is seen, for example, in *Pan o Ihesus cryst* **dampnys** *aberth yn crows may farwe haccra mernans byth ordnys ʒe creatur ny vye* 'When Christ had been condemned that he should die on the cross, a more dreadful death had never been prescribed for any creature' PA 151a. The preterite in the first person singular occurs in *gorhemmyn dev a terrys dre henna y* **fuf dampnys** *the vos neffre yn yfern* 'I broke the command of God; therefore I was condemned to be forever in hell' RD 212-14. Here the verb is a simple past and therefore the preterite is used.

The same kind of distinction can be seen, for example, in the following two examples from *Pascon agan Arluth*: *han corfow esa ynne a ve yn ban drehevys hag eth poran ʒen cyte gans luas y fons gwelys en gwyr ʒe ʒustvnee bos mab du neb o* **leʒys** 'and the bodies that were in them were raised up and went straight to the city; by many were they seen indeed to testify that it was the Son of God who had been killed' PA 210b-d. In this passage *neb o leʒys* must be translated 'who had been killed' as pluperfect. In the following quotation, however, we have a preterite: *na veʒough dyscomfortis Ihesus crist a nazary del welsough a* **ve lethys** *sevys gallas ʒe gen le* 'do not be dismayed; Jesus Christ of Nazareth who was killed, as you saw, has risen; he has gone to another place' PA 255a-b. Here *a ve lethys* is to be translated as a simple past passive 'was killed'.

The use of the verbal adjective together with the preterite of *bos* 'to be' to render the past passive, is perhaps the commonest use of the preterite in the Cornish texts. The preterite of *bos* has other uses, which I should like to examine below. Two in particular do not seem to have been noticed before. Before describing the various uses of the preterite of *bos*, however, it might we wise to list all the forms of the preterite of *bos* 'to be' as they are found in surviving Cornish literature.

The forms of the preterite of *bos*
I have collected the following forms of the preterite of *bos* 'to be' for all persons:

1sg	1pl
buf, buff, buef, bueff, bef, buma, bema	*buen, ben*
2sg	2pl
bues, bys, busta, beste, besta, bos	*bugh, beugh*
3sg	3pl
bue, be, befe, beva, bee	*bons, bonsy, bowns.*

Periphrastic preterite of *bos* 'to be'
Since the earliest Middle Cornish texts the verb *gul* 'to do' has been used as an auxiliary with other verbs both in the present-future, e.g.,

*drove thy'mmo dysempys ha my a **ra** y **dybry** '*bring it to me immediately and I will eat it' OM 247-48

*ov holan ol the dymmyn rag moreth a **wra terry** '*my heart will break all to pieces for sorrow' OM 357-58

*tus dal eff a **ra sawya** '*he will heal blind people' BM 804.

and in the preterite, e.g.,

*an grows I a **rug gorre** war scoth Ihesus 3y don 3y* 'they put the cross on the shoulder of Jesus to be carried thither' PA 162c

*ef a **wruk** ow **husullye** frut annethy may torren* 'he advised me that I should pluck fruit from it' OM 217-18

*Rag ny ren ny redya in teller vith in scripture fatell **rug du schappya** na **furmya** mabden* 'For we do not read in any other place in scripture that God shaped and formed mankind' TH 2.

In Late Cornish the verb *bos* 'to be' forms its future with *gul* 'to do' as an auxiliary:

*ha why a **ra booze** pocara Deew a cothaz ha ha droag* 'you will be like God knowing good and evil' ÉCII: 176

*Mar pethum Francan-belgan me **ra bose** '*If I have it, I shall be Franco-Belgian' BF: 31

*Why **ra boz** e seera, sarra wheag* 'You will be his father, dear sir' ACB: F f 4 *verso.*

The preterite of *bos* is not normally made with the preterite of *gul*. There is one example, however, and it is not in Late Cornish, but in the homilies of John Tregear:

*Evyn an dewetha nois a **rug eff bos** in company gans y aposteleth therag y virnans* 'Even on the last night that he was in the company of his apostles before his death' TH 51a-52.

As far as I am aware, this is the only attested example of the periphrastic preterite of *bos* 'to be'.

The Uses of the Preterite of *Bos*

I attempt below to classify the uses of the preterite of bos 'to be' according to the sense of the various examples. Some of the instances I give might possibly be classified differently.

A With *re* as a perfect: 'has been, have been'

With the perfective preverbal particle *re* the preterite means 'have been, has been':

> *agan cregy ny yv mall rag ny **re be** laddron dres* 'to hang us is just, for we have been wicked thieves' PA 192d
>
> *bythqueth **re bue** vs geneugh war pask my the ase theugh vn prysner ha'y thelyffre* 'you have always had a custom at Passover for me to grant you a prisoner and to free him' PC 2034-36
>
> *my **re bue** war ow ene ovth emloth mayth en pur squyth vskys na yllyn ponye* 'I have been fighting upon my soul so that I was very tired; I could not run fast' PC 2508-10
>
> *me **re bue** peghadoras a peghas marthys yn fras* 'I have been a sinful woman who sinned remarkably greatly' RD 1097-98a
>
> *me **re bue** ree cruel orth crustunyan me a greys* 'I have been too cruel against Christians, I believe' BM 1364-65
>
> *Maria kemer the flogh maria **re buff** re logh in the gever sav mercy y raff pesy* 'Mary, take thy child; Mary I have been too slack in thy regard, but I beg for mercy' BM 3796-800.

This usage with perfective *re* is still attested in *Beunans Meriasek* (1504) but is wholly absent from Tregear's homilies and *Sacrament an Alter* of the second half of the sixteenth century.

B As a perfect without *re*

The perfective particle *re* is omitted after the negative particles *ny* and *na*. It is also omitted after *py*, *ple* 'where?' and some other conjunctions:

> *pedyr te am nagh tergweth bythqueth arluth na **vef** 3ys* 'Peter, you will thrice deny me; never have I been your lord' PA 49c
>
> *In meth an lader arall drok 3en os kepar del **ves** ny 3owtyth du* 'The other thief said: Evil man as you have been, you do not fear God' PA 192ab
>
> *Abel pe **feste** mar bel* 'Abel, where have you been for so long?' OM 467
>
> *py vr **fuf** vy y wythes* 'When have I ever been his guardian?' OM 576
>
> *ny **fuf** den thotho bythqueth* 'I have never been a comrade of his' PC 1238
>
> *creator a brys benen yn yfarn na **feugh** gynen fatel thutheugh why omma* 'O creature from the womb of woman, never have you been with us in hell; how did you come here?' RD 191-93
>
> *ty creator bynyges fattel thuthte gy the'n cres na **fues** gynen yn yfarn* 'you blessed creature, how did you come to peace? You have not been with us in hell' RD 259-61
>
> *a thev ysse **fuef** goky pa na vynnan vy crygy* 'O God, how foolish I have been in that I would not believe' RD 1565-66

a pur harloth ple fugh why 'you utter rogues, where have you been?' RD 2243

ny vef yn scole rum levte bys ynnewer gorʒewar 'Upon my word until last night I have never been in school' BM 102

Bythqueth ny ve thewhy parow 'Never has there been your equal' BK 1256-57

Py fys abarth Marya? 'For Mary's sake, where have you been?' BK 1368

a das kear ny won for thy na ny vef bythqwath ena 'dear father, I do not know the way thither nor have I ever been there' CW 1738-39.

C The preterite as a simple past

The preterite is also used (the positive forms without *re*) to describe something that is in the past. We saw this use in the example cited above from the archangel Michael's speech in *Beunans Meriasek* (BM 4339). Here are some further examples:

lauar thy'mmo ty venen an frut ple russys tyrry mara pe a'n keth eghen o dyfynnys orthyn ny 'tell me, woman, where did you pluck the fruit? If it was from the same kind as had been forbidden to us' OM 209-12

mar pue drok a oberys trogh yhy gans the glethe 'if what I did was wrong, hack her with your sword' OM 291-92

abarth ow thas bynyges th'y thyller arte glenes kepar del ve 'in the name of my blessed father let it adhere to its place again exactly as it was' PC 1152-54

gans ihesu a nazare yn certan a fue trygys 'assuredly he resided with Jesus of Nazareth' PC 1278-79

lyes guyth y wruk bostye thy'so gy del lauara terry the'n dor an temple yn try geth y wul arta maga ta bythqueth del fue 'many times he boasted, as I tell you, of breaking down the temple; in three days of building it again as good as it was' PC 2439-43

thomas lemmyn gueyt crygy an arluth the thasserghy rak omma y fue gynen 'Thomas, now be sure to believe that the lord has arisen, since he was here with us' RD 1345-47

an emperour ef [a] sawse maga tek bythqueth del fue kyn fe y cleues mar bras 'it would heal the emperor as whole as ever he was, though his disease be never so severe' RD 1658-60

ef a fue drok corf yn bys 'he was an evil person in the world' RD 2228

ow stons a fue crous a pren kyns en myghtern den ha dev 'my resting place was a cross of wood, before I was a king, man and God' RD 2579-80

He me yv sawys pur dek neb a fue sur efrethek lues blethen in bysma 'And I am cured very nicely who was a crippled for many years in this world' BM 563-65 *govy na* **vuma** *war kyns hager dyweth yv helma* 'Alas that I was not careful before now! This is a nasty death' BM 4099-100

Dal y **fueff** *lues blythen* 'I was blind for many years' BM 4393

thegen heveleb ny eff a rug Eva an kynsa benyn bethqueth a **ve** 'he created Eve in our likeness, the first woman who ever was' TH 2a

Yma S paule ow rebukya in y epistill thyn Corinthians, neb a **ve** *in kythsam case na* 'St Paul in his epistle to the Corinithins rebukes them, who were in that very same position' TH 33

eff a **ve** *promysiis thethans y ha thega successors neb a* **ve***, neb ew, ha neb a vith in egglos* 'he was promised to them and to their successors, who were, who are and who will be in the church' TH 36a

Origine o mablyan bras, ha eff a **ve** *agy the cc blethan wosa crist* 'Origen was a great theologian, and he lived within 200 years after Christ' TH 45

lemmen te a wele an Crefter a gere Christ o conys, the changia pith ny **ve** *derag dorn* 'now you see the power of the word of Christ working to change that which did not exist previously' SA 62

Lowena thu'm gwelha gour a **ve** *bythquath a Gurnow* 'Joy to my best hero who ever was from Cornwall' BK 1914-15

Lowena thu'm arluth stowt, gallosak drys suel a **ve***!* 'Joy to my stalwart lord, powerful beyond all who ever were!' BK 2546-47

par dell **vema** *vngrasshes lemyn yth oma plagys* 'as I was graceless, now am I plagued' CW 1575-76

Ha e **ve** *enne terebah mernaz Herod* 'And he was there until Herod's death' ÉCII: 198.

Two of the examples above are from the if-clause of a conditional sentence in past time. Some of the others could no doubt also be classified under B as perfects.

D With the sense 'took place, happened, occurred'

The preterite is used to describe a single event or happening. In many cases below the preterite can be translated 'occurred, happened, happened to be':

A[n] peynys a wotheuys ny **ve** *ragtho y honan lemmyn rag pobyll an bys* 'The pains he suffered did not happen for his own benefit but for the people of the world' PA 6ab

yn er na y **fe** *dorgis ha dris ol an bys ef eth* 'then there happened an earthquake and it went through all the world' PA 200b

ragh y **fue** *kyns y vos gurys dew vgens blythen ha whe* 'since, before it was completed, forty six years occurred' PC 350-51

y **fue** *gynen arluth nef ha worthy'n ol a geusys* 'the lord of heaven happened to be with us and he spoke to us all' RD 1229-30

in nos y a **fue** *gena* 'they happened to be with me in the night' BM 1813 *kyn nag esogh why ow consyddra an plag a behosow athewethas in kith scisme a ve in agan mysk ny* 'though you are not considering the plague of sins recently in the same schism which happened in our midst' TH 40a

Ith esaff ow supposya na ve va heb cowse bras an ii the suffra in vn dith, in vn tyller, ha in dan vn persecutor 'I suppose that it did not happen without great cause that the two suffered in one day, in one place and under one persecutor' TH 47

Ow lester a ve lehan drys mor pour thown 'My vessel across the very deep sea happened to be a slab of rock' BK 94-5.

E With the adjective *marow* 'dead' with the sense 'died'

In Cornish *gul marow, guthyl marow*, literally 'to make dead' is sometimes used instead of *latha* 'to kill'. All my examples come from the same text, *Resurrexio Domini*:

*reys yv thy'm agy the lyst emloth worth an antecryst hag ef thu'm **gruthyl marow*** 'I have to fight in the lists against the Antichrist and he has to kill me' RD 223-25

*cryst a fue dre galarow yn grous pren **gurys** pur **varow*** 'Christ was by torment killed utterly upon the cross' RD 962-63

*hag a'n **gruk** ef scon **marow*** 'and quickly killed him' RD1120

*woge y vos **gurys marow** tus yn beth a'n anclethyas* 'after he was killed, people buried him in a sepulchre' RD 1268-69

*an keth profus a whylyes **gurys** yv **marow*** 'the very prophet you were seeking has been killed' RD 1680-81.

Just as *guthyl marow* 'to make dead' is used for 'kill', so *bos* 'to be' and *marow* 'dead' are used together in Cornish to mean 'die'. The language also has a verb *merwel* 'to die',

*may halle dre baynys bras **merwel** rag ʒe gerense* 'that he might by great torments die for thy sake' PA 70d

*ihesus dampnyas the vos gorrys yn grous pren hag ynhy ef a **verwys*** 'he condemned Jesus to be hung on the cross and on it he died' RD 1805-07

*Kin **fyrwys** mab Marya, Du mer e ras, abarth dengys, der thowgys e tathorhas* 'Though the son of Mary died, God of great grace, in his humanity, in his divinity he rose again' BK 308-11.

The collocation *bos marow* seems to be more frequent than *merwel* 'to die' and is particularly common in finite tenses. Here are some examples:

ny vennaf onan sparye **marow vethons** *kyns vyttyn* 'I will not spare any
  of them; they will die before morning' OM 1643-44

marow vethyn *kettep pen nynsus scapya thynny* 'we will die, everyone of
  us; there is no escaping for us' OM 1655-56

me a'th pys scryf ow ene pan **vyf marow** *yn the rol* 'I beseech you, write
  my name in your book when I die' PC 421-22

a nef vhel an tas mer re'th ordene ty ha'th wrek pan **vy marow** *yn y cver*
  'may the great father of heaven welcome you to his court when you
  die' PC 684-86

my re thysyryas fest mer dybry genogh why haneth boys pask kyns ov **bos
  marow** 'I have greatly desired to eat the Paschal lamb with you
  tonight before I die' PC 718-20

agan laha ef yma pup vr ow contradye may coth thotho yn tor'ma **bones
  marow** *hep lettye* 'he is continually opposing our law, so that he
  should now die without delay' PC 2425-28

bys may hallo bos iuggys ha dre lagha bos dampnys the **vos marow** 'so that
  he may be judged and condemned by law to die' RD 1980-82

y a **veth** *purguir* **marov** *rag cafus sur age goys* 'they indeed will die so that
  their blood may be obtained' BM 1598-99

why a **feth** *purguir* **marov** *maras ywe dyenkys* 'you will die if he has
  escaped' BM 3731-32

an iovle agis acectour rebo pan **vowhy marrov** *mar quregh fynsya* 'may the
  devil be your attendant when you die' BM 3523-25

bethen marov *gans flam tan mes ay ganov* 'we will die by the flame of fire
  from her mouth' BM 3945-46

Me a lever thys, Modres, keffrys te ha'n viternas in ol hast a **vith marow** 'I
  tell you, Modred, both you and your queen will die very soon
  indeed' BK 3179-81.

The author of *Origo Mundi* writes *ty a verow sur cowal* 'you will surely die'
OM 2737 and *marrow cowal ty a vyth* 'you will die utterly' OM 2072. There
appears to be complete semantic equivalence between the two lines. The
equivalence is also apparent in *Gwrens e drubut ha'y sute, rag bos maraw bo bewa*
'Let him make his tribute and his suite, to die or to live' BK 1849-50, where
there a contrast is being made between *bewa* 'to live' and *bos maraw* 'to be
dead/to die'. There can be no doubt, therefore, that *bos marow* was thought to
be the semantic equivalent of *merwel* 'to die'.

The preterite of *bos* 'to be' followed by *marow* 'dead', i.e *y fue marow* or *a ve
marow* is not uncommon in the texts and clearly best translated 'died.' I have
collected the following examples:

yn growys gans kentrow fastis peynys bys pan **ve marow** 'fastened to the
  cross by nails, tortured until he died' PA 2d

ellas a vap myghtern y'th tron ellas gueles tol y'th colon **marow** *na vef* 'alas, O son, king upon your throne! To see a gash in your heart, alas that I did not die!' PC 3169-71

out govy na **vuff marov** *kyns doys a dor ov dama* 'Alas, woe is me that I did not die before I came forth from my mother's womb!' BM 795-96

ihesu crist map maria ha genys a lel werheys a **fue marov** *in grovs pren* 'Jesus Christ, son of Mary and born of a pure virgin, who died on the cross' BM 4047-49

In hanov map maria ihesu crist yth yv henna a **fue marov** *anclethyys* 'In the name of the son of Mary, Jesus Christ this is, who died, was buried' BM 4080-82.

Y fue marow is exactly comparable with Welsh *bu farw*, the ordinary way of saying 'died'. There is also in Welsh a preterite form *marwodd* 'died', the equivalent of Cornish *merwys* 'died', the preterite of *merwel*. The parallel between Welsh *bu farw* and Cornish *y fue marow* has not, as far as I am aware, ever been alluded to in print. Interestingly, early Irish uses the copula with *marb* 'dead' to mean 'die' (see DIL s.v. *marb* c.). We thus have Cornish *y fue marow* ' died', Welsh *bu farw* 'died and early Irish *ba marb* 'died.' We are clearly dealing here with a common Insular Celtic syntagm.

F With the verbal adjective to render the past passive
Cornish verbs possess autonomous or impersonal forms, which are passive in sense. The agent, however, is never expressed when the autonomous verb is used. The autonomous verb is for the most part found in the present-future. Moreover, it becomes increasingly rare in the texts, and by the time of John Tregear's homilies (mid-sixteenth century), it seems to have disappeared completely, having been replaced by the verb *bos* 'to be' + the verbal adjective. It is noteworthy for example that the opening line of *Origo Mundi* (probably early fifteenth century) is *En tas a nef* **y'm gylwyr** 'I am called the father of heaven' OM 1, where the verb *y'm gylwyr* is an autonomous form. The first line of *Beunans Meriasek* (1504), however, reads **Me yw gylwys** *duk bryten* 'I am called the Duke of Brittany' BM 1, where the verb is *yw gylwys*, i.e. *yw* the third singular short present of *bos* 'to be' + the verbal adjective *gylwys* 'called'.

The preterite of *bos* is used with the verbal adjective in Cornish to render past passives. This use is by far the commonest occurrence of the preterite of *bos*. Here are a random selection of examples taken from a wide selection of texts:

tergweyth y **fe convyctijs** *evn yw зyn y voleythy* 'three times he was condemned; it is right for us to curse him' PA 18b

te a ve зym **danvenys** 'you were sent to me' PA 101c

may fyth torrow benegis bythqueth na allas e[m]зon han benenas kekyffrys na ve зeзe **denys** *bron* 'when wombs will be blessed that never could bear children and women also whose breasts were never sucked' PA 169cd

*a'n oyl a versy o dythywys thy'mmo vy gans an tas a'y dregereth pan **vef** chacys gans an el* 'about the oil of mercy which had been promised to me by the Father in his mercy when I was expelled by the angel' OM 703-07

*guyn y vys pan **ve gynys** a allo gul thy's servys* 'happy the man when he was born who may do you service' OM 1476-77

*ogh govy pan **vef genys** gans moreth yth of lynwys* 'Oh, alas that I was born; I am filled with sorrow' OM 2193-94

*lauar thy'm del y'm kerry pan vernans a'n geve ef ha fetel **vefe lethys*** 'tell me please what death did he meet and how was he killed' OM 2218-20

*tewel auel vn bobba a wruk pan **fue acussys*** 'he was silent like a fool when he was accused' PC 2385-86

*ragof y **fue ordynys** maga whyn auel an leth* 'for me it was got ready as white as milk' PC 3137-78

*fatel **fue** cryst **mertheryys** rak kerenge tus an beys why a welas yn tyen* 'how Christ was martyred for the sake of the people of the earth you have seen in full' PC 3220-22

*ihesu a **fue anclethyys** hag yn beth a ven gorrys* 'Jesus was buried and put into a tomb of stone' RD 1-2

*ennoc sur yth of hynwys the'n plas ma y **fuf rafsys*** 'I am indeed called Enoch; I was transported to this place' RD 197-98

*A gony pan **vuen genys** warbarth ny a veth kellys* 'Oh, alas that we were born; together we shall be lost' BM 605-06

*der henna y **fuff sawys*** 'by that I was saved' BM 2154

*fetel **vusta delyfrys** laver thymo me ath peys* 'how were you delivered, tell me I beg you' BM 3764-65

*megys **vue** gans boys eleth* 'he was sustained by food of angels' BM 4464

*rag an myseri han anken bras a **ven** ny dris ynna dre begh* 'for the misery and the great misfortune into which we were brought by sin' TH 3a

*eff a **ve promysiis** thethans y ha thega successors* 'he was promised to them and to their successors' TH 36a

*An power han auctorite na, kepar dell **ve** va **fuguris** in la goyth thyn ordyr a prontereth, the Judgia lypers* 'that power and that authority, just as it was prefigured in the old law to the order of priests to judge lepers' TH 38a

*na ankevy an mysery a russyn ny oll the suffra thea an termyn may **fen** ny **debyrthys** theworth an egglos a crist* 'nor forget the misery we all suffered when we were separated from the church of Christ' TH 40a

*Alas, pan woys cristonyan a **ve** scoyllys agy thyn wlas ma, dre agan kentravoggyan agan honyn! Pan a lyas gwethfas a **ve gesys** heb confort! pan lyas flogh omthevas a **ve gesys** heb confort na succur!* 'Alas, what

41

blood of Christians has been shed within this realm, by our own neighbours! How many widows have been left without comfort! How many orphan children have been left without comfort or succour!' TH 40a

pan lyas testament ha blonogath an marow a **ve** *tyrrys ha* **gesys** *heb colynwall gans intentys ha ordynans anethe!* 'How many testaments and wills of the dead were broken and left unfulfilled with their intentions and ordinances!' TH 40a

pan a abbys a **ve twolys** *thyn dore, pan a colyges, pan a chauntreys, a* **ve towlys** *then dore! Pan egglossyow a* **ve robbys** 'what abbeys have been thrown down, what colleges, what chantries have been thrown down! What churches have been robbed!' TH 40a

Rag y bos an gyrryow pleyn ha symply the vos kemerys kepar dell **vonsy** *kowsys* 'Since the words are plain and to be taken simply as they were spoken' TH 53

Dew a cowsas an ger, ha ny a **ve** *gwris: ha Christ a commandias ha y a* **ve** *creatis* 'God spoke the word and we were made; and Christ commanded and they were created' SA 61a

Gogy pan **ves** *denethys* 'Woe to you that you were born!' BK 67

Gogy vith pan **vos** *genys* 'Woe to you that you were ever born!' BK 424

y **festa** *gwryes te gwase lowse gans dew omma* 'You were made, you vile fellow, by God here' CW 158-59

a thorn dew y **festa** *gwryes ynweth ganso exaltys* 'by the hand of God you were made and also exalted by him' CW 309-10

gans an Jowle y **fowns** *tulles* 'by the Devil they were deceived' CW 1003

me a servyas pell an beyse aban **vema** *kyns formys* 'I served the world for long ever since I was created' CW 1974-75

Ha lagagow angie **ve** *gerres* 'And their eyes were opened' ÉCII: 177

Nena a **ve** *Jesus humbregez abera tha wilderness tha voaze temptez gan an Joule* 'Then Jesus was led into the wilderness to be tempted by the Devil' ÉCII: 185

Pe reeg Herod an matern clowaz hemma, e **ve** *troublez ha oll Jerusalem gonz eve* 'When Herod the king heard that, he was troubled and all Jerusalem with him' ÉCII: 194.

G The preterite of *bos* with the sense 'had'

A unique feature of Cornish is that the verb *bos* 'to be' can have the sense 'have, has'. This sense is in origin a development of the Cornish verb *y'm bus* 'I have'. *Y'm bus* consists of three elements, an initial verbal particle, an infixed personal pronoun with dative sense and the relevant part of the verb 'to be.' *Y'm bus* therefore can be analysed as 'to me there is > I have', and is the same in origin as the Middle Breton verb *em eux, em eus*, Modern Breton *em eus*.

In the second person singular the infixed pronoun is *'th* which mutates an initial *b* to *f* or *v*, but the *'th* itself is then lost. Thus the second person singular of the future of *y'm bus* is in origin **ty a'th fyth* but appears as *ty a fyth* or *ty a vyth*. This is identical with *ty a vyth* 'thou shalt be':

> *ha kymmys yn bys vs vas yn meth an ioul **te a feth** '*and as much as is good in the world, said the devil, thou shalt have' PA 16c
> *bonyl **ty a feth** edrek* 'or thou shalt have regret' BM 409
> *Ty **a vith** gu* 'thou shalt have woe' BK 326
> *ha te **a vith** ef heb mar* 'and thou shalt have it without doubt' BK 1077.

As soon the expression *ty a vyth* 'thou shalt be' was understood also to mean 'thou shalt have', all finite forms of *bos* with initial *b-* could by analogy be used with this possessive sense. Here are some examples of various parts of the verb *bos* 'to be' demonstrating this possessive meaning:

> *In meth Ihesus yn vr na mestry vyth **te ny vea** '*Said Jesus, Then you would not have any authority' PA 145a
> *annethe kyn **feste** calge war na ra fethye inne* 'although you may have much of them, be careful that you do not trust in them' BM 2046-48
> *Rag mar tewgh why ha cara an re vsy worth agys cara why, pana rewarde a **vethow** why?* For if you love those who love you, what reward will you have?' TH 22
> *me a levar thys mar pleag yn pan vanar yn **bema** 'I* will tell you, if you wish, how I came to have it' CW 755-56
> *mar **pethama** kibmiez tho gweel Semblanz 'gun Aulsen Coth Brose* 'if I have permission to make comparison with great old Ausonius' BF: 29.

The preterite of *bos* is found with possesive sense, as in the following examples:

> *confortys yv ow colon pan clewys ow teryfas bones leghys the pascyon a **fus** tyn garow ha bras* 'comforted is my heart when I heard tell that the passion you had sharp, violent and great has been lessened' RD 503-06
> *ha ny an jeva promes a brassa royow dell **vouns** y* 'and we had the promise of greater gifts than they had' TH 28
> *yth ew desquethis fatell rug pedyr dos the Rome, ha pan a peldar a ruga bewa ena, ha pan deweth ha martirdom a **ve** va in Rome* 'it is shown that St Peter came to Rome, and how long he lived there, and what end and martyrdom he had in Rome' TH 47a
> *Te a **ve** ken tresow* 'You had other customs' BK 3304
> *ha sure me ew an kensa bythqwath whath a **ve** dew wreag* 'and surely I am the first who has ever had two wives' CW 1453-54

*Ve a glowhas tha Leaue en Loohar; ha me a **vee** owne, rag theram en Noath* 'I heard your voice in the garden, and I was afraid, for I am naked' ÉCII: 178.

It is noteworthy in the above quotations that the preterite when it means 'had' can be classified according to the categories described under **B**, **C** and **D** above. Tregear's *promes a brassa royow dell **vouns** y* 'the promise of greater gifts than they had' refers to something now finished. On the other hand *a ve* in *an kensa bythqwath a **ve** dew wreag* 'the first who has ever had two wives' is perfect in sense. Rowe's *ha me a **vee** owne* 'and I was afraid' (literally 'I had fear') is perhaps an example of the preterite with the sense 'happened, occurred', i.e. 'a state of fear came upon me.'

H The preterite of *bos* with the sense 'became'
A feature of earlier Middle Cornish was that if two verbs follow the same subject the second often appears as a verbal noun. This is noticeable in particular with the verb *dos* 'to come' as in the following examples from *Pascon agan Arluth.*

> *Cryst kymmys payn yn geve angus tyn ha galarow ma **teth** an goys **ha dropye** war y fas an caradow* 'Christ had so much pain, anguish and affliction that the blood happened to drop down his face, the beloved' PA 59ab
> *me a glewas leuerell an arlont y ʒe denne war y ben gans kymmys nell ma **teth** an dreyn **ha cropye** ʒen nempynnyon dre an tell* 'I have heard tell that they pulled the garland with such force that the thorns happened to sink into his brain through the holes' PA 134a-c.

Moreover forms of the verb *dos ha* + verbal noun are very common in conditional sentences after the conjunction *mar* 'if', though the connecting *ha* 'and' is on occasion omitted. As in the two quotations from *Pascon agan Arluth* above, I translate *dos* 'to come' as 'happen' in the following examples:

> *mar **tufe ha datherghy** mur a tus [a] wra crygy* 'if he happen and rise again, many people will believe' RD 7-8
> *mara **tuen ha debatya** mas an nyyl party omma ov teberth purguir ny warth* 'if we happen to debate, in very truth only one party here will be laughing on leaving' BM 3476-78
> *Rag **mar teffa** crist **ha dos** in dallath an bys whare whosa mabden the beha* 'For if Christ had happened to come at the beginning of the world, soon after mankind had sinned' TH 13a
> *Mar **te** the brother **ha gull** trespas war the byn* 'If your brother happen to trespass against you' TH 31a

*pandre vynnough leverall mar **tema disquethas** theugh certyn tacclow arall mere moy agis helma* 'what will you say if I happen to show you certain other things much greater than this?' SA 60

*rag mar **tema ha rowtya** ha ferneuwhy ha stowtya, ny vith mab den na'm dowtya* 'for if I happen to swagger and rave, there will be no one who does not fear me' BK 1639-41.

By using set phrases like *mar te ha* and *mar teffa ha*, which contain forms of the auxiliary *dos* with provected initial, speakers were able to leave the verb itself uninflected as a verbal noun. This made forming the protasis of conditional sentences easier for speakers, since neither mutation nor inflection of the main verb was necessary. It is easier to say *mar teu va ha dasserhy* 'if he happen to rise again', for example, than *mar tassergh ef* 'if he rises again.'

Nance was presumably well aware both of *ma teth ha* 'so that it happened to' and *mar te ha* 'if he happens to' and he seems to gone a stage further. He suggests that *dos ha bos* can mean 'become.' Similarly he also proposes that *mos ha bos* 'go and be' can have the same sense (Nance 1952, *s.v.* 'become'). As far as I can see, there is no warrant for either *dos ha bos* 'become' or *mos ha bos* 'become' in the corpus of traditional Cornish. Regrettably, perhaps, these two Nancean locutions for 'become' *dos ha bos* and *mos ha bos* are well established in revived Cornish.

The English word 'become' has two rather different uses. In the first case 'become' means 'changes state.' One can say, for example, 'If you leave the dough too long, it becomes hard', or 'The book I was writing became too long, so I cut three chapters out.' In the first case one might equally well say 'it goes hard' and in the second one could say 'the book got too long'. In cases like these Cornish tends to use various parts of the verb *mos* 'to go', as is clear from the following examples:

*agan corfow noth **gallas*** 'our bodies have become naked' OM 253

*rak hyreth **galsof** pur claf* 'for longing I have become quite unwell' RD 775

*** galsos** lemmyn pur woky rak na fynnyth thy'n crygy a foul thomas* 'you have now become very foolish, for you will not believe, you fool Thomas' RD 1513-15

*me a glew vn hager noyes yn carn yn mor er y byn yma dour **ow mos** garow* 'I hear a terrible noise on the rock in the sea; the water against it is become rough' RD 2296-98

*ellas ellas yth **oma gyllys** leper* 'alas, alas, I have become leprous' BM 1358-59

*pan vegh in henna golhys yth **egh** gvyn avel crystel* 'when you are washed in that, you will become as white as crystal' BM 1520-21

*kynth **os gyllys** feynt ha guan wath ty a veth confortys* 'though you have become faint and weak, yet you shall be comforted' BM 3672-73

Galsaf dal rag golowys 'I have become blind because of the light' BK 487
rag yth ew ef cothe gyllys 'for he has become old' CW 1791.

There is also the curious use of *gallas* 'has gone' in *gallas an porthow brewyon*
'the gates [of hell] have become fragmented' [literally 'gone to pieces'] RD 126.
There is one example in Late Cornish of the verb *cotha* 'to fall' with the sense
'became':

Ha an Weale a Kothaz scant 'And work became scarce' BF: 15

The second use of 'become' in English occurs when a change of state or
status is implied, e.g. 'she agreed at last and became his wife the following
spring' or 'he wanted to be a highwayman but he became a banker instead.' In
Cornish such a change of status can be rendered by the circumlocution *bos
gwres* 'be made'.

An gere, henew an mab a thu, a ve gwrys kyge, henno den 'The word, that
is the son of God, was made flesh, that is, man' TH 15
an bara ew gwres kig agen arluth Christ 'the bread is made the flesh of
our lord Christ' SA 62
hagen saviour Jesus Christ, ew gwreis kigg ha gois, rag sawya ny 'and our
saviour Jesus Christ, is made flesh and blood, to save us' SA 63.

This is similar, of course, to the English expressions 'is made, was made', for
example, 'And was incarnate by the Holy Ghost of the Virgin Mary, and was
made man' in the Nicene Creed.
Bos gwres 'to be made' can also be used to express the first meaning of
'become', i.e. to change state:

*an corfe a ve gwrys gwan, ha drys the vos gustith the lyas kynda a cleves ha
gwannegreth* 'the body became weak and was led to be subject to
many kinds of sickness and weakness' TH 12
*ny a rede fatell ve crist transfiguris, ha fatell rug y face shynya kepar han
howle ha y thillas a ve gwris maga whyn avell an yrth* 'we read that
Christ was transfigured and that his face shone like the sun, and
his clothes became as white as the snow' TH 56a.

We saw at **D** above how the preterite of *bos* is used in Cornish to refer to a
single event in the past. In such cases it can be translated 'happened, occurred.'
It is not astonishing, therefore, that the simplest way of saying 'became', both
of 1) change of quality ('become hard') and 2) change of status ('become
friends, become man'), is by using the preterite of *bos* 'to be'. Here are some
examples from the Cornish texts of both senses:

1)

y fons vnver yn treȝe kepar ha del wovyny xxx a vone yn vn payment y wrens ry 'they became unanimous among themselves that they would give in one payment 30 pieces of money as he was asking' PA 39cd

Han ȝew na bys pan vons squyth war crist y fons ov cronkye 'And those two were striking Christ until they became tired' PA 132a

namna fue ow colon trogh pan wylys gorre an gu yn golon dre'n tenewen 'my heart almost became split when I saw the spear thrust through his side into the heart' RD 1244-46

Ha pe reeg e penes doganze jorna ha doganze noze, e ve ouga nena gwage 'And when he had fasted for forty days, he became thereafter hungry' ÉCII: 185-86.

2)

yn vr na keskeweȝa y a ve ha specyall bras 'at that hour they became friends and specially great ones' PA 110d

Bythqueth ny vue vays in pov aban vys crystyan heb wov 'Never has there been any good in the country since you became a Christian' BM 3968-69

an second person in dryngys du o ymmortall, eff a ve den mortall 'the second person in the Trinity of God was immortal; he became a mortal man' TH 15.

These two uses of the preterite of *bos* to mean both 'became (speaking of a quality)' or 'became (something)' are not dissimilar to the sense 'occurred, happened', which we noted at **D** above. As far as I am aware, none of these uses, 'happened', 'became' (of quality) or 'became' of status, has been noticed hitherto.

Cornish revivalists use the unattested locutions *dos ha bos, mos ha bos* for 'become' for all tenses. Since neither is attested, neither can be described in any sense as traditional. In the revived language at the moment, if one wants to say 'his face went white' in the past, one says, *y fâss a dheuth ha bos gwydn*. For 'he became a doctor' one says *ev a dheuth ha bos medhek*. It would be more traditional and more authentic instead to say in the first case, *y fâss a veu gwrës gwydn* or more simply *y fâss a veu gwydn;* and in the second case, *ev a veu gwrës medhek* or more simply, *ev a veu medhek.*

The preterite of *bod* 'to be' in Welsh

Welsh has the preterite *bûm, buost, bu,* etc. As we have seen Welsh says *bu farw* 'he died' in the same way that Cornish says *y fue marow* or *ef a veu marow* for 'he died'. Moreover the Welsh preterite is used similarly to its counterpart in Cornish. In Welsh the preterite of *bod* is both a perfect and a simple past. It can, moreover, often be translated both 'happened, came to pass' and 'became' (Morris-Jones: 134-35, § 311), exactly as is the case with the Cornish preterite

47

buf, bus, bue. Modern Breton, on the other hand, has lost the preterite of 'to be' entirely, and now uses the imperfect instead (HMSB: 208 note).

In the matter of the preterite of *bos* 'to be' Cornish is far closer to Modern Welsh than it is to Modern Breton. This is another of the ways in which Cornish agrees with Welsh rather than Breton. It was Loth's view that Breton and Cornish were dialects of the same language:

> Les regrets que peut nous causer l'extinction du cornique sont, en partie, atténués par le fait que les deux languaes brittoniques vivantes en seont très voisines, le breton sourtout qui forme avec le cornique deux dialectes voisin d'une même langue. Le cornique moyen était du breton-armoricain pris son son ensemble que le breton de Quiberon ne l'est actuellement de celui de Saint-Pol-de Léon

> [Our regrets at the death of Cornish are to some degree alleviated by the fact that the two living Brythonic languages are very close to it, Breton in particular forming with Cornish such a close linguistic group that we can consider them as two related dialects of the same language. Middle Cornish is without doubt closer to Breton as a whole than the modern Breton dialect of Quiberon is to that of St-Pol-de-Léon] (RC 18: 401-02).

In the light *inter alia* of the uses of the preterite in Cornish, Loth's opinion may possibly need revision.

SOME CORNISH PLURALS[9]

The Cornish dual

In Cornish parts of the body that come in pairs are often referred to by dual forms, consisting of the numeral *deu* (masculine) or *dyw* (feminine) 'two', followed by the root word with lenited initial. Among such duals we can include those of the masculines *tros*, *troys* 'foot', *glyn* 'knee', *lagas* 'eye' and of the feminines *luf* 'hand', *gar* 'leg', *bregh* 'arm', *scoth*, *scoyth* 'shoulder', *scovarn* 'ear' and *bron* 'breast'. The first thing to be noticed is that the feminine form of the numeral, *dyv*, *dyw*, appears largely to fall together with the masculine form *dev*, *deu*, *dew* and is often indistinguishable from it.

This can most clearly be seen in the dual forms of the word *luf* 'hand':

a) *dyvlef* PC 2937; *dyulef* PC 2375; *dyvluef* PC 3174; *dywluef* OM 1346; *dywle* RD 2590; *thyvle* RD 1542; *thywle* PC 3153, RD 1266; *diula* AB: 242b.

b) *devle* PC 474; *dewleff* PA 156c, TH 15a, 21a; *thewleff* PA 149a, TH 8, TH 8a, 46a, 55a; *ʒewleff* PA 178c; *ʒewle* PA 157a, 158b, 204d, 217c, 219b; *dewla* CW 1531.

c) *dule* PC 583, 1216, 2163, 2499, 2516, 2677, RD 2202, BM 1315, 2991, 3135; *dula* BM 2603; *dula* AB: 86a; *doola* ÉCII: 187; *thulef* PC 2697; *thule* PC 2733, 2740, 2922, 2985.

d) *dowla* SA 60, 60a, 61 x2, 66; *thowla* SA 65.

Nance himself admits that the two forms fall together, when he says 'the texts confuse *deu*-, m. with *dyw*-, f.' (1938: 39). Notice that the forms from SA cited above exhibit the same *dow*- prefix as examples of *dowlyn*, *dowlin* 'knees' cited below. The feminine prefix *dyw*- would not have developed as *dow*-, but the masculine form *dew*- would. The form ‹diwla› is favoured by some revivalists, although it is wholly without warrant in the traditional texts. The nearest form to it is Lhuyd's *diula* (where there is a point under the *u*).

The plural replacing the dual

It is also remarkable how poorly attested many of such duals are. Apart from *dywlef*/*dewla*, *dewlagas* 'eyes', *dewlyn*/*dowlyn* 'knees' which are well attested (see below), the Cornish duals are relatively uncommon in the earliest Middle Cornish. They become increasingly rare and are replaced by their respective plurals in *-ow* or *-yow*. Let us take for instance, the three masculine nouns *tros*

9 First published in *Cornish Studies*. Second series: Nineteen. 2011. Exeter: University of Exeter Press. Pp. 35–59. ISBN 0-85989-866-9

'foot', *lagas* 'eye' and *glyn* 'knee' and the two feminines *gar* 'leg' and *scovarn* 'ear'. I have collected the following examples.

tros 'foot, leg'
a) *devtros* PC 2781; *thewtros* PC 3154; *ij droys* PA 159c.
b) *treys* PA 130d, PC 251, 474, 480, 488, 518, 525, 583, 846, 863, 876, 877, 2163, 2613, 2937, 3172, RD 854, 1266, 1542, 2082, 2501; BM 2603, 2991, 3035, TH 15a, 21a; *dreys* PA 46a, 178d, 236c, 242b; PC 483, 2516, BM 2030, TH 47; *threys* OM 760, BM 2398; *threis* TH 7a; *trys* PC 835, 841, 1216, 2741; *drys* SA 64a; *thrys* RD 2587, SA 64a; *tryes* CW 873, 1763; *drys* SA 64a; *thryes* CW 1748.

Notice also that the vocabulary in the Bodewryd Manuscript vocabulary gives *trooz, traz* 'foot, feet' (RCEV: 98), where the ‹a› in *traz* has a subscript line. This may represent **traiz*, a variant of *treys*.

lagas 'eye'
a) *devlagas* PC 410, 1193, 1395, RD 54, 529, 617; *dewlagas* PA 222b, PC 396, 1066, RD 791; *theulagas* PC 1400; *thevlagas* PC 2102; *thewlagas* OM 2058; *ʒewlagas* PA 83b, 219c; *ij lagas* PA 225a; *deaṳlagaz* AB: 242b.
b) *lagasow* RD 1492, TH 3a x 2, 19a, 21a, 42, 56, BK 2330, 2711; *lagasowe* CW 694; *lagasaw* BK 1975, RCEV: 97; *lagagow* ÉCII: 176 x 2, 177; *lagadzho* AB: 223; *lagazo* AB: 223.

glyn 'knee'
a) *dewlyn* PA 58a, 195a, 196a, OM 1196, PC 3020; *ʒewleyn* PA 54d; *devglyn* PC 247; *dewglyen* CW 188; *thewlyn* BK 514; *thewglyn* PC 136; *dowlyn* PA 137a, 171c, 220b; *dowlin* ACB E e 7; *ij lyn* BM 4457.
b) *glynnyow* BK 3307.

Many examples of the dual *dewlyn*, etc., listed above occur in the phrase *war ben dewlyn* 'on bended knee, on one's knees'.

gar 'leg'
a) —.
b) *garrow* PA 45c, OM 1346, RD 2501, BM 3831; *garrov* BM 711; *arrow* PA 232a.

scovarn
a) —.
b) *scovornow* PC 1361, 1391, TH 21a; *scovurnow* TH 19; *skovornow* BK 1657, RCEV: 97; *skovernow* BK 1917.

It can be seen from the above examples that from the earliest period onwards *treys* is much commoner than *dewdros*. *Dewlagas* is well attested in *Pascon agan Arluth* and the Ordinalia, but is later replaced by *lagasow/lagagow*. The only exception is the one example from Lhuyd, who was probably quoting a medieval source. The dual forms **dywar* 'legs' and **dywscovarn* 'ears' have been taught to generations of revivalists, but neither is actually found in the traditional language. The attested forms are *garrow* and *scovornow* respectively. On the other hand, the dual *dewlyn* is the ordinary form, and *glynyow* is very poorly attested.

'Arm', 'shoulder' and 'breast'
The dual of the feminine bregh is attested with *dyv-*, *dyw-* and *de-* (from earlier **dew-*):

a) *dyvvregh* OM 688; *dywvregh* PC 3159; *thyvregh* PC 1189, RD 1265; *thywvreg* PC 1179; *dibreh* AB: 242b.
b) *ȝefregh* PA 76a; *ȝeffregh* PA 232a.

I know of only one example of the plural of *bregh*: *breihaụ* 'arms' AB: 242c. It is noteworthy that the examples of the dual are from the Ordinalia and *Pascon agan Arluth*, except for one instance from Lhuyd, who was probably quoting a medieval text.

The feminine *scoth* 'shoulder' is attested with *dyw* and *du-*:

a) *dywscoth* PC 3068; *diskodh* AB: 242b.
b) *duscoth* PC 2583; *duscouth* RD 2500.

No dual form is attested with *dew-* or *deu-*. Moreover all duals are from the Ordinalia, except one from Lhuyd, probably quoting a medieval text. In the Bodewryd Manuscript the word for 'shoulder' is given as *skoth* and the plural is *skothow* (RCEV: 97). The glossary cites no dual form.

The feminine *bron* 'breast' is attested in OCV in the phrase *cluit duiuron* 'breast', literally 'framework of breasts'. In Middle Cornish the word appears once in the dual with *de(w)* in *defran* CW 1910. On the other hand, the Bodewryd Manuscript gives *brodn* 'teat' and its plural as *brodnaw* 'teats' (RCEV: 97). The glossary does not mention a dual form.

The Cornish for 'lip, lips'
Cornish has two, albeit related, words for 'lip, lips'. The first word *gueus* 'lip' at OCV 49. Nance in his 1938 dictionary suggests a plural in *-ow* and the dual form **dywweus*. No dual form is attested. The plural form became known from Tregear's homilies after Nance published his dictionary and in fact it ends in *-yow*:

STUDIES IN TRADITIONAL CORNISH

an poyson a serpons yma indan aga tavosow, **gwessyow** *aga ganowow ew lene a wherewder ha paris the cussia ha ty* 'the poison of serpents is under their tongues, the lips of their mouths are full of bitterness and are ready to curse and to swear' TH 7a.

The second word is *guelv, guelv* 'A lip' cited by Lhuyd (AB: 7b, 75a). Lhuyd gives the plural as *guelvanz* (AB: 75a), which may be a misprint for *?guelvau*. Pryce cites *guelv* and gives two plurals. One, *guelvanz* is clearly derived from Lhuyd; the other is *guelawennow* (ACB: Q 2). The singular and plural are given together in the Bodewryd Manuscript as *gwelve, gwelvaw* (RCEV: 97). It is important notice that no dual form of *guelv, gwelve* is attested anywhere.

The Cornish for 'nose'
Revivalists have often been taught that the Cornish for 'nose' is *tron* masc. In fact *tron* 'nose' is unattested in Middle or Late Cornish, being Nance's respelling of *trein* 'nasus' in the Old Cornish Vocabulary (OCV 29). The word ‹tron› is common in Middle Cornish, but it is always the English borrowing meaning 'throne'. The native word for 'nose' is either *dewfryk* or *frygow*, the dual or plural of *fryg* 'nostril' (*friic* OCV 30; *freeg* RCEV: 97). The dual can be seen in:

> *han thew arall kekeffrys bethans gorrys in ye* **thywfridg** 'and as well let the other two be put into his nose' CW 1853-54
> *an eall a ornas thyma pan vo dewath theth dythyow hath voes gyllys alema gorra sprusan yth ganow han thew arall pur thybblance in tha* **thewfreyge** 'the angel ordered me, when your days were over and you gone hence to put a pip in your mouth and the two others indeed in your nose' CW 1927-33.

The form *thywfridg* in the first quotation rhymes with *pur deake* 'very beautifully' at CW 1857, and is presumably a mistake for **thywfrieg* or **thywfreig* (compare *thewfreyge* in the second quotation). The plural is attested in the following:

> *kynth us ganso sawer poys gor dotho nes the* **frygov** 'although it has a nasty smell, set it near your nose' BM 1453-54
> *lemen pan ywe messent me an set ryb the* **frygov** 'and now that it stinks, I will put it up to your nose' BM 3398-99
> **freegaw**, *freeg: nose, nostrils* RCEV: 97
> *ha del ve thym kyns ornys an dayer sprusan yw gorrys in y anow hay* **fregowe** 'and as was commanded me before, the three seeds have been put in his mouth and nose' CW 2086-88.

SOME CORNISH PLURALS

Luf ~ dorn **and** *dewla*

Among the duals that remain vigorous in Cornish we must include *dewla* 'hands' and *dewlyn* 'knees'. The first of these is the dual of *luf, leff* 'hand'. The singular is well attested in Middle Cornish:

*hag yn y **leff** 3yghow yn weth gwelen wyn a ve gorris* 'and in his right hand also a white rod was placed' PA 136d

*hay yll **leff** a ve tackis ord en grows fast* 'and one of his hands fastened firmly to the cross' PA 179b

*rag cole orth vn venen gulan ef re gollas an plas a'm **luf** thyghyow a wrussen pan wruge dres ov defen* 'for listening to the woman he has quite lost the place at my right hand we created, when he disobeyed my prohibition' OM 919-22

*pandra synsyth y'th **luef** lemyn* 'what are you holding in your hand now?' OM 1442

*doro kenter er the fyth ha me a tak y **luef** gleth gans ol ow nel* 'bring a nail upon your faith, and I will fasten his left hand with all my strength' PC 2746-48

*ny thue y **luef** sur the'n tol* 'does his hand indeed not reach the hole' PC 2755

*an **luef** a'm gruk me a wel ha'y odor whekka ys mel ow tos warnaf* 'I see the hand that created me with its scent as sweet as honey coming upon me' RD 143-45

*neffre ny fynnaf crygy ken ben vyth mar mur duwon erna hyndlyf y golon gans ov **luef** dre y woly* 'never will I believe, though I have never so much sorrow, until I handle his heart with my hand through his wound' RD 1529-32

*a thomas doro the **luef** yn woly guynys may fuef* 'O Thomas, put forth your hand into the wound where I was pierced' RD 1539-40

*Sens the vagyl in the **leff** in hanov crist us in neff* 'Hold your crozier in your hand in the name of Christ who is in heaven' BM 3007-08

*Ny a vyn y carhara purguir na ala guaya na **luff** na troys* 'We will imprison him indeed so that he can move neither hand nor foot' BM 3573-75

*ny res desquethes theugh an plagys a russyn ny suffra a thea **leff** du ragtha* 'it is not necessary to show you the plagues which we have suffered at the hand of God for it' TH 51

*glane ef regollas an place am **leff** dyghow* 'he has completely lost the place at my right hand' CW 2214-15.

Gradually, however, from the Middle Cornish period onwards the word *dorn* 'fist' begins to replace *luf* with the sense 'hand':

*Lemen yz **torn** my as re* 'Now into your hand I will give her' CF 17

53

Adam ystyn thy'm the **thorn** 'Adam, stretch forth your hand to me' OM 205

an lost kymmer thethy yn ban y'th **torn** *hep ger* 'by its tail take it up in your hand without a word' OM 1454-55

otte ow fycher gyne yn ov **dorn** *rak y gerghas* 'look, here I have my pitcher in my hand to fetch it' PC 656-57

tan syns y'th **dorn** *an giu na* 'come, take that spear in your hand' PC 3010

lemmyn pup ol settyes **dorn** *yn keth schath ma th'y tenne* 'now let everyone set his hand to drag him in this same boat' RD 2351-52

whath an feith a rug prevaylya woteweth, hag eff an Jeva an **thorne** *vhella han victuri* 'still the faith prevailed in the end, hand it had the upper hand and the victory' TH 34

yth ew recordys fatell rug onyn sodenly apperya the Josue havall the den ha cletha noith in y **dorne** 'it is recorded how one suddenly appeared to Joshua in likeness of a man with a naked sword in his hand.' TH 55a

ha pana substans a cletha o honna essa in **dorne** *henna a rug apperia the Josue?* 'and what substance of sword was that which was in the hand of him who appeared to Joshua?' TH 55a

ty foole prag na bredersys a **thorn** *dew y festa gwryes* 'you fool, why did you not consider that you were created by the hand of God?' CW 308-9

me a lead an voos am **dorn** 'I will lead the girl by my hand' CW 1390

Ev a uaske e **dorn** *uar e dhàgier dho dhestrîa an dhêau* 'He struck his hand upon his dagger to murder the two' JCH § 40 (BF: 19)

Ha leben lez e ora e **Dorn** *a raage ha komeraz weeth dore an gwethan bownaz, ha debre, ha bowa rag nevra* 'And now lest he put forth his hand and take from the tree of life and eat, and live for ever' ÉCII: 184

Bedh **dvrn** *rê ver, dhvn tavaz rê hîr* 'The hand is too short for too long a tongue' AB: 251c

ha Enna ma setha war **dorne** *dyhou an Taz vlnerth* 'and there is seated at the right hand of the Father Almighty' BF: 41

ha gath man do nêv, ha setha war **dorn** *dyhow a'n taz olgallusack* 'and ascended into heaven, and sat at the right hand of the Father Almighty' ACB: E e 4.

The plural of *dorn* with the sense 'hands' is *dewla* as can be seen, for example, in:

In scorgijs prenyer esa yn **dewle** *an ij ethow* 'As scourges there were sticks in the hand of the two Jews' PA 131a

neb a formyas neff ha novr in bys ma gans y **dule** *map den a pry* 'who created heaven and earth, in this world mankind from clay' BM 1314-16 *ef a ve degys inter e **thowla*** 'he was carried in his hands' SA 65

*y varck warnaf y settyas poran gans y owne **dewla*** 'he set his mark upon me with his own hands' CW 1530-31

*E ra ry tha e eelez an pohar an hanesta et ago **doola** y ra tha doone man* 'He will give his angels power over you; in their hands they will carry you up' ÉCII: 187.

Compare also Lhuyd's entry in his Comparative vocabulary: 'Manus ... *A hand* ... C[ornish] Dorn, *plur.* Dṵla' (AB: 86a). When *dorn* means 'fist', however, the plural is *dornow*:

*me a'n dalhen fest yn tyn ha gans ow **dornow** a'n guryn* 'I will seize him very sharply and will squeeze him with my fists' PC 1131-32

*pur ankensy gans **dornow** thotho war an scovornow reugh boxsesow trewysy* 'very painfully with fist give him nasty blows upon the ears' PC 1360-62

*ha ren thotho boxsusow gans **dornow** ha guelynny* 'and let us rain on him blows with fists and rods' PC 1389-90

*eff a ve cuffeys gans **dornow**, kylmys gans lovonow, scurgys, ha plattys war y ben curyn a sperne* 'he was beaten with fists, tied up with ropes, scourged and a crown of thorns put on his head' TH 15a

*me a'n dorn gans ow **dornow** may clamderha rag ewn ueth* 'I will punch him with my fists so that he may faint out of sheer terror' BK 2651-52.

On the other hand, in Middle Cornish 'foot' is *tros, troys* and the plural is *treys*. When, therefore, Cornish wished to speak about 'feet and hands' it uses the plural of *tros* but *dewla* (originally the dual of *luf/leff*). The usage can be seen from the following examples:

*hag ena ij an scorgyas yn tebel gans ij scorgye ha hager fest an dygtyas corf ha pen **treys** ha **dewle*** 'and then two whipped him horribly with two whips and very cruelly they treated him, body and head, feet and hands' PA 130cd

*worth an les y a dollas ij doll yn grows heb ken may ȝello an kentrow bras dre y **ȝewleff** bys yn pen rag y **dreys** y a vynnas telly ȝy worre yn tten* 'acrossways they made only two holes where the large nails might go as far as their heads through his hands; for his feet they wished to pierce to stretch him out' PA 178 b-d

*me a vyn mos the vre ow arluth **treys** ha **devle** gans onement ker yn certan* 'I will go to anoint my lord feet and hands with precious ointment indeed' PC 473-75 *mara'n kefons yn nep chy ha'n kelmyns* **treys** *ha* **dule** *ha'n hembrynkys bys thy'nny* 'if they find him in some house, and let them bind him feet and hands and bring him to us' PC 582-84

yma ow **trys** *ha'm* **dule** *thyworthef ow teglene math ew krehyllys ov dyns* 'my feet and hands are shivering off me so that my teeth are chattering' PC 1216-18

gorre the'n mernans gorre yn pren crous a thysempis ha kelmys **treys** *ha* **dule** 'put him to death, put him on the cross without delay with his feet and hands bound' PC 2161-63

y **dreys** *ha'y* **dule** *yn ten gans kentrow worth an plynken bethens tackys* 'let his feet and hands be tightly fixed to the plank with nails' PC 2516-18

a thomas doro the luef yn woly guynys may fuef dre an golon hag yn **treys** *hag yn* **thyvle** 'Thomas, put your hand in the wound where I was pierced through the heart and in the feet and in the hands' RD 1539-42

scorgis gans an ʒethewon kentrewys **treys** *ha* **dula** 'scourged by the Jews, nailed feet and hands' BM 2602-03

kentrewys gans ʒethewon **treys** *ha* **dule** *eredy gueskis gu in y golon* 'nailed by Jews feet and hands indeed, a lance thrust into his side' BM 2990-92

treys *ha* **dule** *kentreweys berth in grovs inter ladron* 'feet and hands nailed onto the cross between robbers' BM 3035-36

spykys bras a horne dre an **treys** *ha* **dewleff** 'great spikes of iron through the feet and hands' TH 15a

Gans agan gallus ha power, hen ew the venya gans agan **dewleff** *ha* **treys**, *gans agan lagasow ha scovornow, gans agan ganowow ha tavosow, ha gans an partys erell kyffrys abarth corfe hag ena, ny a gottha thyn omry agan honyn the wetha ha the colynwall y commondment eff* 'With our might and power, that means with our hands and feet, with our eyes and ears, with our mouths and tongues, and with the other parts of the body and soul, we should devote ourselves to keeping and to fulfilling his commandments' TH 21a.

The dual *dewla* and the plural of *gar* were also used together, as can be seen in:

a tas whek ol caradow ov **dywluef** *colm ha'm garrow gans louan fast colmennow na allan seuel am saf* 'O dear father beloved father, tie my hands and my legs firmly with a rope, knots so that I cannot stand up' OM 1345-48

SOME CORNISH PLURALS

Similarly the plural of both *gar* and of *tros* are used together in:

> *pyw a thueth a'n beys yn ruth avel gos pen ha duscouth* **garrow ha treys**
> *marth thy'm a'n deusys yma* 'who has come from the world as with his
> head and shoulders red as blood, his legs and feet? I wonder at the
> Godhead' RD 2499-2502.

Cornish, then, commonly uses the dual of the word for 'hand' together with
the plural of the word for 'foot'. In this respect resembles Welsh. 'Hands and
feet' in Welsh are usually rendered *dwylo a thraed*, where *dwylo* is the dual of
llaw 'hand', and *thraed* (< *traed*) the plural of *troed* 'foot'. The syntax is also
similar in Irish where one says *mo dhá lámh* 'my two hands' (dual) but *mo chosa*
'my feet' (plural). It would seem that Cornish *treys ha dewla* is a reflex of a
common Celtic syntagm.

Pedren, pedrennow 'buttock, haunch'
Lhuyd gives *patschan* 'buttock, haunch' AB: 48b. This seems to be a development of **pedren*, possibly via an anomalously assibilated **pejern*. Nance in his
1938 dictionary suggests a dual form **dywbedren* as well as a plural. In fact only
the plural is attested in Middle Cornish:

> *del wascaf y* **peydrennow** *may fo gos y vlewennow ha'y gorf ol kyns es hethy*
> 'as I strike his haunches so that his hair and all his body may be all
> blood before I stop' PC 2094-9
> *Rag esya an* **pedrennov** *ha rag stopya tarthennov yma thywy forten tek* 'For
> easing the buttocks and for stopping tertian agues you have good
> luck' BM 1422-24.

Clun, dywglun, glunyow 'hip, loins'
The OCV cites *penclun* under *clunis* 'hip' (OCV 88). This is for *pen clun* 'end of
haunch'. The OCV also cites the dual of in *duiglun* 'loins' (OCV 84). In Middle
Cornish this would be expected to appear as **dywglun*. Such a form is attested,
although it is written without lenition of the initial consonant cluster:

> *arluth gesugh vy dhe govs ornugh ragthe pob y bovs may fo claff age* **duklyn**
> 'lord, let me speak: order his ?bout for each one, that his buttocks may
> be sore' BM 3310-12.

On the other hand Borlase gives *clenniaw* 'a hip, a thigh', though the form is
clearly plural (Borlase: 381). If *clenniaw* is indeed both plural and genuine, it
appears that in Middle and Late Cornish *clun* 'hip, haunch' used both the dual
and the plural form.

The Cornish for 'cheeks' and 'eyebrows'

The Old Cornish word for 'cheek' is *bogh*, cited as *en uoch* 'the face' (OCV 37); and as *bôh* by Lhuyd, (AB: 45a, 62c). Nance suggests a dual **dywvogh*, which is unattested. The Bodewryd Manuscript give the singular *boah* and the plural *bohaw* (RECV: 97).

The word for 'eyebrow' and 'eyelid' is *abrans*, in which form it occurs at OCV 38 and AB: 158b and 276a. The Bodewryd Manuscript spells the word *abranz* (RCEV: 97) as does Lhuyd (AB: 9b). Nance suggests both a plural *abransow*, **abranjow* and a dual **deu-abrans*. Only the plural *abranzaw* is attested (RCEV: 97)

Further possible duals

The following words refer to body parts which come in pairs. We have no evidence whether they had duals in the traditional language, nor do we know what their plurals were: *ufern* 'ankle'(given as *lifern* in OCV 94); *gwewan* 'heel' (ÉCII: 181), *gueuan* (ACB Q 2); *morthos* 'thigh', given as *morboit* in OCV; as *morrhas* in the Bodewryd Manuscript (RCEV: 98) and as *morraz* by Lhuyd (AB: 28a, 59a). Nance suggests a dual **dywvordhos*, which is unattested. The word *goden truit* 'sole of the foot' occurs at OCV 96. Neither dual nor plural is attested anywhere. In the later language it seems to have been replaced by **goles tros* 'bottom of foot'; this form is cited as *goolas an trooz* in the Bodewryd Manuscript (RCEV: 98) and as *golaz trûz* by Lhuyd (AB: 121c). Again neither the plural nor the dual is attested anywhere in the remains of Cornish.

The word *elin* 'elbow' occurs at OCV 74. At OCV 746 it also means 'corner' (presumably in a church). It also occurs in the phrase *a'th elyn* 'of your elbow' at PC 2310. The word apparently acquired an inorganic initial *g*, appearing as *geelin* in the Bodewryd Manuscript (RCEV: 98) and as *gelen* in Lhuyd (AB: 52c). Lhuyd also gives the simplex as *ilin* (AB: 15c). No instance of either the plural or the dual appears to be forthcoming.

Plurals of words in -or and -er

Nouns of native origin in *-er* or *-or* usually form their plural by the addition of the suffix *-yon*, which is sometimes written ‹yan›. Here are some examples:

'workman': *gueiduur* OCV 225, 226; *guythoryon* OM 2331; *guithòryon* AB: 242c.
'merchant, dealer': *guicgur* OCV 267; *guycoryon* PC 331; *guykcoryon* PC 1304
'preacher': **progother; progothorryan* TH 42
'piper': *peeber* Bilbao Manuscipt; *pyboryon* BM 4563
'priest': *pronter; see next section*
'thatcher': **tyor; tyorryon* OM 2411, 2423, 2486.

SOME CORNISH PLURALS

Lhuyd has the plurals *kothskrefèryon, kothskreforyon* 'historians' (AB: 224 x 2, x 1) and *tregèryon* (AB: 224), *tregòryon* (AB: 224) 'dwellers, inhabitants'. Lhuyd also writes such words with a plural in ˙-yo rather than -yon, e.g. *triʒeryo* 'inhabitants' (AB: 222), *koth-skrefèrio* 'historians' (AB: 224), *ah-skrefèryo* 'genealogists', *lennerio* 'readers' (AB: 222) and *senezerrio* 'members of parliament' (AB: 22). All these forms would seem to be coinages by Lhuyd himself.

Pronter, prontyryon 'priest'
This word is common both in the singular and the plural. I have collected the following examples:

> singular: *pronter* BM 522, 785, 1903, 2550, TH 42a, 48a; SA 62, 66 x 2; AB: 143a; *prontyr* TH 39, 42a, 56; *prounder* OCV 107; *prounter* TH 11, 48a, JTonkin (LAM: 228); *prownter* TH 11; *proanter* WGwavas (LAM: 242); *praonter* AB: 127c.
> plural: *prounterian* JTonkin (LAM: 226); *prontiran* TH 33a; *prontirion* TH 38a; *prontyryan* TH 33a, 49; *prontyrryan* TH 33a, 42a, SA 65a; *bronteryon* PA 89a; *brontyryan* TH 32, 39.

Pronter is probably a reflex of a British form **premitir* < **presbyter*; cf. Old Irish *cruimter* 'priest', itself borrowed via Brythonic (see LHEB: 126, 128).

Borrowings in *-er* and *-or*
Some borrowings in *-er* or *-or* also have plurals in *-yon*:

> 'calculator, mathematician': **calcor; calcoryan* BM 1375
> 'carpenter': **carpenter; karpentorryon* OM 2410; *karpentoryon* OM 2422
> 'palmer, pilgrim': **palmer; palmoryon* RD 1477
> 'soldier': **soudor; soudoryon* BK 3243; *sovdoryan* BM 798, 1354; *sovdoryon* BM 1190, 2493; *sovdoryen* BM 1558.

The English plural in *-s* is also found with two of these:

> 'carpenters': *carpenters* OM 2557
> 'soldiers': *sovdrys* BM 1514, 2349, 2479, 2484, 2487, 3243, 3534, 3543.

The *-s* plural only is found with the word *tormentor* 'torturer':

> 'torturers, executioners': *tormentors* OM 2682, PC 959, 2145, 2513, RD 1917, 2144; *tormentours* PC 1348, 1357, 2045, 2055, 2506; *tormentores* RD 1761, 1876, 2240; *tormentoris* BM 950, 951, 952, 1170, 1171, 1523, 1524, 1525, 1526, 2310; *tormentourys* PC 950.

The singular of the word *gwerryor, gwerror* 'warrior' occurs in *Bewnans Ke* variously spelt five times: *gwerryor* BM 2706; *guerryor* BK 2618, 2628; *gwerror* BK 1997 and *guerror* BK 2598. One might perhaps expect the plural to appear as **gwerryoryon*. In fact only a plural in -s is attested:

> *Lemmyn, ow **gwerrors** gwelha, dun ahanan in un rowt* 'Now, my best warriors, let us go hence in a host' BK 2787-88
>
> *Ow **guerrors** da ha worthy, prederough a'gys huneth* 'My good and worthy warriors, consider your ancestors' BK 2800-01
>
> *Marow ew Lucy heb gyl ha'y **werrors** in katap myl* 'Lucius is dead indeed and his warriors, every thousand of them' BK 2832-33.

There are also some words of native origin for which only an -s plural is attested, the word *aweylar* 'evangelist' for example. The following are the attested plurals:

> *awaylers* TH 53a; *aweilers* TH 42; *aweylers* TH 42, 53, 53a x 2, 54; *aweylors* TH 53.

It is very likely that the plural **aweyloryon* occurred at one time, but it is not attested.

Nouns in -ador

The agent suffix *-ador, -adur* is fairly well attested in traditional Cornish. I have collected the following examples in the singular of words bearing this suffix:

'sleeper': *cuscadur* OCV 397
'doorkeeper': *darador* OCV 764
'sower': *ȝynnadar* AB: 148a, 240c
'weaver': *gweader* WGwavas (LAM: 242); *gueiadar* AB: 163b; *gueadar* AB: 240c
'sinner': *pehadur* PA 8b, TH 38a; *pehadure* TH 9a, 38a
'rower, oarsman': *ruifadur* OCV 273; *revadar* AB: 14a, 138b; *reuadar* AB: 240c
'fisherman': *piscadur* OCV 234; *puscador* TH 45a; *pysgadar* AB: 120c, 240c; *pysgadȳr* (in phrase *pysgadȳr ŷn mȳtêrn* 'kingfisher') AB: 65a
'saviour': *selwadour* BM 539, 4320; *sylwador* PC 304, *sylwadur* RD 480, 800, 1152, 1733, 2486; *sylwader* RD 2008
'saviour': *salvador* CW 1865.

Lhuyd twice uses *deskadzher* 'teacher, professor' (AB: 222, 223). This is a creation of his own and is unlikely to be authentic, since it is clear that the suffix in traditional Cornish is *-ador* rather than **-ager*. Assibilation does not occur in other words when intervocalic -d- is followed by r in the next syllable.

SOME CORNISH PLURALS

We thus also find *peder* 'four' and *gweder* 'glass', both with unassibilated medial *-d-*.
There appear to be only two nouns in *-ador* for which a plural is attested. The first is *pehador, pehadur* 'sinner', whose plural ends in *-yon, -yan*:

peghadorryan TH 10a; *pehadoryon* PA 5c, TH 7a; *pehadoryan* TH 8, 9; *pehadorryan* TH 4a, 8a, 10a; *pehadurrian* TBoson (BF: 41).

The second word is *puscador* 'fisherman', attested in OC as *piscadur*, in Tregear as *puscador* and in Lhuyd as *pysgadar, pysgadyr*. The plural in *-s* is confined to two instances from William Kerew:

*Ha Jesus gwandra reb a môr Alale wellas deaw broderath Simnen criez Peder ha Andrew e broder a towlah rooze en mor, rag tho an giie **poscaders*** 'And Jesus walking by the sea of Galilee saw two brothers, Simon called Peter and Andrew his brother, casting nets into the sea, for they were fishermen' ÉCII: 191
*A meth e thonge, suyow vee, he ee vedn gee[l] thew **poscaders** a deeze* 'He said to them, Follow me, and I will make you fishers of men' ÉCII: 191.

As with *awayler* 'evangelist', so with *puscador* 'fisherman': it is very probable that a plural **puscadoryon* occurred in the language. It is just not attested in our surviving texts.

Nouns in *-yas*
Cornish has a number of agent nouns in *-yas* (Old Cornish *-iat*). I have collected the following examples of such formations in the singular:

'assistant pilot': *brenniat* OCV 275
'redeemer': *dysprynnyas* PC 404, RD 844
'singer, player': *cheniat* OCV 115; *keniat* 261
'horn-blower': *cherniat* OCV 258
'murderer': *denleythyas* TH 32a
'liar': *gouleueriat* OCV 424
'poisoner': *guenoinreiat* OCV 312
'keeper': *guidthiad* OCV 196; *guythyas* OM 692; *gvythyas* OM 74; *gwethyas* CW 368
'speaker of the truth': *guirleueriat* OCV 421
'worker, cultivator': *gunithiat* OCV 338
'enchanter': *wurcheniat* OCV 311 (for **gurcheniat*)
'persecutor': *helhiat* OCV 317
'priest': *oferiat* OCV 106

'overlord, suzerain': *gwarthevyas* BM 7; *guarthevyas* BK 1488, 1525; *guarthyfyas* BK 1788; *gwarthyvyas* BK 1973; *warthyvyas* BK 1923
'leader, conductor': *hebrenchiat* OCV 106, 170
'tailor': *seuyad* OCV 291
'saviour': *sylwyas* PC 252, 394, RD 307, 614, 845, 856, 1722, 2418.

'Priest' and 'judge'

Two nouns in -*yas* are commonly used by revivalists, namely *oferyas* 'priest' and **brusyas* 'judge'. As we have seen, the first of these occurs as *oferiat* 'priest' in OCV, but is wholly unattested in Middle Cornish. Its place is taken by *pronter*, plural *prontyryon*, which is first attested in the OCV, but is common thereafter (see above).

The second word **brusyas* is an invention of Nance's, for it is attested nowhere in the traditional language. The word *brodit* 'judge' occurs at OCV 177, which would have developed in Middle Cornish as **brudyth*; cf. Middle Cornish *prydyth* (BK 2497) < Old Cornish *pridit* (OCV 263). The only word for 'judge' in Cornish is *iug, iudg*:

> *nep a tawo yn pow ma thyrag **iug** ny fyth iuggys* 'whoever remains silent in this country, will not be judged before a judge' PC 2387-88
>
> *ha in pub oys ha tyrmyn eff a ve kemerys ha recevys gans tus da disposis ha tus diskys rag lell **judge** a henna* 'and in every age and period he was taken and accepted by well disposed and educated people as a true judge of that' TH 38
>
> *an egglos an jevas an lell sens an scriptur ha yth ew **iudg** a henna* 'the church possesses the true sense of scripture and is the arbiter of that' TH Note on page 36
>
> *Rag an tyrmyn an prontyr, ha rag an tyrmyn an **judge**, in stede a crist* 'For the time being the priest, and for the time being the judge instead of Christ' TH 42a.

The plural of *iug* is attested once: *Rag lymmyn athewethas pub den sempill heb understonding na skyans a re supposia fatell yllens y bos **iudges** in maters a contra-uercite* 'For now recently everybody simple without understanding or knowledge has been assuming that they can be judges in matters of controversy' TH 37.

The plural of words in -*yas*

The word *guythyas, gwethyas* 'guard' has a plural *guythysy*, attested at OM 2038, and as *gwyththysy* at OM 2397. The singular **gonesyas* 'workman, labourer' is attested only in its Old Cornish form as *gunithiat ereu* 'field worker, farm-worker'. There are several examples of the plural in Middle Cornish, however:

gonesugy OM 2438, 2447, 2489; *wonesugy* OM 2326.

SOME CORNISH PLURALS

None of the singulars *treghyas 'cutter', *gwandryas 'wanderer', *sewyas 'follower, successor' nor *rewlyas 'ruler' is attested in traditional Cornish. The plurals of all four occur, however. The plural of the first is cited by Lhuyd: *trahezi mein* 'stone-cutters' AB: 242c. The plurals of the second and third occur in Tregear's homilies:

> *lymmyn rag henna nyns owgh why strangers ha* **gwandresy**, *mas y thowhy citesens gansans an syns* 'now therefore you are not strangers and wanderers, but you are citizens with them, the saints' TH 33.
>
> *S Hierom inweth in y epistill the Damasus yma ow settya in mes very notably an primasie, ha'n supremite an epscop a Rome, y bosans an successors, hennew an* **sewysy**, *a pedyr* 'St Jerome also in his epistle to Damasus sets out very clearly the primacy and supremacy of the bishop of Rome, that they were the successors, that is the followers, of St Peter' TH 49.

The fourth plural seems to be used as a suppletive one. In Middle Cornish the usual word for 'ruler' apparently is *rewler, rewlar*:

> *Ny yv certen lowenek rag cafus dyn meryasek the voys* **revler** 'We are indeed happy to get Meriasek as our ruler' BM 2716-18
>
> *Eff an grug Souereign* **rewler** *ha pen war oll an pusces in dowre, war an ethen in eyer, ha war oll an bestas in nore* 'He made him sovereign ruler and head over oll the fishes in the water, over the birds of the air, and over all the beasts of the earth' TH 2
>
> *lymmyn in mar ver dell ew an spurissans* **ruler** *ha gouerner an Catholik egglos* 'now inasmuch as the Holy Spirit is ruler and governour of the Catholic church' TH 36a
>
> *Me re dueth theugh gans mer grys rag guthyl both agys brys, par dell ough* **rewlar** *an wlas* 'I have come to you with great speed to do your will, as you are ruler of the kingdom' BK 3067-69
>
> *mar gwreth henna honorys ty a vyth bys venarye ha pen* **rowler** *warnan ny heb dowt in case* 'if you do that you will be honoured for ever and chief ruler over us without doubt in the matter' CW 513-16.

On the other hand the only attested plural of any word for 'ruler' is *rewlysy*:

> *Omma me a vyn govyn vn questyon the vos assoyles, mar te cherite requyria the predyry, the cowsse da, ha the wull da the bub den, da ha bad, fatell yll an* **rewlysy** *an wlas executia Justis war drog pobill gans charite?* 'Here I will pose a question to be answered, if charity requires one to think, to speak well and to do good to everybody, good and evil, how can the rulers of the country execute justice upon evil people with charity?' TH 24a.

STUDIES IN TRADITIONAL CORNISH

It might not be too rash to assume therefore that in Middle Cornish the singular was *rewler,* but the plural *rewlysy.*

'Servant, servants'

The singular **servyas* is unattested. Indeed the usual way of expressing the notion 'servant' is to use *servont, servant.* I have collected the following examples:

> *servont* OM 572, PC 649, BM 2117, 2130, 2436, 2627, 3202, 3656, 4061, 4339, 4379, TH 49; *servonnth* OM 2609; *seruant* TH 21a; *servant* TH 8, 10a, BK 1043, CW 1401, 1487, 2095, 2107.

Servont, servant has a plural *servons, servans, servantes:*

> *servons* BM 2329, 2384; *servans* TH 41; *servantes* TH 35a, BK 313, 755, 761, 3259.

Apparently, however, the commonest way of rendering the plural 'servants' in the traditional language is to use *servysy, servygy,* the plural of the unattested singular **servyas.* I have collected the following examples:

> *pysyn may fyyn* **servysy** *th'agan arluth hep parow* 'let us pray that we may be servants to our peerless lord' OM 235-36
> *gorthyans ha gras the dev ow thas luen a vercy pan danvonas yn onor bras thy'm* **servysi** 'glory and thanks to God my merciful father, when he sent in great honour servants to me' PC 169-72
> *saw ol the len* **servygy** *rak the vones dyvythys yn hanow dev bynygys me a grys the vos deffry* 'but all your loyal servants, because you have come in the name of God, I believe are blessed indeed' PC 279-82
> *an tas dev roy thy'n bos guyv the vos len* **seruysy** *thy's* 'may God the Father make us worthy to be loyal servants to you' PC 712-13
> *guyn vys ynno nep a grys rak the weres yv parys the'th* **seruygy** *yn bys-ma* 'happy he who believes in him, for your help is ready for your servants in this world' PC 2706-08
> *ha gura thy'm moy* **seruygy** 'and make for me more servants' RD 2460
> *ha nep na vynno crygy ny yl bos a'm* **seruysy** 'and whoever does not believe cannot be one of my servants' RD 2469-70
> *yma ov quan rewardya y* **servysy** *rum ene* 'upon my soul, he pays his servants badly' BM 3261-62
> *yma thymo* **servysy** *orth ov gorthya pur vesy* 'I have servants worshipping me very assiduously' BM 3373-74
> *sav mercy y raff pesy hag onen ath* **servysy** *nefra bethe heb awer* 'but I will ask for mercy and will be one of your servants forever without demur' BM 3800-02

rag ov **servesy** *in beas war thu pesy me a ra* 'for my servants in the world I shall pray to God' BM 4275-76

Naha ... derrygy ... **servygy** 'To deny ... his destruction ... servants' BK 673-75

sirvigy *servants: a good word* RCEV: 100

Servisi *and* **Servidzhi**, *Servants* AB: 242c.

It would seem, then, that the default word for 'servant' in traditional Cornish was *servont, servant*. For the plural speakers used either *servons, servans* or, more frequently, *servysy, servygy*.

Population names in *-an* and *-on*

Lhuyd writes *Dân* 'Dane', plural *Dano* (AB: 224) and *Norman* 'Norman', plural *Normanno* (AB: 224). Nance coined the word **Alman* 'German' and in his 1938 dictionary gave it the plural *Almanow*. Caradar wrote *Almannow* 'Germans' (see, for example *KemK*: 36 x 2). In his 1951 dictionary, however, Nance gives the plural *Almanas*. Similarly he recommends *Alban* 'Scot' with the plural *Albanas*, and *Roman* 'Roman', plural *Romanas*. Although I myself used *Romanas* in my 2002 edition of the New Testament, I am not sure that *Romanas* and plurals like it are really legitimate. 'Romans' in traditional Cornish is *Romans*, a form which is attested in three separate texts:

Rag henna yma S Powle in y epistyll then **romans** *in v chaptyr ow leverall* 'Therefore St Paul in his epistle to the Romans says in the fifth chapter' TH 4a

yma du ow tesquethas pandra ony dre y profet Jheremy hag in weth ow cowse dre y apostyll S Pawle thyn **romans** *an iii-a chapter* 'God shows what we are by his prophet Jeremiah, and also speaking through his apostle St Paul to the Romans, the third chapter' TH 7a

yma S pawle in kynsa chapter thyn **romans**, *ow affirmya playn fatell wothya an bobyl mer an gwrythyans a thu* 'St Paul in the first chapter to the Romans plainly affirms that the people knew much of the works of God' TH 14

kepar dell vgy S paul thyn **romans** *ow kull mencion* 'as St Paul mentions to the Romans' TH 14a

Yma S poule in delma ow declaria thyn **romans** 'St Paul thus declares to the Romans' TH 25

in y Exposicion war an vi-as chapter an pistlis a S paull then **Romans**, *scriffes in vaner ma* 'in his exposition upon the sixth chapter of the epistle of St Paul to the Romans, written thus' TH 45

An **Romans** *a vyth wystyys, ymstorvye pan na alhons* 'The Romans will be laid waste, since they cannot starve themselves' BK 2136-37

Merough ple ma an **Romans** *ow settya ragow' myrnans* 'See where the Romans are plotting death for you' BK 2808-09

Ha na ore den veeth durt peniel reeg an kol ma kensa dose, durt an **Romans**
meskez gen a Brittez, po ugge hedna durt an Sausen 'And no one knows
from which this loss first came, from the Romans mingled with the
Britons, or thereafter from the English' NBoson (BF: 29).

The same kind of plural in *-ans, -ons* is to be noticed in other population
names also:

a)
ha vi c. blethan wosa crist an **Saxons** *a ve spredys drys oll an wlas* 'and 600
years after Christ the Saxons were spread across all the country'
TH 51
Me re thanvanas deffry duk an **Saxens**, *Chellery* 'Indeed I have already
sent Childerich, leader of the Saxons' BK 3229-30.

b)
Yma S paule ow rebukya in y epistill thyn **Corinthians** 'St Paul in his
epistle to the Corinthinans rebukes' TH 33
an terribill sentens a S paule in xi chapter in kynsa pistill then **Corinthians**
'the terrible sentence of St Paul in the eleventh chapter of the first
epistle to the Corinthians' TH 51a
Pella agys oll an rema, yma in xi chapter a S paul then **Corinthians** *goodly
ha largy processe ow tochia thin sacrament ma* 'Further than all these,
in the eleventh chapter of St Paul to the Corinthians there is a
goodly and broad discussion of this sacrament' TH 53a
ha not ena only, mas in pistlis a S paule then **Corinthians** 'and not only
there, but in the epistles of St Paul to the Corinthians' TH 57a.

c)
hag in iii-a chapter then **galathians** *yma S Powle ow leverell* 'and in the
third chapter to the Galatians St Paul says' TH 7a
Agan frutys ny ew declaris in v chapter a S pawle then **galathians** 'Our fruit
are declared in the fifth chapter of St Paul to the Galatians' TH 9
Ima S paul ow recordia in v chapter then **galathians**, *Walkyow ha gwandrow
warlyrth an spuris* 'St Paul records in the fifth chapter to the
Galatians: Walk and wander according to the Spirit' TH 16a
ha S pawle a gylwys an **galathians**, *fooles ha tus heb vnderstonding, in
second chaptur in epistill scriffis thyn* **Galathians** 'and St Paul called
the Galatians fools and people without understanding in the
second chapter of the epistle written to the Galatians' TH 29a.

d)
*y ma S paull ow cowse, An aposteleth a crist, ha oll an rena a ve ministers in
egglos a crist thea nyna bys in dith hethow, han charg anetha ow rewlya*

an flok a crist in iiii-a chapter thyn **Ephesians** 'St Paul speaks of the apostles of Christ and all those who were ministers in the church of Christ from then until today, and the charge of them ruling the flock of Christ in the third chapter to the Ephesians' TH 41a

ema Chrisostom ow scryfa than **philipians** *a remembrance, a vea res thetha bos, in keth sacrament na rag an marow* 'Chrysostom writes to the Philippians of the remembrance which they should have for the dead in this same sacrament' SA 66.

The Cornish for 'Britons'

Nance in his 1951 dictionary for 'Briton' suggests either *Brython*, plural **Brythonyon*, or **Bretanyas*, plural **Bretanysy*. None of these forms is actually attested, though Lhuyd writes *Brethyn* 'Briton' (AB: 223, 224) and *Brethon* 'Britons' (AB: 224 x 3). William Gwavas writes *Pow an Brethon* 'Britain' (LAM: 238). Nicholas Boson uses *Brittez* for 'Britons' (BF: 29, 31 x 2).

Since the discovery of *Bewnans Ke*, however, it is clear that the authentic word for 'Britons' in the plural is *Bretons*:

An **Vretons** *– me a theben e kerth, un vaner ha gothow* 'The Britons—I shall cut their heads clean off, just like geese' BK 2430-31

ha dun coyt war an **Vretons** *ha prosternyn an felans the'n myrnans dyhow ha cleth* 'let us attack the Britons and let us lay low the felons to death both right and left' BK 2805-07.

The lenited initial of an *Vretons* in both cases, shows that the plural *Bretons* is a well-integrated element in the Cornish lexicon. We can be sure that *Bretons* is the authentic Cornish plural 'Britons'. The singular was presumably *Breton*.

Conclusions

From our brief discussion above of some duals and plurals in Cornish, some salient facts emerge, which may be of interest to revivalists.

The dual *dewla* 'hands' survives into the Late Cornish period. The singular of *dewla* is increasingly *dorn* rather than *luf*. The invariable way of saying 'hands and feet' in Cornish is *dewla ha treys*, with the dual *dewla* but the plural *treys*. This corresponds to both the Welsh usage, *dwylo a thraed*, and to the Irish usage *mo dhá lámh* 'my two hands' with dual number but *mo chosa* 'my feet' with the plural.

Other surviving duals appear to be *dywvron* 'breasts', *dywglun* 'loins' and *dewlyn* 'knees'. Otherwise the plural is mostly used with bodily organs in pairs: *scovornow* 'ears', *lagasow* 'eyes', *garrow* 'legs', *pedrennow* 'buttocks', *gwelvow* or *gwessyow* 'lips' and probably also *scothow* 'shoulders'. Revivalist should also note that 'ears' appears as *scovornow*; **scovarnow* is unattested.

Words in *-er/-or* and *-ador/-adur* originally had plurals in *-yon*. These however yield to plurals in *-s*, and thus we find *aweylers* 'evangelists', *gwerryors/gwerrors* 'warriors' and *poscaders* 'fishermen'.

Curiously, the plural of *rewler* 'ruler' may well have been *rewlysy*, rather than *rewloryon* or even *rewlers*. The word *servont*, servant seems to have had two plurals: *servons/servantes* and *servysy/servygy*. *Servysy/servygy* seems to have been the more frequently used.

Population names in *-an*, *-on* invariably form their plurals with *-s* rather than *-as*: *Romans*, *Saxons*, *Corinthians*. *Brethon* 'Britons' (singular *Brethyn*) is used by Lhuyd. A plural form *Brittez* 'Britons' is used three times by Nicholas Boson. Perhaps the most authentic word for 'Briton, Britons' is **Breton, Bretons* in BK, and 'the Britons' is an *Vretons*.

ADJECTIVAL AND ADVERBIAL PREFIXES IN CORNISH[10]

Speaking of the adjective in Cornish Nance says:

> In the positive degree this normally follows the noun: **cümyas tēk**. In cases where the adj. comes first it may be considered as compounded or hyphenated with the noun, **pür, brās, cot, cam, gow, gwȳr, gwan, tebel, drōk, fals, hager, hȳr**, are oftenest so used (CfA: 11).

Nance says that the preceding adjective is 'compounded or hyphenated' with the noun. 'Prefixed' is perhaps a better term.

As we shall see, Nance in his list has omitted some further adjectives that may precede their noun. Moreover he does not mention that the behaviour of prefixed adjectives may vary. Most, though not all, can be used after a noun, so that, for example, one can say *hyr-penys* 'long abstinence' but also *termyn hyr* 'a long time'. Many can also be used predicatively. For example, one can say *camwyth* 'evil deeds' but also *henna nyns yw cam* 'that is not wrong'. Other adjectives can also be prefixed to verbs and thus acquire adverbial function, e.g. *drok dywethe* 'to end badly', *tebel fara* 'fare badly'. Still others, when prefixed change their sense, e.g. *gwan* 'weak' but *gwan hanow* 'evil name', and *pur* 'pure, utter' but *pur tha* 'very good'. Further a number of English borrowings can be prefixed to adjectives and verbs, e.g. *overdevys* 'overgrown' and *bad-ober* 'bad work, crime'. Finally there remains the question of how far prefixed adjectives lenite the initial consonant of the word to which they are attached.

Let us look at the prefixed adjectives in turn to see how each one is used in the traditional language.

Adjectival Prefixes in the Cornish Texts

drok-, drog- 'bad, evil, wicked'
This is commonly functions as an adjective prefixed to its noun:

> A out warnes **drok venen** worto pan wrussys cole 'damn you, evil woman, that you paid attention to him' OM 221-22

10 First published in *Cornish Studies*. Second series: Twenty-one. 2013. Exeter: University of Exeter Press. Pp. 33–75. ISBN 0-85989-886-7

pan rellens remembra ha lamentya aga pehosow haga **drog bewnans** *esans ow ledya* 'when they remember and lament their sins and their evil lives which they were leading' TH 6a

mar ny fystyn pup huny why as byth **drog vommennow** 'if everyone does not hurry, you will get evil blows' OM 2323-24

Ser duk me a weyl tevdar ha parcel a **throk coscar** *pur thevrey orth y sewa* 'Sir duke, I see Teudar and a group of evil fellows indeed following him' BM 2358-60

In meth an lader arall **drog ʒen** *os kepar del ves* 'The other thief said, 'you are an evil man as you have been' PA 192a

Thymmo heb mar, te **drog-den**, *ny vethyth gowr* 'To me indeed, you evil man, you will not be a husband' BK 2960-61

Gans an eʒewon war hast **drok ʒewas** *a ve dyʒgtys* 'By the Jews in haste an evil drink was got ready' PA 202a

vyngens re'n geffo amen ha **drok thyweyth** 'may he suffer vengeance, amen, and an evil end' RD 2085-86

A **throg thewath** *re wyrwhy!* 'May you die an evil death!' BK 473

yma eff ow dysky fatell ra **drog gerryow** *ha* **drog prederow** *deservya condemnacion* 'he teaches that evil words and evil thoughts will deserve condemnation' TH 9

pan ello ow corf yn pry guyth vy rak an joul **drok was** 'when my body goes into the earth, protect me from the devil, the evil fellow' RD 1563-64

kemereugh corf a'n **drok was** *vgy ow flerye gans blas yw myligys* 'take the body of the evil fellow that is stinking with an accursed odour' RD 2159-61

gallas genaf ve **droag lam** *poran rag an ober na* 'I have suffered an evil fate precisely for that deed' CW 1687-88

kepar hag ef on crousys ha dre wyr vreus quyt iuggys rak agan **drok ober** *kens* 'like him we are crucified and by true judgement condemned for our evil deeds ere now' PC 2900-02

kepar dell ra an laddron, advltrers, denlath, hag oll an **drog pobill** *erell* 'as the thieves do, adulterers, murderers and all the other evil people' TH 24

Gallas Lucifer **droke preve** 'Lucifer, the evil snake, has gone' CW 335

them shape ow honyn ytama why a weall omma treylys **drog pullat** *ha brase* 'to my own shape, behold me, you see me transformed, an evil fellow and a great one' CW 925-27

So rag an wyckyd han **drog requestys** *ma eff a ve grevously rebukys ha reprovys* 'but for these wicked and evil requests he was grievously rebuked and reproved' TH 46a.

Drok-, drog- may also be prefixed to verbs and verbal nouns, as is clear from the following examples:

dre laha y coth dotho **drok dywethe** 'by law he ought to meet an evil end' PC 1827-28

me a'm bues gallos i'n bys ha'm yskerans a **throkfar** 'I have power in the world and my enemies will fare badly' BK 1411-12

gueyt an harlot na scapyo **drok handle** *del om kyry pan gyffy dalhen ynno* 'make sure that the scoundrel does not escape mistreatment, as you love me, when you get your hands on him' PC 990-92

hy re ruk ov delyfrya mes a preson mam kerra le mayth ena **drokhendelys** 'she has delivered me from prison, dearest mother, where I was being mistreated' BM 3758-60

y thadder yw **drok tylys** *pan y'n lathsons dybyte* 'his goodness has been badly repaid since they have killed him without mercy' RD 3096-97.

The jussive particle *re* may separate *drok-* and the verb *fara* 'to fare' as can be seen in: *A, harlot,* **drog re fary** *gans the govanscosow gow!* 'Oh scoundrel, may you fare badly with your lying excuses!' BK 459-60.

In the above examples *drog-* often lenites initial *b* and *gw*, and it may also lenite *d > th*. It seems, however, that initial *p* is not usually lenited after *drog-*. We thus find the following: *drok pyn* 'evil torment' PC 2108, 2726; *drog pys* 'badly paid, angry' PC 3089; *drok pryson* 'evil prison' RD 2002; *drok pobyll* 'evil people' BM 1325; *drog pobyll* 'idem' TH 18, 25, 29a, 40, 40a; *drog pobill* 'idem' TH 24, 24a x 2, 25 x 4, 31a x 3; *droke polat* 'evil fellow' CW 769; *drog pullat* 'idem' CW 927; *drog polat* 'idem' CW 1441, 1485; *drog prederow* 'evil thoughts' TH 9; *droke preve* 'evil snake' CW 335. Indeed I can find no example anywhere of *drok-, drog-* leniting following *p > b*.

This prefixed *drok-, drog-* is thus the ordinary way of saying 'badly' in Cornish. The adverbial particle *yn* is never attested with *drog* itself. *Yn ta* 'well' is common in the texts, but **yn trog* 'badly' is wholly unattested. The only attested example of 'badly' not involving a prefixed adverb in Cornish is probably *rag eff a recevyas Corf Dew* **warlerth badd maner** 'for he received the body of God badly' SA 65a.

Drok, drog is also used as an adjective predicatively with parts of the verb *bos* 'to be'. Particularly common is the use with the pronominal forms of the preposition *gans* to mean 'be sorry, regret' (all our examples of this latter idiom contain the first person singular):

mar **pue drok** *a oberys trogh yhy gans the glethe* 'if what I did was evil, cut her with your sword' OM 291-92

a ihesu whek re iovyn **drok yv** *gyne na venta kammen tryle yn maner tek* 'dear Jesus, by Jove I regret that you will not convert nicely at all' PC 1291-94 *thomas ty yv me a grys an gokye den yn beys ha henna* **yv drok** 'Thomas, you, I believe, are the silliest man in the world and that is bad' RD 1453-55

thomas ty yv muskegys hag yn muscokneth gyllys **drok** *yv gynef vy lemmyn* 'Thomas, you are mad and sunken in insanity, I regret' RD 1127-29

Drog yv *genef gruthyl den* 'I regret having created man' OM 917

drok yv *gynef bones mar lyes enef ow mos the'n nef* 'I am sorry that so many souls are going to heaven' RD 298-300

drog yv gena doys oma 'I regret coming here' BM 457

Drog o *the gan owth owtya* 'Evil was your song as you yelled' BK 27.

Drok, drog is also used in adjectival phrases of the kind *drog y gnas, drog aga gnas* 'evil natured'. There are two instances in PC:

arluth lauar dyssempys thy'nny mars yv both the vreys ha bolenegoth a'n tas my the wyskel gans clethe nep vs worth the dalhenne scherewys **drok aga gnas** 'Lord, tell us immediately whether it is your wish and the Father's will that I should strike with a sword those who are seizing you, evil their nature' PC 1137-42

a peue den **drok y gnas** *ny alse yn nep maner pur wyr cafus mar mur ras rak sawye tus dre vn ger* 'had he been an man of evil nature, he could not in any way indeed have had such great grace to cure people by a single word' PC 2969-72.

In the Cornish texts *drok, drog* also functions as a noun 'evil, disease', for example in the following examples:

ol en da han **drok** *kepar ʒe ihesu beʒens grassys* 'for all the good and the evil alike let Jesus be thanked' PA 24d

kyns yn ta ef a ylly tus a bup **drok** *ol sawye* 'ere now well he could cure people of all ill' PA 194b

kemys **druk** *vs ov cothe ha dewethes hag avar yma ken thy'm the ole* 'so much evil is occurring both late and early, I have reason to weep' OM 628-30

gul **drok** *thy'so ny vynna* 'I will not do you any harm' RD 1815

gothvos ynweth decernya omma ynter **drok** *ha da yv ov ewnadow pup vr* 'also to be able to distinguish here evil from good is my desire always' BM 28-30

an wethan ma ew henwys gwethan gothvas **droke** *ha da* 'this tree is called the tree of the knowledge of evil and good' CW 375-76

ha why ra boaze pocara Deew a cothaz Da ha **Droag** 'and you shall be like God knowing good and evil' Rowe

Nessa, urt an Skavaoll Crack-an-codna iggava setha war en Cres an awles ewhall (cries tutton Harry an lader) heb **drog** *veeth* 'Next, because of the precarious stool he sits on in the middle of the high cliff, called the hassock of Harry the thief, without any harm' BF: 12

Na tedna ny en Antoll, buz gwitha ny vrt **droag** 'Do not lead us into temptation, but deliver us from evil' BF: 55.

Drok, drog is not generally used, however, as an attributive adjective after its noun. There are no examples of **den drog* 'evil man,' **benen throg* 'evil woman', **pollat drog* or **ober drog* 'evil work' for example. The only exception to this rule that I can find is the following from BM:

Nefra cosker ongrassyas menogh a ra bostov bras neb tebel dorne pan vo grueys mas **hap drok** *orthugh a skyn gase farwel me a vyn molleth du in cowetheys* 'Ever an ungracious crowd will often make great boast when some evil trick is done. But an evil fortune will descend upon you. I shall take my leave. God's curse on the company' BM 1282-87.

Note: this one example is slighty doubtful, however, for a number of reasons. The noun *hap* is not otherwise attested in Cornish, although *parhap* 'perhaps' occurs twice (OM 1352, CW 661), moreover the usual word for 'but' in BM is *sav*, not *mas*. It is not impossible that the original text here was something like: **par hap drok orthugh a skyn* 'perhaps evil will fall upon you'. In which case we would have no example in Cornish of *drok* after the noun it qualifies.

In Middle Breton, as in Cornish, the word *drouc* can be used either as a noun meaning 'evil, wickedness' or as a prefixed adjective in such compounds as *drouc-preder* 'evil thought', *drouc-speret* 'evil spirit' and *drouc-ober* 'evil deed'. *Drouc* does not seem to be used after the noun it qualifies. In Welsh *drwg* 'bad, evil' can also be a noun meaning 'evil, wickedness' and an adjective 'evil, wicked'. When prefixed, it often appears as *dryg-*, e.g. *drygddyn* 'evil person', *drygliw* 'bad colour, stain' and *drygair* 'bad name, ill report'. *Drwg* can also, however, be used after its noun, e.g. in such expressions as *dydd drwg* 'evil day', *ffrwyth drwg* 'evil fruit'. Notice incidentally that Welsh exhibits vocalic alternation in *drwg* by itself but *dryg-* in compounds. Such alternation is absent from both Breton and Cornish.

The Irish congener of *drok* is *droch-*, which is a prefixed adjective only, e.g. *drochétach* 'poor clothes', *drochmenma* 'bad mood, dejection', *drochduine* 'evil person', etc. *Droch-* cannot be used predicatively, nor as a noun. It would seem therefore that the common Celtic usage was to prefix the reflexes of **druko-* to the noun qualified. The Welsh syntax of allowing *drwg* to follow its noun seems not to be favoured in the other insular Celtic languages, though we may have one example in Cornish.

tebel- 'evil, wicked'

This word seems to be a learned borrowing from Latin *debilis* 'weak, poor'. When used as a noun it means 'devil, evil one':

besy yw 3ys bos vuell ha seruabyll yth seruys manno allo an **tebell** *ogas 3ys bonas trylys* 'it is vital for you to be humble and diligent in your service so that the devil may not be turned near towards you' PA 19cd

poken yma an **tebell** *war agan dalla* 'or the devil blinds us' TH 51

der temptacon an **teball** *ow hendas adam pur weare eave re gollas der avall an place gloryous pur sure* 'through the temptation of the devil my grandfather Adam, he indeed has by an apple lost the glorious place surely' CW 2133-36

hedre vo yn the herwyth fythys nefre ny vethyth gans **tebeles** *war an beys* 'while you carry it never will you be overcome by evil ones in the world' OM 1464-66

hag y res gover fenten marth erhyth thotho hep fal may hallo tus ha bestes ha myns a vynno eve may whello an **debeles** *ov gueres menough thethe* 'and a stream of spring will flow, if you bid it without fail, so that man and beast and whoever wishes may drink, so that the evil ones may see my frequent help to them' OM 1845-50

Tebelas 'devils, evil ones' RCEV: 99.

Tebel and *yn tebel* are both used adverbially to mean 'severely, wickedly, horribly':

hag ena ij an scorgyas **yn tebel** *gans ij scorgye ha hager fest an dygtyas corf ha pen treys ha dewle* 'and then two scourged him horribly with two scourges and very grimly they treated him, body and head, feet and hands' PC 130cd

War aga dewlyn y 3e 3erag Ihesus re erell aga fen y a sackye hag a gewsy pur **debell** *worth Ihesus rag y angre* 'Upon their knees others came before Jesus; they shook their heads and spoke very wickedly to Jesus to annoy him' PA 195ab.

The commonest use of *tebel-* is as an adjective prefixed to a substantive:

Out warnas, **tebal-venyn!** 'Damn you, evil woman!' BK 1210

a **teball** *benyn heb grace ty ram tullas ve heb kene* 'O evil woman without grace, you have deceived me without cause' CW 854-55

an dragon yv **tebelvest** 'the dragon is a nasty animal' BM 4128

Inweth **teball** *vewnans a thora dampnacion thyn rena vgy ow teball vewa* 'Also evil life brings damnation to those who live wickedly' TH 16a

sav ny vyn awos trauyth gage y **tebel crygyans** 'but he will not for anything forsake his evil belief' PC 1813-14

tebel den *ef mar ny fe ny ny'n drosen thy'so gy* 'had he not been a wicked man, we would not have brought him to you' PC 1975-76

Gans gloteny ef pan welas cam na ylly y dolla en **tebell el** *a vynnas yn ken maner y demptye* When he saw that he could not seduce him by gluttony the devil tried to tempt him by another means' PA 13ab

ena wy a gyff in lel guas ovth eria heb question esel yv then **tebel el** 'there you will find indeed a fellow defiant without question; he is a limb of the devil' BM 967-69

Inna yth ew scriffes fatell rug an wyly serpent an **tebell ell** *dos the eva* 'in it is written that the wily serpent, the devil came to Eve' TH 3

yma agys yskar an **teball ell** *kepar ha lyon ow huga* 'your enemy the devil is like a roaring lion' TH 3a

Fy the Jovyn, **tebel-el!** *Henna ew dyowl pur* 'Fie to Jove, an evil angel! He is an utter devil' BK 134-35

rag ef o **tebel ethen** *neb a glewsys ov cane* 'for he was an evil bird that you heard singing' OM 223-24

martesyn y a yll skynnya in myschew an parna may teffans ha tenna re erell dre aga **teball examplis** *ha gwrythyans* 'perhaps they can descend into mischief of that kind so that they may draw other people by their bad examples and deeds' TH 25a

me ny'th sense guel es ky denagh the **tebelvryans** 'I will not esteem you more than a dog; deny your evil deeds' BM 3501-02

maras yns fur y a nagh in vr na **tebel wythres** 'if they are wise then they will renounce evil deeds' BM 4122-23

pan rens y ry thotheff **teball gyrryow,** *eff ny re aga theball gortheby* 'when they used wicked words against him, he did not answer them wickedly' TH 23

skettyaf the ben ha'th coloven theworth the scoyth gans the gonha kepar ha goyth, te mab hora, **tebal-voran!** 'I will smash your head and your skull from shoulder and neck like a goose, you son of a whore, an evil hussy!' BK 2159-65

The'n cans myl deawl reg yllough ha byner re thewellough, why, na **tebal nawothow!** 'May you go to the hundred thousand devils and may you never return, you nor bad news!' BK 744-46

Aron whek pyth a cusyl a reth thy'm orth am vresyl a son a'n **debel bobel** 'Dear Aaron what advice do you give me against the dispute of the murmuring of the wicked people?' OM 1813-15

moyses kemer the welen ha ty ha'th vroder aren arag an **debel bobal** *guask gynsy dywyth an men* 'Moses, take your staff and you and your brother Aaron before the wicked people strike with it twice the rock' OM 1841-44

yssyw hemma trueth bras bos the corf ker golyys gans **tebel popel** *ogh ogh* 'what a great pity this is that your dear body has been wounded by evil people, alas, alas!' PC 3182-84 *an falge dragon* **tebel preff** *ny gara gueles y grueff desawer vest yv honna* 'the treacherous dragon, evil reptile, I do not wish to see its face; it is a noisome beast' BM 4133-35

tebel seruont *a leuer mar serf ef bad y vester ke the honan ha gura guel* 'a wicked servant says, if he serves his master badly, "Go thyself and do better."' PC 2283-85

me yv vexijs anhethek gans **tebel speris** *oma* 'I am continuously vexed by an evil spirit here' BM 2630-31.

Notice that the compound *tebel-el* is used by several writers to mean 'devil'. Variously spelt *tebel el, tebell el, tebell ell, teball el, tebell el,* this expression is attested 23 times in the texts.

Tebel- is also prefixed to verbs where it bears adverbial sense as 'badly, wickedly, severely':

> *Inweth teball vewnans a thora dampnacion thyn rena vgy ow* **teball vewa** 'Also evil living brings damnation to those who live wickedly' TH 16a
>
> *a ihesu gouy ragos mar* **tebel dyghtys** *the vos* 'O Jesus, alas for you so wickedly treated!' PC 2633-34
>
> *Ay re* **deball dowethy** 'Oh, may you end badly!' CW520
>
> *mar calla y* **tebelfar** *drefen y voys sur heb mar erbyn fay crist dyspusant* 'if I can, he will fare ill because of course he is powerless against the faith of Christ' BM 2281-83
>
> *darne ov fobyl yv marov ha me* **tebelwolijs** 'part of my men are dead and I am badly wounded' BM 2489-90
>
> *pan rens y ry thotheff teball gyrryow, eff ny re aga* **theball gortheby** 'when they used wicked words against him, he did not answer them wickedly' TH 23
>
> *Ha pan ruga suffra myrnans, ny rug eff aga latha y, naga* **theball henwall** 'And when he suffered death, he did not kill them, nor call them evil names' TH 23
>
> *Whath kyn feva lyas tyrmyn assays ha* **teball pynchis**, *whath an feith a rug prevaylya woteweth* 'Yet though it was often tried and badly afflicted, still the faith prevailed in the end' TH 34.

When prefixed *tebel-*, as can be seen from the examples above, usually lenites *b > v* and *gw > w* in the next word. *Tebel-* also appears on occasion to lenite initial *p-* to *b-*.

As has been noted above, *yn trog* 'badly' is unattested in traditional Cornish. 'Badly' must be expressed by either *drog-* or *tebel-* prefixed to its verb.

Rarely *tebel* is used adjectivally after the noun it qualifies:

rag dewes mar nystevyth yn certan y a dreyl fyth hag a worth **dewow tebel**
'for if they do not get drink certainly they will change allegiance
and will worship evil gods' OM 1816-18

ham kyke yv **escar teball** *pur ysel me an temper* 'and my flesh is an evil
enemy; I shall tame it full low' BM 162-63

prest an **eʒewon debel** *ʒe Ihesus esens a dro* 'always the wicked Jews were
about Jesus' PA 140d

Re an **eʒewon tebell** *a leuerys heb pyte a wottense ow kelwel hely 3030 3y
wyʒe* 'Some of the wicked Jews said without pity, "Behold he is
calling on Elijah to preserve him."' PA 203ab.

In all these four cases above the word *tebel, tebell, teball* is in final position in
the line and is necessary for rhyme. We can assume that *tebel* was not usually
put after its noun in the spoken language.

gwan-, gwadn 'weak, bad'

Gwan 'weak' as a prefix means 'evil, bad, poor (in quality)':

surely ymowns in **gwan cas,** *mas y a rella gans speda ha in du tyrmyn
repentya ha gull penans* 'surely they are in a bad position, unless
with haste and in due time they repent and do penance' TH 32a

*Ellas emperour debyta mar mennyth oma latha flehys bythqueth na pehes yma
dywhy* **guan cusel** 'Alas, merciless emperor, if you will here kill
children that never sinned, yours is wicked advice' BM 1591-94

Arte Iudas ow tryle **gwan wecor** *nyn geve par ny yl den vyth amontye myns
a gollas yn chyffar worth ihesus ef a fecle* 'Again Judas turning—as a
bad dealer he had no equal; no one can compute how much he lost
in the transaction—to Jesus he spoke falsely' PA 40ac

Ha ʒenz hedna, an **guadn-ʒyrti** *ʒenz e follat a ƀestrîaz an dên kôt en guili*
'the wicked wife with her paramour killed the old man in the bed'
AB: 252a

Ha nessa metten an **guadn-ʒyrti,** *hei a ƀalasvaz ƀv 'u̜îl krei* 'And the next
morning the wicked wife, she began to make an uproar' AB: 252a

*pew vs in agan mysk ny mas eff a gylwe y gentrevak hay kyscristian foole
vncharitably bo nampith a throg ha* **gwan hanow** *arell?* 'who among us
does not call his neighbour and his fellow Christian a fool
uncharitably or some other unpleasant and evil name' TH 28a

moy ew ow **gwan oberowe** *hag inwethe ow fehasowe es tell ew tha vercy dew
thym tha ava* 'greater are my evil deeds and also my sins than is
your mercy to forgive me, O God' CW 1169-72

henna o **gwan obar** *gwryes* 'that was an evil deed done' CW 1268

*nefra ny wren rejoycya mes pub ere oll ow murnya heb ioy vyth na lowena der
tha* **wadn ober** *omma* 'never shall we rejoice but always will be

lamenting withut any joy or happiness through your evil deed here' CW 1272-75

henna o **gwadn ober** *gwryes* 'that was an evil deed done' CW 1679

Me yv parys arluth da sav **guan revle** *yma oma na yllyn lefya kyn moys* 'I am ready, my good Lord, but this is a bad rule that we cannot have lunch before departing' BM 3924-26

yth ombrovas **gwan dyack** *mayth of poyntyes 3a bayne bras* 'I have proved myself a poor manager, so that I am condemned to great torment' CW 920-21.

In the two examples from AB *guadn-ɜyrti* is a compound of *gwan, gwadn* and *gwreg ty* 'house-wife' (seen in CF: 14), where *gw-* remains unlenited after *gwadn*. In *gwan wecor* (< *gwecor, gwycor* 'dealer') on the other hand *gwan-, gwadn-* appears to lenite following *gw > w*. There is no evidence that *gwan-, gwadn-* mutated *c > g*.

I have no examples of *gwan-, gwadn-* prefixed to verbs. *Gwan, gwadn* is, however, used adjectivally after its noun, e.g.

du assus lues **den gvan** *sawys genogh in bys ma* 'God, how many weak people have you cured in this world!' BM 757-58

lues **den guan** *in bys ma pur guir eff a confortyas* 'many weak people in this world in truth he comforted' BM 4480-82

in nomine patris et filij virtu crist rebo yly a **dus gvan** *dygh in tor ma* 'in the name of the Father and the Son may the virtue of Christ be a salve, O weak men, for you at this time' BM 555-57.

Gwyr 'true'

Gwyr 'true' is used as a predicative adjective:

guyr *yv y vones arluth ha'y ober a pref henna* 'true it is that he is lord and his works prove that' PC 213

mester genough ym gylwyr hagh arluth henna yv **guyr** 'I am called master by you and lord and that is true' PC 873-74

reys yv bos **guyr** *an awayl* 'the gospel must be true' PC 924

ru'm fay **guyr** *yv agas cous* 'upon my faith, what you say is true' PC 1345

ty a yl y atendye bos **guyr** *ow cous kettep ger* 'you can observe that what I say is true, every word' RD 477-78

hep dout mars yw **guyr** *henna me a vyn mos alemma* 'without doubt if that is true, I shall go from here' RD 1236-37

ha na ylla possibly bos **gwyre** 'and it cannot possibly be true' TH 20

Gweyr *ew henna, by my sowl!* 'That is true, by my soul!' BK 767

dr' erama creege hedna tho bose **gweer** *eu skreefez enna* 'that I believe what is written there to be true' BF: 31.

Pur wyr means 'very truly, in very truth':

*yn clewsons ow leuerell **pur wyr** y fenne terry an tempel cref* 'they heard him saying very truly that he would destroy the mighty temple' PA 91ab

*Kayphas **pur wyr** a sorras hag eth pur fol yn vr na* 'Caiaphas very truly became angry and went quite mad then' PA 94a

*ytho bethyth mylyges **pur wyr** drys ol an bestes* 'therefore you shall be accursed very truly above all animals' OM 311-12

*otte omma ve kunys ha fast ef gynef kelmys **pur wyr** a das* 'behold here it is, firewood and it tied tightly by me very truly, O father' OM 1299-301

*nep re ordenes y lathe **pur wyr** y fythons dampnys the tan yfarn droka le* 'whoever have ordered that he be killed very truly will be condemned to the fire of hell, dreadful place' PC 3092-94

*rak **pur wyr** dasserghys yw* 'for very truly he has risen' RD 1004

*yth egen yn cres almayn orth vn prys ly yn **pur wyr** pan fuf gylwys* 'I was in the middle of Germany at lunch very truly when I was summoned' RD 2148-50

*my a wor **pur wyre** yn ta py ma an mester trygis* 'I know well very truly where the master lives' BM 38-39

*yn ov scole ny ve bythqueth ȝyso gy **pur wyre** cowyth yn discans nag yn dader* 'in my school there has never been anyone like you very truly in learning and goodness' BM 204-06

*yma pensevyk an gluas dysplesijs **pur guir** genas* 'the prince of the country is displeased with you very truly' BM 489-90

*yma duk oma in vlays drehevys sur er the byn ha ganso **pur guir** ost brays* 'a duke here in the country has risen surely against you and with in very truly a huge host' BM 2301-03

*lues den guan in bys ma **pur guir** eff a confortyas* 'many weak persons in this world he comforted very truly' BM 4480-81

*Christ mab an ughella Tas ew Du **pur wyer*** 'Christ the son of the most high Father is God very truly' BK 170-71

***Pur wyer** ny'th car neb lyes rag the debal-vanerow* 'Very truly quite a lot of people do not love you because of your evil ways' BK 1064-65

*Nu'm ankevyr ve **pur wyr** hedre vo nef in e le* 'I shall not be forgotten very truly, as long as heaven remains in its place' BK 1471-72

*The leud desyr a'm cuth **por wyer*** 'Your lewd desire grieves me very truly' BK 2952-53

***Por wyer** o'm gallos ema kekeffrys gul drog ha da* 'Very truly it is in my power to do both evil and good' BK 3112-13

*heb dallath na dowethva **pur wyre** me ew* 'very truly I am without beginning nor ending' CW 2-3 *ty a thebar in tha wheys theth vara **pur wyre** nefra* 'you will eat your bread very truly in the sweat of your brow for ever' CW 949-50

*vnna a gyke pub huny gans peagh **pur wyre** ew flayrys* 'in it everyone of flesh very truly stinks with sin' CW 2247-48

*der temptacon an teball ow hendas adam **pur weare** eave re gollas der avall an place gloryous* 'through the temptation of the evil one my grand-father Adam very truly has lost through the apple the glorious place' CW 2133-36.

Pur wyr (*pur guir, purguir, pur wyre, pur wyer, pur weyr, pur weare, por wyr, por wyer*) is very common in traditional Cornish. I have counted 188 examples. *Gwyr* is also frequently used as a noun meaning 'truth':

gwyr re gwesys yredy yn meth crist mygtern oma '"You have spoken truth," said Christ, "I am a king."' PA 102d

*lauar **gwyr** ʒymmo vn ger mar sota mab den ha du* 'tell me truth, one word, if you are man and God' PA 129c

*yma thy'mmo mur dysyr a wothfes ortheugh an **guyr*** 'I have a great desire to know the truth about you' RD 194-95

guyr a geusyth ievody 'you speak truth indeed' RD 653

*tav ty wrek gans the whethlow ha cous **guyr** del y'th pysaf* 'silence, you woman, with your stories and speak truth as I beg you' RD 901-02

*agan arluth yw marow ellas **guyr** a lauaraf* 'our Lord is dead, alas; I speak truth' RD 907-08

*me a leuer an **guyr** thy's* 'I will tell you the truth' RD 1061

*Rag purgacion theworth pegh a thee dre neb menes eral pella ys an **gwyre*** 'For purgation from sin comes by other means more than the knowledge of the truth' TH 14

*thea tirmyn pedyr bys in dith hethow an **gwyr** a ve derives a thorne the thorne* 'from the time of St Peter until the present the truth was transmitted from hand to hand' TH 48

*why a levar **gwyre** benyn vas* 'you speak truth, good woman' CW 675

*tha thew nyng eis otham vythe awoos cawas agen pythe me a wore **gwyre*** 'God has no need to receive our wealth, I know as truth' CW 1132-34

*devethys tha baradice me a wore **gwyre** yth oma* 'I know as truth that I have come to paradise' CW 2129-30

*E ve welcumbes, me ore **gwir*** 'He was welcomed, I know as truth' LAM: 224.

A frequent use of *gwyr* as a noun is seen in the expression *the wyr* 'truly, indeed':

y won the wyr dev an tas re sorras dre wyth benen 'I know truly that God the Father has become enraged through the work of a woman' OM 255-56

lemyn my a wor the wyr bos ov thermyn devethys 'now I know truly that my time has come' OM 2343-44

crys my the wyr the thasserghy 'believe that truly I have risen' RD 868

na nyl susten na pegans ny yllen dendyl the guir 'neither food nor income could I earn indeed' BM 696-97

der an sperys sans kerra concevijs y fue the guir 'through the most beloved Holy Spirit he was conceived truly' BM 858-59

settys rag th'agan dyseysya me a wor the wyr e vos 'I know that he is ready truly to discomfit us' BK 2240-41.

This nominal sense of *gwyr* can also be seen in the expression *yn gwyr* 'in truth, truly':

gans luas y fons gwelys en gwyr ʒe ʒustynee bos mab du neb o leʒys 'by many they were seen indeed to testify that it was the son of God who had been killed' PA 210cd

Onan ha try on yn gvyr en tas ha'n map ha'n spyrys 'One and three we are indeed, the Father and the Son and the Spirit' OM 3-4

yma ken thy'm the ole daggrow gois in gvyr hep mar 'I have reason to weep bitter tears of blood indeed' OM 630-31

tyr segh yn guel nag yn pras mar kefyth yn gvyr hep gow ynno gueet in ta whelas bos the'th ly ha the'th kynyow 'if indeed you find dry land in field or in meadow without doubt be careful to seek food for your lunch and for your dinner' OM 1137-40

pan pyn a gotho thotho lauar en guyr thy'm certan 'what punishment would be fitting for him, tell me truly for sure' OM 2233-34

dew vody tha ough yn guyr 'you are two good people indeed' OM 2461

an nyl torn y fyth ro hyr tres aral re got in guyr 'at one moment it is too long, at another moment too short indeed' OM 2548-49

drethos the gy y fyth ol ny yn guyr sawys 'through you all, we, indeed will be healed' PC 295-96

sur ol the wovynnadow ty a fyth yn guyr hep gow 'surely all your requests you will indeed have without falsehood' PC 599-600

ov hanov in guir heb mar yv costyntyn the nobil 'my name indeed of course is Constantine the noble' BM 1155-56

me a wor in guir heb mar benytho arluth ath par pur thefry nygyn bethen 'I know truly of course that we will not have a lord like you ever indeed' BM 4266-68

In gweyr heb mar, henna ew laver kymmyn 'Truly of course, that is a common saying' BK 757-58 *hy ew esya tha dulla es adam in gwyre yn ta* 'she is easier to deceive than Adam well truly' CW 472-73.

Note: Nance mistakenly took the collocation *yn guyr* in the texts to stand for *yn* the adverbial particle (which is followed by mixed mutation) + *guyr* as an adjective. He thus rewrote *yn guyr* as *yn whyr 'truly', a form which is unattested. *Yn guyr* means 'in truth', not 'truly'. Nance's *yn whyr is a mistake. *Gwyr* is occasionally used as an attributive adjective after its noun:

*hag ow bostye y bos ef **cryst guyr** vn vap dev a nef* 'and boasting that he was true Christ, the only son of the God of heaven' PC 1576-77

*nynsus **ger guir** malbe dam wath in ol the daryvays* 'there is still not a true damn word in all you say' BM 864-65

*me, myghtern Cragow, Corssyth, gans Arthor in **quarel gwyr** a vith paris corf ha pyth* 'I, Corsyth, king of Cracow, with Arthur in true contention will be ready body and wealth' BK 1462-64

*An lavar kôth yu **lavar guîr*** 'The old saying is a true saying' AB: 251c

*Enna ew ol guz **dega gwîr*** 'That is all your true tithe' Gwavas, LAM: 244.

As an attributive adjective, however, *gwyr* is most usually prefixed to its noun with lenition of the following initial consonant:

*dre **guyr vrus** sur y cothe dotho gothaf bos lethys* 'by rightful judgement surely he ought to be killed' OM 2237-38

*certan **guyr vres** yv honna* 'that certainly is rightful judgement' PC 515

*eugh sacryfyeugh in scon yn meneth the'n tas a'n nef hag ol agas **gvyr thege*** 'go, sacrifice quickly on the mountain to the Father of heaven with all your true tithe' OM 438-40

*my a'th worth gans ol ov nel y'm colon pur trewysy hag a offryn thy's whare warbarth ol ov **gvyr thege** yn gorthyans thys y lesky* 'I will worship you with all my strength in my heart very seriously and will offer you straight away together all my true tithe to burn it for you as worship ' OM 510-14

*rag bos a abel **gvyr thege** ef a'n gefyth yn dyweth an ioy na thyfyk nefre* 'because there is a true tithe from Abel, he will get in the end the joy that never ends' OM 515-17

*dvn yn vn rew scon hep lettye er byn ihesu neb yv **guyr dev** ow tos the'n dre* 'let us go in a group soon without delay to meet Jesus, who is true God, coming to the town' PC 239-42

*ellas bythqueth kyns lemmen y vos **guyr dev** ny wythen* 'alas, we never knew before now that he was true God' PC 1913-14

*Nyng es **gwyer Thew** saw onyn* 'There is no true God but one' BK 194

*e vos **gwyer Thew** ne brevith bys venytha, te pen cog!* 'you will not ever prove that he is true God, you blockhead!' BK 230-31

*Try personne eternal yns hag un **gwyer Thew** byttygyns* 'They are three eternal persons and one true God nonetheless' BK 253-54

*me re peghes marthys trus **guyr gos** dev pan y'n guyrthys* 'I have sinned wondrous perversely when I sold the true blood of God' PC 1505-06

*Martesyn te a lavar, fattellans bos gwyer? e vosama ow gweles an shap, an not an **gwyer gois** agen arluth Christ?* 'Perhaps you will say, how can they be true? That I see the shape and not the true blood of our Lord Christ?' SA 62a

*na ve y vose **guir sans** mar lues merkyl dyblans byth ny russe* 'were he not a true saint, he would not have done so many manifest miracles' BM 2051-53

*Meryasek del oys **guir sans** lemen prest sav ov bevnans* 'Meriasek, as you are a true saint, now readily save my life' BM 2175-76 .

John Boson writes *Deiu guir* 'true God' BF: 55, and Gwavas writes *an Deu guir* 'the true God' LAM: 238. Earlier writers write *guyr dev* without lenition, and *gwyer Thew* with it. The lenited form is almost certainly correct. In revived Cornish 'true God of true God' of the Nicene creed has been translated as *gwyr Dew a wyr Dew*, for example in LPK: 23. In the light of the three instances of *gwyer Thew* in BK, this should perhaps now be emended to *gwyr Dhew a wyr Dhew*.

Hager 'ugly, foul'

This is used as an adjectival prefix:

*Kensa, vrt an **hagar auall** iggeva gweell do derevoll warneny* 'First because of the storms he causes to rise up against us' BF: 9

***Hager awell**, ha auel teag* 'Bad or foul weather, and fair weather' ACB: F f *verso*

*hena o **hagar vargayne*** 'that was a grim bargain' CW 791

***hager vernans** an par-na ef a'n gefyth* 'a hideous death like that he will get' RD1984-85

*yn beys na allo den vyth gul **hager vernans** thy'mmo rak ow colon ow honan gans ov hollan me a wan* 'lest anyone in the world inflict a hideous death on me I will pierce my own heart with my knife' RD 2040-43

*ny rebue tus ongrasyas ha re vsias **hager gas** raffna ladra pur lues feyst* 'we have been graceless people and have used a foul case to ravage, to rob very many indeed' BM 2142-44

*yma ov tegensywe **hager gowes** war ov feth* 'a foul shower is threatening upon my faith' OM 1079-80

*ha saw ny gynes yn weth na'n beyn mar **hager thyweth** na mar garow* 'and save us with you as well that we do not have such a foul death and so violent' PC 2894-96 *govy na vuma war kyns* **hager dyweth** *yv helma* 'alas I was not aware before; this is an ugly death' BM 4099-100

An **hagar musi** *na ens vâze* 'The evil girls they are not good' BF: 58

martezen (ameb ev) ma nebònen en nessa tshei, a 'ryʒ uelaz aʒen **haʒer oberou** 'perhaps, he said, there is someone in the next house, who has seen our evil deeds' AB: 252a

Ase rusta **hager prat***!* 'What a nasty trick you have played!' BK 84

rag henna scon yʒ eth ef ʒe wrek pylat mayʒ ese han tebel el **hager bref** *yn y holon a worre war y mester venions cref y to Ihesus mar laʒe* 'therefore quickly he went to Pilate's wife where she was, and the devil, foul reptile, put in her heart that severe vengeance would come upon her husband if he were to kill Jesus' PA 122bd

Lebben an **hagar-breeve** *o moy foulze avell onen veth ell an bestaz an gweale a reege an Arleth Deew geele* 'Now the evil serpent was more false than any one of the beasts of the field which the Lord God had made' ÉCII: 174

henna vea **hager dra** 'that would be a foul business' CW 259

Gallas genaf **hager dowle** 'I have suffered a nasty fall' CW 420.

Rowe uses the expression *hagar-breeve* five times. This is, of course, exactly the same word as *hager bref* in PA and it indicates that *p* is lenited to *b* after *hager* in this word at least; though *p* is unmutated in *hager prat*. It seems *b* becomes *v* after in *hager vernans* and *hagar vargayne*; *c* is lenited in *hager gas* and *hager gowes* while *t* is lenited in *hager dra* and *hager dowl*. The differing treatment in *hager thyweth* and *hager dyweth* is noteworthy.

Hager may be used predicatively:

gouy vyth rak edrege bos mar **hager** *ow gorfen* 'alas for regret that my end is so foul' PC 1529-30

hager *lower os me avow* 'you are fairly hideous, I admit' CW 480

blewake coynt yw ha **hager** 'he is oddly hirsute and ugly' CW 1586.

It is also very rarely used after its noun:

Ay a vynta ge orth mab dean pan vo gwryes a **slem hager** *occupya rage sertayne ow rome* 'Do you wish that man, when he has been made of foul slime, should occupy my place indeed?' CW 254-56.

fals, falge 'false, perfidious'

This is used as a prefixed adjective:

Me, Hirtacy, mightern Partys, a veth iwys orth Arthor, an **fals brathky** 'I Hirtacy, the king of the Parthians, indeed will venture against Arthur, the treacherous cur' BK 2636-39 *pan faryng vs y'n temple gans ihesu an* **fals brybor** 'how are things in the temple with Jesus, the false vagabond?' PC 374-75

An **fals brybours** *dre bur tholowrs ru'm grug muscog* 'The false vagabonds by sheer affliction have driven me mad' BK 747-49

Mar kowsyth moy a Arthor o'm goith ve, te **fals bribor!** *neffra ny thibbryth bara* 'If you speak more of Arthur in my presence, you false vagabond! never shall you eat bread' BK 3185-87

Yma in pov **falge cregyans** *ov cul dym angyr an iovle* 'There is in the country a false belief that is giving me the devil's anger' BM 1161-62

ihesu parde a nazare an **fals crystyon** 'Jesus by God from Nazareth, the false Christian' PC 1111-12

na ny gotha thetha settya in rag na mentenya **fals discans** *thyn bobill* 'nor should they set out nor maintain false teaching for the people' TH 32a

nyns a den vyth vynytha a'n keth re-na the'n tyr sans marnas calef ha iosue rag y the vynnas gorthye **fals duwow** *erbyn cregyans* 'no one of those same with go to the Holy Land except Caleb and Joshua because they wanted to worship false gods contrary to belief' OM 1879-82

Gwayt e worthya pub termayn ha nagh Astrot ha Jovyn ha'th **fals duwaw** *in pub tu* 'Take care to worship him always and deny Astrot and Jove and your false gods on every side' BK 221-23

Fals du *ema ow conys* 'He worships a false god' BK 399

dyllyrf thy'nny baraban ny ol a'th pys dre the voth ha crous ihesu an **fals guas** *yntre dismas ha iesmas* 'deliver to us Barabas, we all beseech you by your will and crucify Jesus, the false fellow, between Dismas and Jesmas' PC 2484-87

Out warnogh wy **falge guesyon** 'A curse upon you, you false fellows' BM 3803

a **fals harlot** *gowek pur* 'O false villain, utter liar' RD 55

Te **falge horsen** *nam brag vy* 'You false whoreson, don't threaten me' BM 3491

my re gyrhas thy's the dre mab adam a[n] **fals huder** *may hallo genen trege* 'I have fetched home to you the son of Adam, the false deceiver, that he may dwell with us' OM 564-66

re fethas an **fals ievan** *hythyw ter-gwyth yn certan* 'he has conquered the treacherous demon three times today' PC 154-55

rak **fals iudas** *nep a'm guerthas ogas yma* 'for false Judas who has betrayed me is near' PC 1101-02

ty re worthyas war nep tro an **fals losel** 'you have worshipped on some occasion the false scoundrel' PC 2692-93

gorreugh an **fals nygethys** *gans abel a desempys the yssethe* 'put the false renegade immediately to sit with Abel' OM 914-16 *lauer thymmo ty lorden ay covs ty falge negethys* 'speak to me, you churl, of his words, you false renegade' BM 776-77

da vye kyns dos sabovt dyswruthyl an fals profes 'it would be good before the Sabbath comes to destroy the false prophet' PC 561-62

Bethow ware a fals prophettys 'Beware of false prophets' TH 19a

Na'ra chee boaz faulz teaze bedn tha contrevack 'Thou shalt not be a false swearer against thy neighbour' Rowe

iudas ny gosk vn banne lymmyn dywans fystyne thu'm ry the'n fals yethewon 'Judas is not sleeping at all but is hastening immediately to betray me to the false Jews' PC 1078-1080.

It should be noted that as a prefix *fals-* does not appear to lenite a following consonant. *Fals* sometimes follows its noun:

a pe danvenys thetha rag dyswruthyl der cletha an anfugyk fals na'm car 'were he sent to them to destroy by the sword the false wretch who loves me not' BK 2722-24

Modreth kyns ol y fynhas ahanowgh an darivyas, an fykyl fals 'Modred first of all wanted account of you, the false hypocrite' BK 3264-66

Iudas fals a leuerys trehans dynar a vone en box oll beȝens gwerthys 'False Judas said, "Three hundred pence of money—let all the box be sold."' PA 36ab

ha gwra avoydya talys nowith ha fanglys termys, ha bostow a sciens fals 'and avoid new stories and fancy terms and boasts of false science' TH 18a

a dus fals y redoȝye an purre laddron yn pow 'from false men they had come, the veriest thieves in the country' PA 90d.

Fals- is sometimes used adverbially before a verb:

ha genes mollat pup plu drefen fals brugy map dev map maria 'and be accursed in every parish because you have falsely judged the Son of God, the son of Mary' RD 2198-200.

Otherwise 'falsely' is expressed in Cornish by the English borrowing:

trueth vye den yw gulan falslych y vones dyswrys 'it would be a shame for an innocent man that he should be falsely killed' PC 2437-38

ef a whylas ihesu Cryst myghtern a nef ha falslych y'n iuggyas ef gans cam pur bras 'he sought Jesus Christ, the king of heaven, and falsely he judged with very great injustice' RD 2261-64

Mar pe oll an epscobow an bys re an par na, kepar dell esta se falsly ow reportia y the vos, pandra rug an sea postall a rome theth hurtya ge 'If all the bishops in the world were like that, as you falsely report that they are, in what did the apostolic see of Rome hurt you?' TH 48.

*Yn fals 'falsely' is unattested.

Cam 'crooked, wrong'
Cam is an adjective meaning 'crooked, wrong'. It can be used attributively after its noun:

A **consler cam**, pyth ew cusyl orth an wrusyl? 'You crooked adviser, what's to be done against the insubordination?' BK 967-69

ny vyn an vyl **harlot cam** awos an bys dywethe 'the crooked scoundrel won't die for all the world' PC 2914-15

a molath then **horsen kam** ha thage inweth gansa 'Oh, a curse on the crooked scoundrel, and on you too with him' CW 806-05

me a wra then **horsen cam** boos calassa presonys 'I will make the crooked villain be more harshly imprisoned' CW 2037-38.

Cam is also used as a noun meaning both 'crooked person, criminal' and 'wrong, crime':

syttyough dalhennow yn **cam** a leuer y vos map dev 'seize the miscreant who says he is the son of God' PC 1125-26

ma stryf yntre an thev **cam** ny wrons vry my the crye 'there is a dispute between the two scoundrels; they don't care that I am calling' PC 2248-49

ha falslych y'n iuggyas ef gans **cam** pur bras 'and falsely he judged him with very great injustice' RD 2263-64

A wek wegov agys mam thywhywhy y fye **cam** boys lethys am govys vy 'O sweet darlings of your mother, for you it would be a crime to be slain for my sake' BM 1653-55

yth ogh kerhys dymovy repreff na **cam** nygis beth 'you have been brought to me; you will suffer neither reproof nor wrong' BM 1769-70

byth ny ra **cam** the neb den gallus an iovle pup termen dretho a veth confundijs 'never does it wrong to anyone; the power of the devil will always be confounded thereby' BM 2031-33

thynny prest y fye **cam** mar ny rellen y gorthya 'for us it would ever be a sin if we did not worhsip him' BM 3755-56

ymowns ow kull inivri ha **cam** the crist 'they commit injury and wrong to Christ' TH 17a

a rug agan savyour, a supposta, inivry ha **cam** an parna then stall po cheare an scribys han phariseis 'did our Saviour, do you suppose, show injury and wrong of that kind to the stall or chair of the scribes and the pharisees?' TH 48a *ha'm bos parys the sconya pub* **cam** *der weras Jesu a'n prennas tyn* 'and that I am ready to reject all wrong by the help of Jesus who redeemed us dearly' BK 2028-30

"Eth esough why ow cul **cam** *thotho ef suer,"* e meth a '"You do him wrong surely indeed" he said BK 2232-33

Marya, an gwelha mam, in cheryta ragaf pys, ma'm bo gevyans ol a'm **cam** 'Mary, the best of mothers, in charity pray for me, that I may receive pardon for all my wrongdoing' BK 2827-29.

Cam- has been used as a prefix meaning 'crooked, wrong' since the Old Cornish period. One of the earliest compounds is the word *camniuet* 'yris uel arcus [rainbow]' OCV 436. The second element is *-niuet*, probably the plural of *nef* 'heaven'. The same word appears in Late Cornish as *Cabm-thavaz* (ACB: F f), where *cam* has been pre-occluded to *cabm-* and the second element has apparently been reshaped on the basis of the word *davas* 'sheep'. This is presumably as a result of the association of the rainbow with 'fleecy' clouds.

Here are some further compounds containing *cam-* as the first element:

An avel worth y derry wose my thy's th'y thefen ty re **gam wruk** *eredy* 'By plucking the apple after I had forbidden it to you, you indeed have sinned' OM 279-81

ty a **gam wruk** *yn tor-ma mes a egip agan dry* 'you did wrong now bringing us out of Egypt' OM 1646-47

ny the **gamwul** *y won guyr* 'I know truly that we have done wrong' PC 1065

rak ty th'y **gam worthyby** *ty a vyth box trewysy* 'because you answered him impertinently, you will get a nasty slap' PC 1268-69

yn ta ef re'n dyndylas pan **cam worthybys** *cayfas cafus drok hag yfle grath* 'well he has deserved it, to reeive harm and revenge since he answered Caiaphas impertinently' PC 1402-04

ha gava tha ny gon **Kabmoth** [i.e. *cabmweyth*] 'and forgive us our trespasses' Keigwin

camhinsic *injuriosus* 'injurious' OCV 306

camhinsic *injustus* 'unjust' OCV 403

henno myrnans in crowsse, dre paynys an parna gans **cammensyth** *procurijs* 'that was death on the cross by pains of that sort procured by injustice' TH 15

eff a suffras lyas kynde ha sorte a **kammynsoth** 'he suffered many kinds and sorts of injustice' TH 15a

tav se the vyn ty phelip rak pur wyr ty a **gam dip** *warnotho ef* 'silence your mouth, you Philip, for in truth you are mistaken about him' RD 995-97

may whrussons **cam dremene** *sur y vyllyk an prys* 'when they sinned surely they will curse the time' OM 337-38

as wrussough **cam tremene** 'how greatly you have sinned' RD 40
yma an apostyll pedyr ow leverall omma an very cawsse praga vgy tus ow
camvnderstondia *scripture* 'the apostle Peter explains here the very
cause that people wrongly understand scripture' TH 18.

It should be noted that *camhinsic* 'unjust' in Old Cornish and *cammensyth*,
kammynsoth 'injustice' in Tregear are all based on *cam-* and the root **hins*, **hens*
(Welsh *hynt* 'way', Breton *hent* 'way'). The simplex **hins*, **hens* is unattested in
Cornish. Notice also that Lhuyd uses the expression *kabmdybianz* 'mistaken
opinion' AB: 223, which is based on the verb seen in Tregear's *ty a gam dip*.

Cowl 'completely'

As an independent adverb *cowl* 'completely' usually appears as the disyllabic
cowal:

vynytha ny efyth coul marrow **cowal** *ty a vyth* 'never will you drink soup;
   you will be completely dead' OM 2701-02
ty a verow sur **cowal** *awos the thev nay vestry* 'you will die completely in
   spite of your God and his power' OM 2737-38
er the pyn cousaf **cowal** *marth a'm bues a'th lauarow* 'I shall speak against
   you completely; I am astonished at your words' PC 2391-92
syns war the keyn an grous pren yma lour the saw thy'so pur **cowal** *ty a
   ynny* 'bear on your back your cross; sufficient for you is your
   burden—completely you will go on it' PC 2586-88
A'n mor the gela **cowal** *pur theffry ef a'n ystyn* 'from one sea to the other
   indeed it encloses entirely' BK 1199-200.

When used as a prefix the form is either *cowl-* or *col-*:

nebas lowre a vyth an gwayne pan vo genas **cowle comptys** 'little enough
   will the gain be when you have reckoned it all fully' CW 794-95
aban omma **cowle dyckles** *hag a paradice hellys me a vyn dallath palas*
   'since I am entirely without resources and driven from paradise, I
   shall begin to dig' CW 1031-33
pur wyr leskys ef a vyth rag **cowlenwel** *both the vrys* 'in truth it will be
   burnt to fulfill the desire of your heart' OM 433-34
cresseugh **collenweugh** *kefrys an nor veys a dus arte* 'increase, also fill the
   earth with people again' OM 1211-12
yn lyfryow scryfys yma bos **collenwys** *lowene a ganow a'n fleghys da* 'in the
   scriptures it is written that joy is fulfilled from the mouths of good
   children' PC 435-37
lemyn na fo ol ow bouth **cowlynwys** *thy'mmo lemyn sav the voth the gy
   arluth bethens gruys yn pup termyn* 'now let not all my will be

fulfilled for me, O Lord, but let your will be done at all times' PC 1037-40

y vothe re bo **collenwys** *genan ny pub pryes* 'may his will be fulfilled by us always' CW 2471-72.

ha pen vo hy **cowle devys** *hy a vyth pub eare parys tha thone an oyle a vercy* 'and when it is fully grown it will ever be ready to bear the oil of mercy' CW 1938-40.

Lel 'loyal, true'

Lel 'loyal, true' is sometimes used predicatively after a noun:

travyth ny wreth gorthyby er byn **dustenyow lel** 'you do not answer anything against reliable witnesses' PC 1317-18

hag ena gwrewh aga lyskye dowt dew genow tha serry mar ny wreen **oblacon leall** 'and there burn them lest God be angry with you if we do not make true oblation' CW 1073-75

moyses mar sos **profus lel** *rys yv thy'so dyogel ry dour thy'nny the eve* 'Moses, if you are a true prophet, you must give us water to drink' OM 1799-801

bersabe ov **fryes lel** *rys yv gruthyl dyogel both agan arluth sefryn* 'Bathsheba, my faithful spouse, indeed it is necessary to do the will of our sovereign lord' OM 2187-89

guel yv vn den the verwel ages ol an **bobyl lel** *the vos keyllys ru'm laute* 'upon my word better it is for one man to die than for the faithful people to be lost' PC 446-68

the vroder ov **servont lel** *prag nag vsy ef genes* 'your brother, my loyal servant, why is he not with you?' OM 572-3

eugh ow dew el thu'm **seruons lel** *yn pryson evs* 'go my two angels to my loyal servants who are in prison' RD 315-16.

More usually, however, *lel* is prefixed to both nouns and verbs. Here are some examples of prefixed *lel* as both an adjective and an adverb:

rak certan kemmys a'n crys ha a vo **lel vygythys** *sylwel a wra* 'for certainly as many as believe him and are duly baptized he will save them' RD 1142-44

a pedar byth da the cher faste the gy the vreder yn **lel grygyans** 'O Peter, be of good cheer; do you confirm your brothers in the true faith' RD 2367-69

henna yv an **lel cregyans** *del deske sans eglos dyn ny* 'that is the true faith as holy church teaches us' BM 1319-1320

yth eseff prest ov cresy y vos **lel du** *genys ay vam maria* 'I believe firmly that he is true God born of Mary his mother' BM 834-36 *ef re thyndyles yn ta gothaf mernens yn bys-ma mara pethe lel iuggys* 'he has deserved to suffer death in this world, if he is properly judged' PC 1342-44

del on ny the lel bobil devethys yth on warbarth rag enour dis ha gorthyans 'as we are your loyal people we have come together for your honour and worship' BM 1173-75

scryffes yma thym pub tra a thallathfas an bys ma may fova leall recordys 'I have written everything from the beginning of this world that it may be truly recorded' CW 2171-74

nefre me ny fanna cur marnes a vn ena sur du roy thym y lel revlya 'never do I wish for a cure but of one soul surely; God give me to rule it rightly' BM 2845-46

enoch yth ew owe hanowe leal servant than drengis tas 'Enoch is my name, loyal servant to the Father, the Trinity' CW 2094-95

der thowgys e tathorhas e honnyn par del vynnas, ha'y lel servantes dyspernys 'through godhead he arose as he himself desired and his his loyal servants redeemed' BK 311-13

Jesu Christ, mab Marya, roy thym gras the'th lel-servya! 'Jesus Christ, son of Mary, grant me grace to serve you faithfully' BK 781-82

me a goth in pur thefrye gorthya dew an leall drengis 'I ought in very deed worship God, the true Trinity' CW 1955-56.

It is clear from *lel vygythys, lel grygyans, lel bobil* and *leall drengis* that lenition where possible is customary after *lel-*.

Lun, leun, luen, lene 'full, complete'

ha the wull lene amyndys ha pe sufficient raunsyn rag pehosow 'and to make full amends, and to pay a sufficient ransom for sins' TH 12a

the kekemmys na'm guello hag yn perfyth a'n cresso ow len benneth me a pys 'for as many who do not see me but believe perfectly my full blessing I shall request' RD 1554-56

pesef agys leun vanneth 'I beg your full blessing' BM 211

Meryasek welcum yn tre ham luen vanneth y rof 3ys 'Dear Meriasek, welcome home and my complete blessing I give you' BM 216-17

Tays ha mab han speris sans wy a bys a levn golon 'Father and Son and Holy Spirit, you will beseech with your whole heart' PA 1a

mar pesy a leun golon whare sawijs y fe3e del vynna crist y honon 'if he prayed with a full heart, straightway he would be healed, as Christ himself wished' PA 25cd

ha henna sur my a greys a luen colon pur theffry 'and that I believe surely indeed with my whole heart' OM 1263-64

a thev a nef the pysy a luen colon gueres ny 'O God of heaven—I beseech thee with all my heart—help us' OM 1607-08 *a bur fals dyscryggygyon tebel agas manerow na gresough a* **luen golon** *bos an tas dev hep parow* 'O you false unbelievers, wicked your ways, that you do not believe with all your heart that the Father is God without equal' OM 1855-58

gorthyans the'n tas arluth nef a'm **luen golon** *my a bys rag* **luen gallosek** *yw ef* 'glory to the Father, lord of heaven, I pray with all my heart, for he is wholly powerful' OM 2087-89

pyiadow a **luen colon** *a wor the ves temptacion na vo troplys y enef* 'pray with the whole heart puts temptation to flight that his soul be not troubled' PC 24-26

gaf thy'm lemmyn yn tor ma a **luen golon** *me a'th pys* 'forgive me now at present, I beg you with the fullness of my heart' PC 1445-46

me a'n pys a **luen golon** *yeghes thy'mmo a thanfon* 'I will beg him with all my heart to send me good health' RD 1715-16

ha fasta sy the vreder yn **luen grygyans** 'and confirm your brothers in full faith' RD 1163-64

eua war an beys meystry **luen gummyas** *yma thy'mmo* 'Eve, I have mastery, full licence over the world' OM 409-10

Me, Ethyon, duk Boecy, war the enmy a rys gans **lune devocyon** 'I, Ethyon, duke of Boethia, will attack your enemy with full devotion' BK 2673-76

rak me a wor lour denses marnes dre an **luen dvses** *omma ny sef* 'for I know that much manhood will not stand here except through the full divinity' RD 2514-16

luen dyal *war ol an beys ny gemeraf vynytha* 'full vengeance upon all the world I shall never take' OM 1233-34

rag why re sorras an tas m'agys byth **luen edrege** 'for you have angered the Father so that you will have full regret' OM 346-47

Dev a ros thy's an naw ran rag bewe orto certan dre y **luen grath** *ha'y versy* 'God gave you the nine parts to live on indeed through his full grace and his mercy' OM 493-95

guelas ow map y carsen a tas dre the **luen weres** 'I should like to see my son, O Father, by your full help' RD 442-43

Lowena ha **lune-rowath** *theso war ver lavarow* 'Joy and complete respect to you in few words' BK 1578-79

ihesu kyn wruk the naghe **luen tregereth** *me a pys* 'Jesu, though I did deny you, I beg full mercy' RD 1147-48

Lowena ha **lun yehas** *thu'm arluth ha gormolys* 'Joy and full health to my lord and praise' BK 2677-78

It is apparent from the above examples that *a luen golon* was the customary way in Middle Cornish of saying 'with all one's heart'.

Lun- is not infrequently prefixed to verbs:

a'n beth the vos datherghys y **luen crygy** *me a wra* 'that you have risen from the grave, I will believe it fully' RD 481-82

yn wlas na ow **len grysy** *tus yv tanow* 'in that land few men believe fully' RD 2461-62

pyv penagh a **len grysso** *yn weth bysythyys a vo a vyth sylwys* 'whoever believes fully and shall be baptized, will be saved' RD 2467-68

reys yv thy's ynno crysy ha **luen fythye** *yn teffry* 'you must believe in him and trust fully' OM 1508-09

rag y gerensa eff Du en tas ew **lene pacifies**, *satisfies ha greis contentys gans mab den* 'for his sake God the Father is fully pacified, satisfied and made content with man' TH 10a

Maria mam ha guerhes me a vyn the **luenbesy** 'Mary, mother and virgin, I will beseech thee fully' BM 3591-92

E coyth thotha gothvas gras ha'y **lunworthya** *pub termyn* 'One should give him thanks and worship him fully always' BK 321-21

ha gans ow ru in ow thermyn me a'th **luenworth** 'and with my royal power in my time I worship thee fully' BK 1224-26.

Mur, muer **'great, grand'**
Mur is sometimes used as an attributive adjective after its noun:

ystyn quaral na relha erbyn Myghtern **Bretyn Veor** 'lest he extend a quarrel agains the King of Great Britain' BK 1423-24

laddron mur *us in pov ma lues den ov tustruya* 'there are great robbers in this country destroying many people' BM 2059-60

rag y fynner mara kyller gans **paynys mer** *ow dyswul glan* 'for one will, if possible, destroy me utterly by torments' PC 2600-02

Trueth mur *yv ahanas* 'It is a great pity for you' BM 1992

indelle te a alse gul **worschyp mur** *theth nesse* 'thus you could provide great honour for your relatives' BM 2039-40.

It is also commonly used as a noun in the expression *mur a* 'much of, many of':

anotha y ma notyes **mur a ӡadder** *yn povma* 'much goodness is noted of him in this country' BM 188-89

yn y golen fast regeth **mur a gerense** *worӡys* 'into his heart much love has gone towards you' PA 115c

the vap den y tysquethas pur wyr **mur a kerenge** 'to mankind he showed indeed much love' RD 2637-38

may hillyn gwelas ha percevya fatell esa the crist **mer a garensa** *worthan ny pan ruga suffra kymmys paynys ragan ny* 'so that we can see and perceive that Christ showed much love towards us when he suffered so many torments for us' TH 15a *mur a onour te a fyth te yw mygtern cvrvnys* 'much honour you shall have; you are a crowned king' PA 136c

Mab marya mur a beyn a woȝevy yn vr na 'The son of Mary then suffered much pain' PA 54a

hen o ȝoȝo mur a bayn 'that was for him much anguish' PA 137d

agys sperys sur an pren in anken ha mur a beyn 'their spirit will pay for it indeed in misery and great torment' BM 1893-94

serpent rag aga themptya mer a bayne es thyes ornys 'serpent, for having tempted them much pain is ordained for you' CW 906-07

my a re gans mur a ras whare lemyn strokyas vras 'I will give quickly now with much grace great blows' PC 2715-16

mear a rase thewhy sera 'much thanks to you, sir' CW 702

Ko anberra der e derggawe gen mear a worianze 'Go into his gates with much worship' BF: 39.

It is also extensively used as a prefixed adjective

ena ty a yl dysky martegen the vrys mur dader 'there you can learn, if it be minded, great goodness' BM 60-1

yma notijs sur ha covsis mur thadder an keth den na 'there is noted indeed and spoken much goodness of that same man' BM 2772-74

Ihesu crist mur gerense ȝe vab den a ȝyswe ȝas 'Jesu Christ showed great love to mankind' PA 5a

iouyn roy theugh mur onour 'may Jove grant you great honour' PC 1712

The'n tas dev yn mur enor war y alter my a wor grugyer tek hag awhesyth 'To God the Father in great honour I place upon his altar a fine partridge and a skylark' OM 1201-03

my a's guyth gans mur enour na vo harth den yn bys ma kyn fe myghtern py emprour aga gorra alemma 'I shall keep them with great honour so that no one in the world, be he even a king or an emperor, will be bold enough to remove them from here' OM 2051-54

Lowena thys corf heb par ha mer honour 'Joy to you, O person without peer' BK 72-73

try person in idn dewges ow kysraynya bys vickan in mere honor ha vertew 'three person in one godhead reigning together forever in great honour and power' CW 6-8

kyn fena lethys marow dre mur peyn ha galarov ny'th tynahaf bynary 'though I be killed dead by great torment and affliction, I will not ever deny you' PC 905-07

yn mur payn pan y'th welaf ellas dre kveth yn clamder the'n dor prag na ymwhelaf 'in great pain when I see you, alas for anguish in a faint why do I not fall down?' PC 2592-94

hag ena ow brodar cayne me an gweall ef in mer bayne 'and there my brother Cain, I see him in great torment' OM 1831-32

Arluth a ver ryelder, the arghadow a vith gwrys 'O Lord of great majesty, your command shall be done' BK 402-03

Arluth ker thy's mur worthyans rag hyr lour ev ov bewnans 'Dear Lord, to you much worship for long enough is my life' OM 847-48

lemmyn cryst agan arluth mur worthyans thys del theguth worth agan dry alemma 'now Christ our lord great worship to you as is fitting, bringing us out of here' RD 149-51

The crist ihesu mur worthyans ha thys meryasek nefra 'To Christ Jesu much worship and to you, Meriasek, forever' BM 3846-47

An arlythy kepar dell goyth a the deffry pen ow arloyth th'y anterya, gans melody ha mer worthyans 'The lords as is fitting will go indeed to bury the head of my lord with melody and great respect' BK 2903-08

mear worthyans theis ow formyer ha gwrear a oll an beyse 'much worship to thee, my creator, and maker of all the earth' CW 1415

mere worthyans than drenges tase 'great worship to the Trinity, father' CW 1940

meare worthyans thyes arluth nef 'much worship to thee, Lord of heaven' CW 2478.

It seems that there is indeed a syntactic difference between *mur a gerense* 'much love' and *mur gerensa* 'great love', though the meaning is effectively the same.

Mur is also used adverbially before a verb and a verbal adjective:

du asota mur presijs dres ol breten heb awer 'My God, how greatly praised you are throughout all Brittany freely' BM 230-31

Mearthysaysys of drys pub gyst 'I am greatly afflicted beyond all joking' BK 1227-28.

pur 'pure, very'

When it is used attributively after a noun *pur* means 'pure, utter'.

ny eve cydyr na gwyn na dewes marnes dour pur 'he drank neither cider nor wine nor drink except pure water' BM 1969-70

a pegh golhys dre goys pur wy a fya tek sawys 'were you washed in pure blood, you would be cured beautifully' BM 1496-97

en eʒewon a arme treytour pur y vos keffys 'the Jews kept crying out that he had been found an utter traitor' PA 119c.

It is also used attributively before nouns with the sense 'pure, sheer':

eff a suffras lyas kynde ha sorte a kammynsoth ha paynys intollerabill ha turmontys yn y pur ha innocent corffe 'he suffered many kinds and

95

sorts of iniquity and unbearable pains and torments in his pure and innocent body' TH 15a

*eugh yn fen ȝe bylat agis Iustis rag me an syns **pur ȝen** len* 'go quickly to Pilate, your justice, for I consider him a pure honest man' PA 113ab

*yth esen dre **pur hyreth** war the lergh ovth ymwethe* 'we were for sheer longing pining for you' RD 1169-70

*a **pur voren** plos myrgh gal ty a verow sur cowal awos the thev nay vestry* 'O utter dirty wench, disreputable girl, you will die utterly in spite of your God and his power' OM 2736-38

*Reys o ȝoȝo dysqueȝas ȝe **pur treytours** y ȝewle* 'he was compelled to show his hands to utter traitors' PA 157a

*dre **pur natur** ha reson pan wreth hepcor an bevnens hep guthyl na moy cheyson a hugh an eleth ha'n sens ty a thue the nef thu'm tron* 'by pure nature and reason when you relinquish life without making any more ado you will come to heaven to my throne above the angels and the saints' RD 458-62.

It is commonly used adverbially before adjectives to mean 'very':

*A vroder ov banneth thy's rag the gusyl yv **pur tha*** 'O brother, my blessing to you, for your counsel is very good' OM 1827-28

*saw yma thym ahanes dowte **pur vras** a anfugye* 'but I have very great fear of you of mischief' CW 575-76

*gonys a wreugh **pur vysy** thy'm del hevel fossow da gans lym ha pry* 'you will make for me very busily as it seems sound walls with lime and mortar' OM 2448-50.

Interestingly, Tregear does not use *pur* to mean 'very'. Instead he uses the English word itself:

*Du a wellas pub kynd a ruga gull, ha yth ens **very da*** 'God saw everything that he had made, and they were very good' TH 3

*fatell rug agan savyour govyn worth pedyr **very ernysch**, mar sega eff worth y gara eff moy ys onyn arell an aposteleth* 'that our Saviour asked Peter very earnestly whether he loved him more than any other of the apostles' TH 43-43a

*ny a ra whare persevya nag o offence bean mas **very grevaws** ha poos* 'we will soon perceive that it was not a small offence but very grievous and serious' TH 4

*S Hierom inweth in y epistill the Damasus yma ow settya in mes **very notably** an primasie* 'St Jerome as well in his epistle to Damasus sets out the primacy very notably' TH 49

ADJECTIVAL AND ADVERBIAL PREFIXES IN CORNISH

S Ireneus martyr benegas in weth, **very ogas** eff a ve then tyrmyn an
abosteleth 'St Irenaeus, a blessed martyr also, he was very near to
the time of the apostles' TH 18a

han kyth tra na a yll bos prevys **very pleyn** dre an scripture 'and the same
thing can be proven very plainly by means of scripture' TH 42a

Pan danger ewa the reylya in moyha spytfully a ylly bos, ha gans **very vylle**
termes ow Jestia gansa 'What danger is it to rail most spitefully as
possible and with very vile terms to make mock of it?' TH 55a.

Tregear also uses the English word very to mean 'very, self same' in such
expressions as y very corffe 'his very body', an very gyrryow 'the very words',
and an very substans 'the very substance'. This usage is found in BK and CW as
well.

Revivalists, when using the word pur as a leniting prefix meaning 'very',
pronounce the word with the same vowel as pur 'clean', i.e. with a fronted long
[y:]. This, I believe, is probably a mistake. There has always been good
evidence that pur 'very' had a reduced vowel, which was either schwa or short
o. There is one Late Cornish example of per:

Nenna e eath car rag Frink rag debre an Tacklow ewe **per trink** 'Then he
went away to France to eat the things that are very bitter' LAM: 226.

In Late Cornish 'very' is also sometimes written por:

Eth o ve **por loan** tha gwellas why a metten ma 'I am very glad to see you
this morning' ACB: F f verso

Rag fraga an arleth ni ewe deawe **por tha** 'For why our Lord is a very good
God' BF: 39.

Moreover Lhuyd makes it clear that the vowel of 'very' was schwa or a
rounded vowel. Under Optimus 'best' he gives the Cornish forms as Guella &
guel'ha, **por-dha** AB: 108c. In his Cornish Grammar he has two entries: Por, **pur**
and pyr, Very; **Por-chal**, Very blind AB: 232 and Of Quality. Por, Very; **Por dha**
and pordha AB: 249. Lhuyd's pur in the entry from AB: 232 he has presumably
got from the Middle Cornish written sources. Lhuyd also cites the sentence
Yma e **pyr havel** dhys 'He is very like thee' AB: 242b, where pyr is a Lhuydian
spelling for por. In the preface to his Cornish grammar, Lhuyd in his own
Cornish writes por 'very' eighteen times, inter alia in por dhâ 'very well', por
Spladn 'very clear' and por uîr 'very truly' (AB: 222-24).

Although Nance did not realize that prefixed pur- should have a reduced
vowel, he himself used prefixed por < pur in Unified Cornish porres 'dire
necessity, urgency', which derives from pur + reys 'necessity'. This is common
in the texts; here are a few examples:

rag an lahys ȝynny es a vyn y dampnye **porres** 'for we have laws that will of necessity condemn him' PA 32c

Mas lemmyn rys yv **porris** *batayles kyns ys coske* 'But now it is very necessary to struggle before we sleep' PA 51a

rag sustene beunans thy'n rys yw **porrys** *lafurrye* 'to sustain life it is essential for us to work' OM 682-83

Eff a res **purris** *bos y very corfe eff hay gois in dede* 'It must of necessity be his very body and blood' TH 52

An Tas ha'n Mab der reson **porrys** *ew Du* 'The Father and the Son by reason must be God' BK 264-65.

It is also possible that *por* < *pur* occurs in the adverb *poran* 'exactly', but the second element is not clear. The pronunciation of Middle Cornish *pur* 'very' as *por* has now been amply corroborated by examples in BK:

Mars eugh the Arthor **por** *wyr* 'If you go to Arthur very truly' BK 1357

por *theffry ny vith kerys neb mar te va re venowgh* 'in very truth nobody is loved if he come too often' BK 1600-01

Bethans **por** *war!* 'Let him be very wary!' BK 1739

por *gentyll ew ha'y uos presyus hag honorys a ve va guyw* 'he is very noble and his blood is precious and it was worthily honoured' BK 2014-17

Henna ew kowsys garow hag a golan stowt **por** *wyer* 'That is roughly spoken and from a proud heart very truly' BK 2404-05

neffra ny vith da e ger, na vith **por** *wyer* 'never will his mood be good, it will not very truly' BK 2762-63

ha **por** *harth the'n senators trybut Bretayn presant a in dyscharg thymmo nefra* 'and very courageously to the senators Britain's tribute, present it to discharge my debt for ever' BK 2840-42

The leud desyr a'm cuth **por** *wyer* 'Your lewd desire grieves me in very truth' BK 2952-53

Ny thebbra' boys na nu'm deg troys, ny raf **por** *wyr* 'I shall not eat food, nor shall foot carry me, I shall not in very truth' BK 2967-79

Me a ra, syra, **por** *wyr* 'I shall, sir, very truly' BK 3028

Mar ny vethaf curunys, in tan **por** *doun te a lysk* 'If I am not crowned, in very deep fire you will burn' BK 3095-96.

On occasion the scribe of BK writes *pour* rather than *por*. This suggests that the word may sometimes have been pronounced with a long [u:]:

Ow lester a ve lehan drys mor **pour** *thown* 'My vessel was a stone slab across a very deep sea' BK 94-5

*Pan desefsan bos an lorden **pour** galarak, grassa the Christ a re an pyst* 'When I should have thought that the fellow would be very wretched, the idiot gave thanks to Christ' BK 719-23
***Pour** awherak ha prederak ove, by God!* 'Very wretched and anxious am I, by God' 77-80.

This pronunciation is perhaps attested in BM also: *Plos marrek **pour*** 'utterly dirty knight' BM 2444, although here *pour* comes after its noun.

Sans 'holy'

Sans 'holy' as an attributive adjective usually follows its noun, in the expression *speris sans, spyrys sans, spuris sans, Speres zance, Spiriz Sanz* 'Holy Spirit' PA 1a, OM 85, BM 212, TH 5a, BF: 41, 56, etc., etc Lhuyd also writes *skriptor zanz* 'holy scripture' AB: 223. When used in conjunction with *eglos* 'church', however, the adjective *sans* is always prefixed:

> *yth esough ov kuthyl ges a thu hag e **sans eglos*** 'you are making mockery of God and his holy church' PC 332-34
> *aspyen gvas gans pors poys mar kyllyn den **sans eglos*** 'let us look for a chap with a heavy purse, a man of holy church' BM 1875-76
> *hythyv an dus **sans eglos** pan lafuryens rag benefys ware y feth govynnys py lues puns a yl bos anethy grueys* 'today the people of holy church, when they labour for a benefice immediately is asked how many pounds can be made from it' BM 2826-30
> *te neb vgy ow defya ydols yth esas ow robbya **sans egglos*** 'you who defie idols you rob holy church' TH 14a
> *in ascra agan mam **Sans egglos*** 'in the bosom of our mother, holy church' TH 41
> *an dus coyth auncient ow tochya an primacie, bo an vhell ordyr a **sans egglos*** 'the old ancient people concerning the primacy, or the high order of holy church' TH 46
> *Onyn an **sans egglos** ew gilwis Vigilius a martyr* 'One of holy church is called Vigilius, the martyr' SA 64.

Notice also that John Boson prefixes *zans* to *Carrack* 'rock' in *Ma canow vee wor Hern gen Cock ha Rooz Kameres en **zans Garrack** glase en Kooz* 'My songs is about herrings by a boat and net taken in the holy green rock in the wood' BF: 43.
The different position of *sans* in *Spyrys Sans* but *sans eglos* may be a reflection of the usage in ecclesiastical Latin, where 'Holy Spirit' is usually *Spiritus Sanctus* but 'holy church' is *sancta ecclesia*, e.g. in the Apostles' Creed: *Credo in Spiritum Sanctum, sanctam ecclesiam catholicam* 'I believe in the Holy Spirit, the holy catholic church'.

Hen 'old', coth 'old', hyr 'long', cot 'short', gow 'falsehood'

Hen 'old' is not common in Cornish, being replaced in most contexts by *coth* 'old'. It does, however, occur once as an attributive adjective after its noun:

> *duen alemma verement brays ha byen **tus hen** guelhevyn an pov* 'lets us go hence truly, great and small, elders, nobles of the country' BM 2927-29.

It occurs as a prefixed adjective only in words for 'grandfather, forefather.' We thus find:

> *avus **hendat*** 'grandfather' OCV 129
> *whath kenthew ow **hendas** cayne pur bad dean lower accomptys* 'yet though my grandfather Cain is a very bad man enough accounted' CW 1446-47
> *haw **hendas** cayme whath en bew* 'and my grandfather Cain still alive' CW 1480
> *cayne whath kenthota ow **hendas*** 'Cain, yet though thou art my grandfather' CW 1660
> *Rag kepar maner dell rug eff temptia agan **hendasow** ny Adam hag eva* 'For just as he tempted our ancestors Adam and Eve' TH 3a
> *Ny a rug peha kepar hagan **hendasow**, ny a rug an pith nag o da na mytt ragan the wull* 'We sinned as our ancestors sinned, we did that which was not good nor meet for us to do' TH 9a
> *abavus **hengog*** 'great-grandfather' OCV 130
> *cayne ow **hengyke** ew marowe* 'Cain my great-grandfather is dead' CW 1702.

Coth as a prefixed adjective occurs only, it seems, in the compound *cothwas* 'old fellow, old man':

> *hemma yv an keth ihesu a leuer y vos map dev map iosep an **coth was** gof* 'this is the same Jesus who says he is the son of God, the son of Joseph the old fellow of a smith' PC 1693-95
> *Gans gweras ahanowgh why ow eskar a vith lethis, an **coethwas**, my nu'm bues dowt* 'With your help my enemy will be killed, the old fellow, I have no doubt' BK 3246-48.

Nance says *hyr* is commonly used as a prefixed adjective, but the only example known to him would have been: *crist ker regyn danvoneys oma prest theth confortya kynth eses ovt[h] **hyrpenys*** 'beloved Christ has sent us here always to comfort you, though you be doing long fasting' BM 3883-85. A further instance of prefixed *hyr* is now known from *Scon te a vyth gorthybys heb **hyrwyge*** 'You will soon be answered without long delay' BK 152-53. Here *hyrwyge*, which is not otherwise attested, is apparently a compound of *hyr* 'long' and *gwega 'to wind, to meander'; cf. gweg 'bindweed, vetch'; Welsh gwyg 'vetch', Bret. gweg 'vetch'.

Cot 'short' as a prefix is attested only in one phrase:

> an moar brase yn **cutt termyn** adro thom tyre a vyth dreys 'the sea in a short time shall be brought round my land' CW 88-89
>
> yma thymma hyrathe bras rag gothevas pandra vea in **cutt termyn** ages negys 'I have a great longing to know in a short time what your business would be' CW 590-92.

I can find no other examples of cot in this or other compounds.

Nance lists gow as a prefixed adjective, but this is a mistaken, since gow- is a noun, not an adjective. When used as a prefix it is rare, for it seems to be attested twice only. The first instance is Old Cornish **gouleueriat** falsidicus 'liar' OCV 424; and the second, yma ree ov leferel heb ty vyth na **govlya** delyfrys der varia fetel ywa dyogel 'some are saying without an oath or perjury that he has been delivered safely by Mary' BM 3739-42.

Rag, therag 'before'

The prepositions rag 'before' and thyrag 'before' are sometimes compounded with leverel 'to say' to give ragleverel, theragleverel 'to predict, to mention beforehand':

> An seth yw **rag leueris** as gwyskis tyn gans mur angus war hy holon 'the predicted arrow struck her sharply with great grief upon her heart' PA 224ab
>
> Trega suer ew an Spurys a ve **thyrag leverys** 'The Spirit, which was mentioned before, is a presence' BK 268-69
>
> yma ynweth S paull ow scriffa the timothe hay exortya eff ernyssly in study an scriptur haw ry thotheff gans oll an rema an rulle **the rag leverys** 'St Paul also writes to Timothy and earnestly exhorts him in the study of scripture and gives him with all these the rule mentioned above' TH 18a
>
> dell ew **therag leverys**, eff a asas thynny lays rag synsy 'as has been mentioned before he left us laws to keep' TH 40.

Lhuyd uses the expression raglaveryz 'aforementioned' seven times in the preface to his Cornish grammar. Lhuyd may well have heard raglaveryz (cf. rag leueris in PA) or it may a coinage of his own on the basis of Welsh rhagddywedyd and rhagfynegi 'to foretell, to mention before'.

STUDIES IN TRADITIONAL CORNISH

Prefixed adjectives and adverbs borrowed from English

Bad 'bad'
Bad 'bad' occurs four times in *Jowan Chy an Hordh* (JCH §§31-320 in the expression *bad-ober* 'bad deed, crime'. It is also attested in the phrase *warlerth* **badd** *maner* 'in a bad manner' SA 65a and **bad** *dean* 'bad man' CW 1447. In these two cases it is not certain that we are dealing with true compounds, since both may simply be undigested borrowings from English

Chyf 'chief'
Chyf 'chief' is widely used in Cornish as a prefixed adjective:

> *Na rug Du dynvyn y* **chyff apostill** *pedyr the the rome* 'Did God not send his chief apostle to Rome?' TH 46a
> *Me yv* **chyff arluth** *rohan* 'I am chief lord of Rohan' BM 1936
> *Ith off gelwys costentyn in rome* **chyff cyte** *an beys emperour curunys* 'I am called Constantine, crowned emperor in Rome, chief city of the world' BM 2513-15
> *poran in Rome, neb ew an pen ha* **chife cyte** *an bys* 'in Rome to be exact, which is the head and chief city of the world' TH 47a
> *ov benneth thy's belsebuk del ose pryns ha* **chyf duk** 'my greetings to you, Beelzebub, as you are prince and chief duke' PC 1925-26
> *yma ov conys thyuwhy* **chyf guythoryon** *ol a'n gulas* 'you have working for you the chief workers of all the kingdom' OM 2330-31
> *henew the leverell, may fo agan* **chiff ioye** *ha delite settys in du* 'that is to say that our chief joy and delight should be set on God' TH 21-21a
> *Rag an ena, an pith ew an* **chyff part** *a vabden* 'For the soul, that which is the chief part of man' TH 12
> *whath an rema ew an* **chiffe partys** *anetha vs omma ow folya* 'still the those which are the chief parts of them follow here' TH 36
> *An* **chiff poynt** *a ra den tyrry charite ew murdyr* 'The chief way in which a man can break charity is murder' TH 27.

It is clear from the first two examples above that Rome was regularly in Middle Cornish referred to as *chyf cyte an bys* 'chief city of the world'

over 'over'
The English borrowing *over* was used adverbially as a prefix before verbs:

> *Arthur a vyn e vettya in hast ha'y* **oversettya** 'Arthur wishes to meet him in haste and to overcome him' BK 2393-94
> *eff a rug* **ouerwelas** *an dignite han beautye a sans egglos* 'he oversaw the dignity and the beauty of holy church' TH 31

*the kafus an cure ha the **ouerwelas** ha gouerna y egglos bys gorfen an bys* 'to obtain the cure and to oversee and govern his church until the end of the world' TH 41a

*why am gweall, **overdevys** yth ama warbarth gans bleaw* 'you see me, I am overgrown with hair' CW 1507-09

***overdevys** oll gans henna yth os gans bleaw* 'moreover you are all overgrown with hair' CW 1604-05

*defalebys ove pur veare hag **overdevys** gans bleawe* 'I am greatly deformed and overgrown with hair' CW 1665-66.

It is likely that *casula **ofergugol*** 'chasuble' OCV 789 is a compound of Old English *ofer* 'over' and *cugol* 'hood' < *cuculla*.

At first sight the English word 'open' seems to be a prefix in ***opyn guelys** yv omma nag us du mas ihesu ker* 'it is openly seen here that there is not God but beloved Jesus' BM 4152-53. It is more likely, however, that *opyn* is free-standing adverb that happens to be placed immediately before the verbal adjective. The same adverb occurs immediately after the verbal adjective in *kerys oys purguir gans du **prevys open** oma yv theragon in teller ma* 'you are very truly loved by God; it is openly proven here in this place before us' BM 675-77.

Conclusions

Nance is largely correct when he lists as the commonest prefixed adjectives *pur, bras, cot, cam, gow, gwyr, gwan, tebel, drog, fals, hager, hyr*. *Gow*, as we have seen, is not an adjective. Nance does not, however, mention *cowl-, lel-, lun-, mur* nor *sans* as prefixes. Neither does he cite either of the borrowings *chyf-* or *over-*, both of which are used as prefixed adjectives in the traditional language. This latter omission is presumably the result of his customary purism.

The examples from the texts cited above give us an insight into how the various prefixed adjectives and adverbs were used in the traditional language. Probably the most important points for us as revivalists to remember are the following:

1) that *drog-* 'bad' and *fals-* 'false' almost invariably precede their noun or verb. They do not follow. Furthermore neither of the two adverbs **yn fals* 'falsely' nor **yn trog* 'badly' is attested in the traditional language. 'Falsely' in Cornish is either *fals-* or *falslych*; 'badly' is either *drog-* or *tebel-*.

2) that *pur* 'very' was pronounced with a short *o* or schwa, and in the revived language should perhaps be written *por*.

"IF" IN CORNISH[11]

Conditional Sentences

Conditional sentences are usually in two parts. One part or clause usually contains a word meaning 'if' and sets out a condition. The other clause describes the result of the condition. The *if*-clause is known as the protasis, and the other clause is called the apodosis. I shall be using these terms.

Real Conditions 1

Let us take for example a simple English sentence: 'If I see John tomorrow, I will give him the money.' 'If I see John tomorrow' is the protasis, 'I will give him the money' is the apodosis. In Cornish 'if' is most commonly rendered *mar* or *mara*, both of which cause hard mutation or provection. If we want to render 'If I see John, tomorrow, I will give him the money' into Cornish we can say, for example, *Mar qwelaf Jowan avorow, me a re an mona dhodho*. Notice that the initial of *gwelaf*, the first person singular of the present-future of *gweles* 'to see' is hardened, devoiced or provected to *qw* after *mar*. Notice also incidentally that for 'money' I say *mona*. In traditional Cornish the word for 'money' is always *mona*. In traditional Cornish *arhans* never means 'money,' but rather 'silver.'

To say 'I will give him' I say *me a re*, the present-future of *ry* 'to give'. One can also, and more idiomatically say *me a vydn ry*. The accepted doctrine in Unified Cornish was always that *me a vyn* meant 'I want to,' but this is only partially true. In traditional Cornish when *me a vyn, ev a vyn*, etc. are followed by a verbal noun, the sense is usually simply a future, with little if any sense of volition. We know this from numerous examples in the texts. For example, when in *Origo Mundi* Abraham is about to kill Isaac he says to him: *gans ov clethe sur the **lathe** scon **me a vyn** *'with my sword soon surely I will kill you' (OM 1362-63). Abraham doesn't want to kill Isaac, his only son. He must, because God has told him to. He intends to, but there is no volition. There are plenty of further instances. Notice for example the following sentence from Lhuyd: *Ny **vedn** e nevra **dvz** vêz a ʒýndan* 'He will never get out of debt' (AB: 230c). He wants to get out of debt. The year is 1707 and he is afraid of debtors' prison; he just hasn't got the money. *Ny vedn e nevra dvz means* 'He won't ever come' not 'He doesn't want to come'. In traditional Cornish if one wants unambiguously to say 'I want to do something' one says *me a garsa gwil neb tra*.

I just now translated 'If I see John' as *Mar qwelaf Jowan*, but there are easier ways. One can use an auxiliary verb. The verb *gwil* 'to do' is one possibility and this is common in some texts. I prefer most frequently to use the verb *dos* 'to

11 Delivered as a paper at Skians Conference 2014, Cornwall College, Camborne. October 2014.

"IF" IN CORNISH

come' followed by *ha* 'and' and the verbal noun. One can thus say *Mar tov* or *Mara tov ha gweles Jowan, me a vydn ry an mona dhodho.* This use of *dos* + *ha* in conditional sentences is common in traditional Cornish at all periods. It is well worth imitating in the revived language and it has the advantage that the provection which follows *mar* or *mara* is already in place on the relevant part of the present-future of *dos*. Here are some examples from the texts of the present-future of *dos* in conditional sentences:

mar tue nep guas ha laddre en gueel theworthyn pryve meth vyth ol d'agen ehen 'if some fellow steals from us the rods surreptitiously, it will be a disgrace to all our kindred' OM 2064-66

mar tu fe ha datherghy mur a tus a wra crygy ynno y vos dev a nef 'if he rises from the dead, many men will believe in him, that he is God of heaven' RD 7-9

mara tuen ha debatya mas an nyyl party omma ov teberth purguir ny warth 'if we argue, only one side here indeed will be laughing when we depart' BM 3476-78

Mara tof ha trewelas, ny vyth mab den ou gwelas rag arsevnans ha terrur 'If I rage, no human being will dare look at me for ?persecution and terror' BK 1402-04

the le inclynacion an geffa den the begh, the voy ha the vrassa ew y begh mar te ha gull an dra 'the less inclination a man has for sin, the more and the greater is his sin, if he does the thing' TH 4a

Mar ten ny ha leverell nag ony pehadoryan, yth esan ow desyvya agan honyn han gweroneth nys ugy genyn, mar ten ha menegas agan pehosow du ew lene a vercy, just ha fethfull the gava thyn agan pehosow ha thegan glanhe a bup filth, ha mar tene leverall na russyn peha, ny a ra eff gowak hay er nyns ugy innan ny 'If we say we are not sinners we deceive ourselves, and we have not the truth; if we confess our sins, God is full of mercy, just and faithful to forgive us our sins and to cleanse us from all filth; and if we say that we have not sinned, we make him mendacious and his word is not in us' TH 8

pandre vynnough leverall mar tema disquethas theugh certyn tacclow arall mere moy agis helma 'what will you say, if I show you certain further things much greater than this?' SA 60

mar te wonen ha leverol dr'olga tavaz an Brittez cooth tose tho an ewhelder ma aweeth, mar pee angy mar fortidniez, 'th era ve mar pel durt naha an dadn an tavaz a dama ha a pow, uz rag e crenga dr'oma parrez tho leveral andelna aweath 'if someone says that the language of the ancient Britons could have come to this height also, if they had been so fortunate, I am so far from denying my mother tongue and my country, that for its sake I am prepared to say so also' BF: 31.

Real Conditions 2
In the clause *Mar qwelaf Jowan avorow* the verb is present-future. In *mar tov ha gweles Jowan* the verb is also present-future. There is one verb in Cornish, however, where the present and the future are represented by different tenses of the verb, and this distinction must be maintained in conditional sentences. Look at the following two sentences in English: a) 'If you're hungry, eat something'; b) 'If you're hungry later, I'll make you a sandwich'. In English the protasis in both is identical, even though a) refers to the present and b) refers to sometime in the near future. In Cornish, however, the two clauses must be translated differently. Let's look at the first sentence.

The word in traditional Cornish for 'hunger' is *nown*. This word is rare. It occurs once in Old Cornish, and three times in Middle Cornish, of which two examples are in *Bewnans Ke*. In traditional Cornish the ordinary way of saying 'I am hungry' is *me yw gwag*, literally 'I am empty', e.g. *Gwag ove, rave gawas haunsell?* 'I am hungry, shall I have breakfast?' (ACB: F f *verso*); *Ha pe reeg e penes doganze jorna ha doganze noze, e ve ouga nena gwage* 'And when he had fasted for 40 days and 40 nights, he was then hungry after that' (ÉCII: 185–86). If, therefore, we want to say, 'If you're hungry, eat something', a good way would be: *Mars os gwag, gwra debry neb tra*. Notice of course, that *mar* becomes *mars* and *mara* becomes *maras* before vowels in *bos* 'to be' and *mos* 'to go.' So *Mars os gwag* or *Mars osta gwag* are correct. Here are a very few examples from the texts of the present of *bos* being similarly used in the present in conditional sentences:

> *Mars os mab du leun a ras an veyn ma gura bara ȝis* 'If you are the son of
> God, full of grace, make bread for yourself from these stones' PA llc
> *moyses mars os profus lel rys yv thy'so dyogel ry dour thy'nny the eve* 'Moses,
> if you are a true prophet, you must indeed give us water to drink'
> OM 1799-801
> *Mars ew gwyer the lavarow ny won ple halla' mos rag annetter* 'If your
> words are true, I do not know whither I can go for anxiety' BK
> 504-06
> *mestresy mars ogh parys mones deglos ny a vyn thy anclethyes in certyn an
> corff uskys* 'gentlemen, if you are ready, we will go to church indeed
> to bury the body speedily' BM 4469-72
> *Ha mars owhy desyrus the gafus exampill in matyr ma, na rewgh mas meras
> war an pow ha gwlasow, ha war an bobyll vs in captiuite gans an turk bras*
> 'And if you are anxious to find an example in this matter, merely
> look at the country and the kingdoms, and at the people who are in
> captivity under the Great Turk' TH 49a.

In the sentence 'If you're hungry later, I'll make you a sandwich' the speaker is talking about the immediate future and in Cornish the future must be used. First, however, consider the word 'later.' One sometimes hears people saying *dewetha* for 'later' but this is difficult to defend. *Dewetha* is an adjective, but in 'if you're hungry later' the word 'later' is an adverb. In traditional Cornish *dewetha* means 'latest, last', e.g. *pan vo an dewetha gyrryow clowis a onen a vo in y gwely marnance ha paris the verwall* 'when the last words of someone on his deathbed and ready to die are heard' SA 59. *Dewetha* is never found used as a comparative. For the adverb 'later' it is better in Cornish to use *wosa hebma, wosa hemma* or *moy adhewedhes*.

If we want to say 'If you're hungry later,' because we are referring to the future, we must use the future of *bos* 'to be', i.e. *mar pedhyth gwag wosa hebma* or *mar pedhyth gwag moy adhewedhes*. For 'I will make you a sandwich' i.e. 'I will make a sandwich for you', we can say *me a vydn gwil baramanyn dhis*. Notice that when talking about something for someone the correct preposition, I think, is *dhe* not *rag*. In the *Creation of the World*, for example, Eve is trying to get Adam to eat from the forbidden tree and she says to him: *merowgh merowgh orth hemma tomma gaya avail theys* 'look, look at this; here is a nice apple for you' CW 736-37. Here are a few examples from the texts of the future of *bos* after *mar* or *mara*, referring to future time:

> *mars* **mara pe3a** *degis gans y dus nan caffan ny yn vr na byth leuerys ef 3e sevell dre vestry* 'but if he is carried off by his men, so that we cannot find him, then it will be said that he rose again by supernatural power' PA 240cd
>
> **mara pethaf** *bev blethen my a'n taluyth thyugh ru'm pen* 'if I live for a year, I will repay you by my head' OM 2386-87
>
> *certan* **mar pyth** *e lethys y tue uyngeans war the wour ha war the fleghys keffrys* 'certainly if he is killed, vengeance will come upon your husband and upon your children also' PC 1948-50
>
> **Mar petha** *ve lyftys in ban theworth an nore, me a vyn tenna pub tra oll thymmo ve ow honyn* 'If I am lifted up from the earth, I will draw all things unto myself' TH 53a
>
> **mara pethowgh** *repentys an kethe plage a wra voydya* 'if you repent, the same plague will depart' CW 2344-45.

Unreal Conditions

So far we have been dealing with very straightforward conditions, e.g. 'If I see John, I'll give him the money'. Such sentences are known as real conditions. But there is another class of sentences in which the condition is more hypothetical, e.g. 'If she were to offer me the job, I would not accept it' or 'If she had offered me the job, I wouldn't have accepted it.' These are called unreal conditions, and in English they can be immediately recognized by the auxiliary verbs 'would' or 'should' in the apodosis. 'If she were to offer me the job, I would not accept it' is an unreal condition in future time. 'If she had offered me the job, I would not have accepted it' is an unreal condition in past time.

In Cornish unreal conditions are formed in the following way. 'If' is *a* rather than *mar* or *mara*. *A*, like *mar* or *mara*, hardens or provects the following consonant. The verb in the protasis appears in the past subjunctive and in the apodosis in the conditional. In *Resurrexio Domini* for example, Matthew says to Thomas about the risen Christ: *hythew a tryckes yn tre thyragos ty a'n guelse byw yn poynt da* 'today if you had remained at home, you would have seen him before you alive and well' RD 1381-83.

This is a little too complicated, perhaps, but unreal conditions do not need to be so difficult. In the first place notice that in Cornish (and in other Celtic languages) unreal conditions in past time and unreal conditions in future time are formed in exactly the same way. This means that the time being referred to is to be understood from the context. In the second place, although 'if' is rendered *a*, with most verbs *mara* can also be used with unreal conditions. Third, just as *dos* is used in the protasis in real conditions, *dos* can also be used in unreal conditions. Fourth, we can also use the conditional of *mynnes* in the apodosis or we can use the conditional of *gwil* 'to do'. Let's look therefore at those two sentences, 'If she had offered me the job, I wouldn't have accepted it' and 'If she were to offer me the job, I wouldn't accept it.'

Because there is no difference in syntax in Cornish between unreal conditions in the past on the one hand, and in the future on the other, we can render these two in the same way: *Mar teffa hy ha profya an soodh dhybm, ny vynsen hy recêva.* For 'to offer' I use *profya*, a verb found in *Origo Mundi*, *Beunans Meriasek* and the *Creation of the World*. One might also use *offra* which is found in Tregear and in *Sacrament an Alter*. For 'to accept' here I use *recêva*. This is one of the verbs used in traditional Cornish when accepting or refusing a job. In *Beunans Meriasek*, for example, the Second Bishop says *war epscop venetensi meryasek yv dewesys sav eff ny vyn del glowys y receva eredy* 'As bishop of Vannes Meriasek has been chosen, but he will not accept it indeed, as I have heard' BM 2874-77. One could also use the verb *kemeres*, as we shall see in later example.

Here are some examples from the texts of *mar* with the past subjunctive of *dos* in unreal conditions:

> *y wreg ȝe re aneȝe mos ȝen dre ha degylmy an asen ha dry ganse ha leuerell yredy mar teffa tus ha gweȝe bos ȝe ȝu ȝe wull gynsy* 'he made some of them go to the town and untie the ass and bring it with them and say indeed, if men were to prevent it, that God had business with it' PA 27c-d

> *Rag mar teffa crist ha dos in dallath an bys whare whosa mabden the beha ha the vos kyllys, tus a russa supposia mar teffa du aga suffra the vsya aga naturall powers y a vynsa optaynya salvacion in ta lovr heb gweras vith arell in party du* 'For if Christ had come at the beginning of the world, shortly after mankind had sinned and been lost, men would suppose, if God had allowed them to use their natural powers, they would have obtained salvation well enough without further assistance on God's part' TH 13a

"IF" IN CORNISH

Mar teffa an epscobow han brontyryan in tyrmyn passis, in weth an dus leg, dysky ha practysya aga duty haga vocacyons, dre an exampill ma surly ny russa an egglos a crist dos then dishonor han disordyr a wylsyn ny 'If the bishops and priests in the past and also the laymen had taught and practised their duty and vocations, by this example surely the Church of Christ would not have come to the dishonour and disorder which we have seen' TH 39

mar teffa an holl brodereth obeya according then commondmentys a thu, ny vynsa den vith styrrya na gwaya warbyn an colleges po company a prontyrryan 'if all the brotherhood had obeyed according to the commandments of God, no one would have stirred or moved against the colleges or company of priests' TH 42a.

Unreal conditions with *bos* 'to be'

In unreal conditions the verb *bos* 'to be' requires separate treatment. The conditional of *bos* of course is *bien, bies, bia,* etc. and this is used in the apodosis without any auxiliary verb. When *bos* is the verb in question in the protasis of an unreal condition, traditional Cornish normally uses *a* rather than *mara*, and this is followed as one would expect by the past subjunctive of *bos: ben, bes, be,* etc. but with provected initial. So one would, for example, say *A pe va obma dhyragof, ny vynsen y aswon* 'if he were here in front of me, I wouldn't recognize him'. Or *A pe hedna gwrës yn ewn, an negys a vynsa spedya* 'If that had been done properly, the business would have succeeded'. Here are some examples from the texts of *a* 'if' followed by the past subjunctive of *bos* 'to be':

Hag a pe yndella ve neffre ny vean fethys 'And if it were thus, never would I be defeated' PA 73a

a pe profus bynyges yn sur ef a wothfye y bos hy peghadures 'if he were a blessed prophet, surely he would know that she was a sinner' PC 489-91

saw an corf na byw a pe an emperour ef sawse maga tek bythqueth del fue kyn fe y cleues mar bras 'but if that person were alive, he would heal the emperor as fairly as ever he was, though his sickness be so great' RD 1657-60

ha lyas myghtern ema, a thothya thymo whare in suer heb mar, a pe danvenys thetha rag dyswruthyl der cletha an anfugyk fals na'm car 'and there are many kings who would come to me forthwith indeed of course, if word were sent to them to destroy by the sword the false wretch who does not love me' BK 2719-24.

Na ve

In the phrase *a pe* the verb *pe* is the third person singular of the past subjunctive of *bos* with provected initial consonant; unmutated the same verbal form is *be*. In traditional Cornish this *be* can be used after *na* 'if not' which is followed by

109

soft mutation or lenition. The expression *na ve* means' if it were not, if he were not, had it not been for'. Here are some examples from the texts of *na ve* 'were it not for, had it not been for'.

> *maria* **na ve** *the rays gon guyr y fyen dyswreys* 'Mary, had it not been for your grace, I know truly we would have been killed' BM 3704-04
> *lues oma deworijs gans an dragon ongrassijs* **na ve eff** *sur a vya* 'had it not been for him, many here by the horrid dragon surely would have been devoured' BM 4178-80
> **na ve** *creya warnogh why kellys ol y fyen ny yowynk ha loys* 'had it not been for calling upon you, we all would have *been lost, young and old*' BM 2169-71
> *ha* **na ve** *agan savyowre crist intendys the ry the pedyr specyall auctorite, a vgha na ve agan savyowre crist intendys the ry the pedyr specyall auctorite, a vgh aga* [leg. *y*] *hensa, pana othom vea cowse hemma* 'and if our Saviour Christ had not been minded to give Peter special authority above his fellows, what need would there have been to speak thus?' TH 44a.

This phrase *na ve* 'were it not for, had it not been for' can also be used with a following verbal noun to render negative unreal conditions of other verbs (and indeed of *bos* itself). So, for example, if one wanted to say 'If I had not heard it with my own ears, I wouldn't have believed it' one might say *Na ve me dh'y glowes gans ow scovornow ow honen, ny vynsen y gresy*. Notice incidentally that for 'my ears' I say *ow scovornow*. In traditional Cornish the plural of *scovarn* 'ear' is *scovornow* not **scovarnow*; moreover the dual form **dywscovarn* is unattested.

Here are a number of instances from the texts of *na ve* followed by a verbal noun to express unreal conditions:

> **na ve** *y vose guir sans mar lues merkyl dyblans byth ny russe* 'if he were not a true saint, clearly he would not ever have done so many miracles' BM 2051-53
> *Surely, ny vynsan cresy an aweyll,* **na ve** *an catholyk egglos* **the ry** *thym experiens* 'Surely I would not have believed the gospel, if the catholic Church had not given me proof' TH 37a
> *An kyth office ma ny vynsa pedyr kemeras* **na ve crist the ry** *thotha an auctorite kepar dell ew therag declarys in ii-de an actus appostlis* 'This same office Peter would not have accepted had Christ not given him the authority as has been explained previously in the second chapter of the Acts of the Apostles' TH 44a
> *Me a thothya gans an ger, na ve ow maw* **thu'm lettya**, *drog-chawns th'y ben!* 'I would have come immediately, had my servant not prevented me, evil fortune upon his head!' BK 469-71.

"IF" IN CORNISH

In later Cornish in unreal conditions the past subjunctive in the protasis is replaced by the conditional. There are not many examples; in fact the only example I can find is in Nicholas Boson's *Nebbaz Gerriau dro tho Carnoack*. Speaking of John Keigwin Boson says: *Mar kressa an dean deskez feer na gwellaz hemma, [ev] a venya kavaz fraga e ouna en skreefa composter* 'If that learned wise man were to see this, he would find reason to emend it in orthography' (BF: 27). Here *Mar kressa* is Middle Cornish *mar qwrussa*, the conditional of *gwil*, rather than the expected past subjunctive *mar qwrella*. The same substitution of conditional for past subjunctive can also be seen in two instances of *na via* for *na ve* in the *Creation of the World*. Here they are:

> *na vea me theth cara* ny vynsan theth cossyllya tha vos bargayne mar vras gwryes 'if! didn't love you, I would not have advised you that such a great bargain be made' CW 669-71
> *na vea me theth cara* ny vynsan awos neb tra yn ban tha vos exaltys 'if I didn't love you, I would not wish for anything that you should be highly exalted' CW 699-70.

REFLEXIVE VERBS IN CORNISH[12]

A transitive verb is one which can take a direct object, for example, in the sentence 'David loves Rebecca' *David* is the subject, *loves* is the transitive verb and *Rebecca* is the direct object. If the object of the verb refers to the same person or entity as the subject, the sentence is reflexive, for example, 'Rebecca loves herself'. That is the way we make reflexives in English, by using the reflexive pronoun, *herself, himself, yourself, myself, themselves*, etc. Notice, however, that in English the pronouns *herself, himself, yourself*, etc., are not always reflexive. They can also function as emphatic pronouns, for example: 'Who told you that?' 'I heard it from Rebecca herself', where *herself* is emphatic, not reflexive.

The foundation text of Unified Cornish, and therefore of the Cornish revival in general, was *Cornish for All*, published by R. Morton Nance in 1929. It has been republished several times since. In *Cornish for all* Nance has a short section on reflexive verbs, in which he says several things. First he tells us that verbs are rendered reflexive by the addition of the prefix *om*[2] and he adds a superscript [2] after it to indicate that the prefix causes second state or soft mutation—or more correctly, lenition.

What Nance says is true. The prefix *om*[2] does indeed render a verb reflexive and it does lenite the initial consonant of the verb. Here are some examples:

Confortya 'to comfort' > ***Omgonfortyough**, arluth whek, ha pub tra ol a vith da* 'Be of good comfort, dear lord, and everything will be good' BK 1019-20.

cregy 'to hang' > *Arthur a verew mar harlot avel fals Judas Scaryot, a **omgrogas** orth scawan* 'Arthur will die like a villain as did false Judas Iscariot who hanged himself upon an elder tree' BK 2535-37

*****dyvlamya** 'to excuse' > *saw whath rys ew mos thotha hag **omthyvlamya** orta* 'but still it is necessary to go to him and apologize to him' BK 448-49

gweres 'to help' > *cooth ew eve hag avlethis pan na ylla **omweras** y vaw ny vidna boos* 'he is old and stiff; since he cannot help himself, I will not be his servant' CW 1152-54

gul 'to make' > *An debel dus a gewsys ʒynny sur yma laha may rys y vonas leʒys rag mab du ef a **omwra*** 'The evil men spoke: We have indeed a law by which he must be killed, for he pretends to be the son of God' PA 143ab

---

12 Delivered as a paper at Skians Conference 2015, Tremough. September 2015

gwetha, gwytha 'to keep' > *lemmyn gans ol y vestry ragon ny wor omweʒe* 'now with all his power he cannot protect himself from us' PA 194c

parusy 'to prepare' > *gorten oma ov sovdrys ha warbarth* **omparusen** 'let us wait here, my soldiers, and let us prepare ourselves together' BM 3243-44

prevy 'to prove' > *yth* **ombrovas** *gwan dyack mayth of poyntyes ʒa bayne bras* 'I have proved myself a poor dealer, so that I have been consigned to great torment' CW 920-21

sawya 'to save' > *mars oge cryst map dev ker* **ymsav** *scon yn nep maner na vy marow* 'if you are Christ, the son of beloved God, save yourself quickly that you do not die' PC 2891-93.

Nance also says that the prefix *om*[2] 'also has a mutual and reciprocative sense.' Perhaps 'reciprocal' might be a better word. Nance is undoubtedly right, however. Here are some examples:

acowntya 'to give an account of' > *Arlothas, guyn avel gurys, dun the'n chamber, me a'th pys, may hyllyn* **omacountya** 'Lady, white as crystal, let us go to the bedroom, that we may give an account of ourselves' BK 2981-83

sewya 'to follow' > *guyryoneth a reys bos dreys aberueth yn mater ma ha lendury kekeffrys rag* **ymsywe** *y a wra* 'truth must be brought into this matter and justice also for they follow one another' PC 2447-50

cusulya 'to advise' > **ymcusylle** *gureny ny pyth yv guella the bos gurys* 'let us take counsel together what is the best thing to be done' RD 561-62

knoukya 'to knock' > *yma theugh mur a thylyt a* **vmknouke** 'you take great delight in fisticuffs together' PC 2323-24

tewlel 'to throw' > *Lucto & [luct]or ... To wrestle, to struggle ... C[ornish] Dho* **ymdoula** AB: 81c.

Nance also says 'in **om·dhon** and a few other verbs the prefix takes the accent to give a special meaning; **om·lath**, to fight is further distinguished from **omla·dha**, to kill oneself, by having no inf. ending' (CfA: 23). Nance here, I believe, is partially correct and partially mistaken. He is wrong, I believe, about the position of the accent and he seems to have been led astray by the pair *omlath* 'to fight' as against *omladha* 'to kill oneself'. The original form of the root of *omlath* is *ladh*. We know this because the Welsh equivalent is *lladd* 'to strike, to kill' (*Gwae fy llaw lladd fy arglwydd* 'Alas my hand that I struck my lord' in *Canu Llywarch Hen*) and exactly the same compound *ymladd* 'to fight' occurs in Welsh. The variant *omlatha* is based on a later formation where the verbal noun has the suffix *-e*, *-a*. In Cornish the stress normally falls on the penultimate syllable. Thus if the verbal noun is a monosyllable, e.g. *ladh*, when

113

compounded with *om-* the verb becomes *omlath*, which is naturally stressed on the syllable next before the last, i.e. on the prefix *om-*. The variant verbal noun, however, *lathe, latha*, when prefixed, gives us the reflexive, *omlatha* 'to kill oneself', stressed on the second syllable. Here are some examples of both:

A)
omlath 'to fight': *gor ost genes yrvys da the* **omlath** *del y'm kerry* 'take a host with you, well armed to fight, as you love me' OM 2141-42
da yth **omleth** *a feyys* 'fighting well I fled' BM 2491
nyg esan ow **omloth** *warbyn agan iii yskar, an bys, an kyge, han teball ell* 'we do not fight against our three enemies, the world, the flesh and the devil' TH 9a

B)
omlatha 'to kill oneself': *rak hacre mernans certan eys* **emlathe** *y honan ny gaffe den my a grys* 'for I believe that no man could get a nastier death than to kill himself' RD 2072-74.

The position of the accent is a function of the number of syllables in the verbal noun; it has nothing, I believe, to do with variation in sense. The variation between *lath* and *latha* is not remarkable. Variant forms of the verbal noun are not uncommon in Cornish, for example, in *cows* 'to speak' and *kewsel, cowsel* 'to speak'. Moreover as far as *omlath* is concerned, it should be noted that Lhuyd cites both *Dhv hemladh* and *Emladha* 'To fight' (AB: 249c), where the verbal noun of the verb meaning 'to fight' has in one case two and in the other three syllables. Notice incidentally that *omlath* is a reciprocal verb 'to strike one another, to fight', whereas *omladha* 'to kill oneself' is a simple reflexive.

Nance also believes that *omthon* from *don* 'to carry' gives us the sense 'to conceive, to bear young' and that this "special meaning" is a product of the initial stress. Since, however, *don* is a monosyllable, one would expect *omdhon* to be stressed on the prefix. I do not believe, that there is any difference in stress between *omthon* 'to conceive, to bear young' and the simple reflexive *omthon* 'to carry oneself, to behave'. Here are some examples of both:

A)
omthon 'to carry oneself, to behave':
Tevdar wek manly **omdok** *ha byth na spar guthel drok* 'My dear Teudar, bear yourself manly and never spare to do evil' BM 2344-45
Coyth ew e ben ha'y **omthon** *ha'y antall* 'Clever are his head and his behaviour and his snares' BK 998-99
Suer eth uu glew a **omthyg** *guew* 'Surely he is acute who behaves worthily' BK 2207-08

B)

omthon 'to conceive, carry young'

en deʒyow a vyth guelys hag a ʒe sur yntreʒon may fyth torrow benegis bythqueth na allas e[m]ʒon 'the days will be seen and indeed are coming among us when wombs will be blessed that could never conceive' PA 169cd

*Tha an Venen e cowzaz, Me vedn meare cressha tha dewhan ha tha **humthan*** 'To the Woman he spoke: I shall greatly increase your birth-pangs and your labour' ÉCII: 181.

In the interests of full disclosure, I should point out that I myself followed Nance in this matter and have claimed in print that there is a difference in stress between **om·dhon** 'to breed' and **omdho·n** 'to behave' and as a noun 'behaviour'. This incorrect assertion of mine can be found in *Desky Kernowek*, page 150. I recommend to anyone who possesses a copy of the book to cross out the offending sentence.

Before I leave this matter I should like to make a further point. In *omlath* 'to fight' the final segment follows an unstressed vowel. It was in origin a lenis and is, I believe, to be understood as voiceless, i.e. *omlath* not *omladh*. Historic lenes are voiced in Cornish after stressed vowels because of the relatively greater sonority of the stressed vowel. They are, I believe, voiceless after unstressed ones because such vowels are preceded by correspondingly less sonority. This explains the difference in the final segment in *wheg* 'sweet' but *carrek* 'rock'; *mab* 'son' but *epscop* 'bishop'. In accordance with this structural variation I prefer to write *ev* 'he, him' but *genef* 'with me'; and *bydh* 'will be' but *nowyth* 'new'.

Nance speaks of special senses after the prefix *om²-*. The position of the accent in these cases is a red herring, but it is true that *om²-* can alter the sense of the simplex so radically that it becomes a different verb and must be treated as a separate lexical item. I will call this function of *om²-* its lexicalizing effect. We have already seen it in *omthon* 'to conceive, to breed'. There are further verbs that are lexicalized by the addition of the prefix *om²-*. *Tenna*, for example, means 'to pull, to draw' but *omdenna* means not 'to draw oneself' but 'to withdraw' and even 'to contract, to shrink'. Moreover *omdenna* can take a direct object. Here are some attested examples:

*hedre vons y ow plentye ihesus yn dour a scryfas ha dre virtu an scrife peb ʒe ves a **omdennas*** 'while they were laying a charge, Jesus wrote in the earth and by the virtue of the writing everyone withdrew thence' PA 33cd

*an lyfwoth gurens **ymdenne*** 'let the flood-stream withdraw' OM 1093

*guel vya dyugh **omdenna** adermen ha pesy grath* 'it would be better for you to withdraw in time and beg for grace' BM 3474-75

*Assof engrys! The ves **omden!** '*How angry I am! Withdraw hence!' BK
2156-57

*Truru triueth eu [owth] **ombdina** [y'n] geueth try ru* 'Truro, it is a pity,
when shrinking will have three rows' Carew: 217

*Whath awoos oll hemma ny rug eff **omdenna** y favore thewortans y* 'Yet after
all this he did not withdraw his favour from them' TH 23.

Kemeres means 'to take' but *omgemeres* means 'to undertake, to be responsible
for'. I know of only one example:

*me a **omgemer** ragogh hagis menten benytha* 'I will take responsibility for
you and will support you always' BM 1882-83.

Another aspect of *om²-* not mentioned by Nance, as far as I am aware, is this:
it can be prefixed to a verb without altering the sense at all. Such verbs are
remarkably numerous. Here are some examples:

A *mar ny wreth **ymamendye** ef a wra tyn the punssye may leuerry ogh ellas*
'if you do not improve, he will punish you severely, so that you
will cry Oh! Alas!' OM 1526-28/ *mara mynne **amendye** guel vye y
thylyfrye hep drocoleth thyworthy'n* 'if he were to improve, it would
be better to let him go without harm from us' PC 1862-64; *vnwyth a
caffen hansell me a russa **amendie*** 'if I could only have breakfast, I
should improve' BM 110-11.

B *y weles me a garse owth astel **ymthreheuel*** 'I should like to see him
attempting to rise' RD 394-95/ *sav me warlergh **drehevel** a's dyerbyn
dyougel yn galile ol warbarth* 'but I after arising will meet them all
together surely in Galilee' PC 896-98; *yma an gvyns ov **terevel** fol* 'the
wind is rising wildly' BM 601-02.

C ***ymthysquethas** ny vynna the plussyon auelough why* 'he would not
wish to appear to dirty fellows like you' RD 1496-97/ *ny wruk dev
thy'm **dysquethas** byth ny'n cresons ef neffre* 'God did not appear to
me; never will they believe it' OM 1439-40; *Nena Herod, pereeg e
prevath crya an deez feere, e a vednyaz thoranze seer puna termin reeg an
steare **disquethaz*** 'Then Herod, when he had invited the wise men
privately, he enquired earnestly of them at what time the star
appeared' Kerew; *Ha potho angye gellez carr, mero, elez neeue a
desquethaz ha Joseph a ve hendrez andelma, save aman ha kebar an flô
yonk ha e thama ha ke tha Egyp* 'And when they had gone, behold,
angels of heaven appeared while Joseph was dreaming thus: Arise
and take the young child and his mother and go into Egypt' Kerew.

D *ny a vyn **ompredery** forth rag y treyla defry ken plesijs me ny vethe* 'we
will consider a way to make him change indeed; otherwise I shall
not be pleased' BM 2857-59/ *arluth pan dyffy ʒet pow **predery** ahanaff*

gura 'lord, when you come to your kingdom, think of me' PA 193b; *In kynsa oll the aswon agan honyn ha **predery** a behane onny ha pandra o agan dallath* 'First of all to recognize ourselves and to consider of what we are and what was our beginning' TH 6.

E *dallaz avar in frez darwar oun na porzo ef **emsettye** worzesy kam na vezo* 'begin early; be assiduously careful that he is not alarmed, so that he does not dare in any way to oppose you' CF 27-30/ *Orth pylat ol y **setsans** ha warnoʒo a rug cry rag Ihesus crist ʒen mernans y a vynne porrys dry* 'They all opposed Pilate and made a cry against him, for they wished indeed to bring Jesus Christ to death' PA 117ab; *mata orthen ny na **set** sav dascor ol the vona* 'friend, do not oppose us but hand over all your money' BM 1916-17; *Plos marrek pour dar seposia prest a reta omma **settya** orth emperour* 'You utterly filthy knight, what, do you presume indeed to oppose an emperor?' BM 2444-47; *nyns us in beys genesyk thym a **setya*** 'there is no man born in the world who would oppose me' BM 3211-12; *A aswonsyn ve the stat, ne **setsan** warnas algat, na russan rag meth an bys* 'Had I known your state, I should not have opposed you, I should not at all, for shame in the world' BK 606-08.

We have seen that *om²-* can render a verb reflexive. It can also make a verb reciprocal. It can also radically change the sense of a verb. It can moreover have no effect upon the sense at all. It must, I think, be admitted that the prefix *om²-* as a reflexiving prefix is at best rather uncertain in its function. Speakers of Cornish seem to have been aware of this ambiguity, and from the period of the Ordinalia onward they sometimes reinforced reflexive *om²-* with the reflexive pronoun:

*lemmyn **y honan** ny yl sur **ymsawye*** 'now he cannot indeed save himself' PC 2877-78

y honan yth ymwanas gans y gollan marthys scon 'he stabbed himself with his knife very quickly' RD 2065-66

*rak hacre mernans certan eys **emlathe y honan** ny gaffe den my a grys* 'for I believe that no man could get a nastier death than to kill himself" RD 2072-74

*ny a gottha thyn **omry agan honyn** the wetha ha the colynwall y commondment eff* 'we ought dedicate ourselves to keeping and fulfilling his commandment' TH 21a

*ymons **ow homdenna aga honyn** theworth aucthorite an Epscop a rome* 'they withdraw themselves from the authority of the bishop of Rome' TH 50a

*rag **omsawya ow honyn** keffrys ow gwreak haw flehys an lester a vythe genyn der weras dew vskes gwryes* 'to save myself, also my wife and

117

my children the ark will be made by us with the help of God quickly' CW 2373-76.

Now it is only a short move from marking a reflexive verb with *om*[2]-reinforced by *y honen*, say, to dispensing with the prefix *om*[2]- entirely. And reflexives of this kind are well attested, being normal in John Tregear's homilies (*ca* 1555) and thereafter. It is likely that they had been in speech for much longer. I have counted over 40 examples in Tregear. Here are some examples from Tregear together with one each from SA, Kerew and Pryce:

> *rag ny ny russyn gull agan honyn* 'for we did not make ourselves' TH 1
> *whath te neb vgy ow dysky re erall nyg esas ow dysky the honyn* 'yet you who teach others, do not teach yourself' TH 14a
> *hag anethe hy kemeras dynsys ha joynyas y honyn then dusys in vnite a person* 'and from her he took human nature and joined himself to the Deity in the unity of person' TH 12a
> *pana cas vsy an re na inna neb a rug seperatya aga honyn ha naha an catholyk egglos* 'in what plight are those in who have separated themselves from and have denied the catholic Church?' TH 32a
> *kyn ruga offra y honyn the vos recevys obediently, whath ny ve recevys erna ruga suffra penans hyre* 'though he offered himself to be received obediently, yet he was not received until he suffered long penance' TH 39
> *ha theworta why a rug devydya agys honyn* 'and from it you have divided yourselves' TH 48
> *onyn an chyff duty ew the preparya agan honyn the vos worthy rag receva an Sacrament an aulter* 'one of the main duties is to prepare ourselves to be worthy to receive the sacrament of the altar' TH 51a
> *ha dir sarchia an scripture eth esa ow trylya ow honyn then Arluth Christ* 'and by searching the scripture I turn myself to the Lord Christ' SA 64a
> *Ha lavarraz thotha moth osta Maab Deew towle tha honnen doare* 'And said to him: If you are the son of God, cast yourself down' ÉCII: 187
> *dreffen en tacklow broaz, ma angy mennow hetha go honnen* 'for in great things they often stretch themselves' ACB: E e 4 *verso*.

Nance refers neither to reflexives in which the reflexive pronoun reinforces *om*[2]-, nor to reflexives made by using the reflexive pronoun by itself. Nance was very much a purist. It is probable therefore that was reluctant to acknowledge the use *y honen*, *ow honen*, etc., in reflexives because he thought that such syntax was based on English. The reinforcing use of *y honen*, etc., after a verb with *om*[2]- is present already in the texts, though it is not common. The use of *y honen*, etc., as the sole indicator of a reflexive is found only in Tregear and in Late Cornish, and Unified Cornish was based on Middle Cornish, in particular

118

the Passion Poem; and anyway Nance did not see Tregear until very late in his life, when Unified Cornish was already well established. He probably thought reflexives with *y honen*, etc., were in imitation of English reflexives with 'himself,' etc.

It could be argued that expressions like *an mytern a ladhas y honen* 'the king killed himself' are based on English. But it possible that purist objections to such syntax may be a little over-hasty. English is a Germanic language, and as such it is related fairly closely to Dutch and German, and less closely to Icelandic, Danish, Swedish, etc. The Continental Germanic languages distinguish the reflexive pronoun from the emphatic. In German, for example, 'the king himself' (emphatic) is *der König selbst*. But in German 'the king killed himself' is *der König tötete sich*. *Selbst* (emphatic) and *sich* (reflexive) are kept separate in German. The same distinction holds for all the other Continental Germanic languages. In Old Norse, from which the Nordic languages have developed, the reflexive pronoun was *sik*. In a reduced form this pronoun survives in the English word 'to bask'. This is a Norse word in origin, having been borrowed into English from the Danish spoken in the Danelaw. 'To bask' is development of Norse *baðask* 'to bathe' < *baða* + *sik*, and originally meant 'to bathe oneself'.

English is unique in the Germanic languages, in that it has conflated the reflexive and emphatic pronouns, absorbing the reflexive into the emphatic. This is also the case in the insular Celtic languages, though they are not closely related to English. In Welsh, for example, one says *Mae'r brenin ei hun wedi dod* 'The king himself has come,' where *ei hun* 'himself' is emphatic. But one also says, for example, *Mae'r dyn yn ei weld ei hun* or *Mae'r dyn yn gweld ei hun* 'The man sees himself' where *ei hun* is reflexive. The same is also true in Scottish Gaelic and in Irish. In Irish, for example, if one wants to say 'The king himself killed himself' one can say *Mharaigh an rí féin é féin* where *féin* is used both emphatically and reflexively. The more idiomatic way of saying the same in Irish is *Chuir an rí lámh ina bhás féin* 'The king put a hand in his own death', but the simpler way is perfectly accurate.

If Nance and revivalists who followed him are reluctant to use expressions like *An mytern a ladhas y honen* for 'The king killed himself,' on the grounds that such syntax is based on English, they may be right. But it is equally possible, and perhaps more likely, that *An mytern a ladhas y honen* is not based on English at all, though it resembles the English idiom. On the contrary the English syntax of 'The king killed himself' may in fact have been borrowed from insular Celtic with which English has been in contact for centuries. If this is so, English expressions like 'Rebecca loves herself' owe the ultimate origin of their syntax to the ancestor of Cornish.

AUXILIARY VERBS IN CORNISH[13]

1. CORNISH VERBS USED AS AUXILIARIES

Auxiliary verbs are of the greatest importance in Middle and Late Cornish. Indeed the inflected forms of most Cornish verbs are very poorly attested because inflected forms are to a great extent confined to the auxiliaries. It is useful, therefore, to see which verbs can function as auxiliaries in traditional Cornish and how they are used. The following can have auxiliary function, although naturally enough, not all are equally important: *bos* 'to be'; *cara* 'to love, to like'; *cotha* 'to fall, to be incumbent'; *dos* 'to come'; *gallos* 'to be able'; *gasa* 'to let'; *gothvos* 'to know'; *gul* 'to do'; *mynnes* 'to wish'; *res* 'is necessary'; *tylly* 'to pay, to be worth' and *usya* 'to use, to be accustomed to', *y'm bus* 'I have'. The scope and use of all these will briefly be examined in turn below.

2. *BOS* 'TO BE'

Long form of *bos* + *ow* + verbal noun as periphrastic present
The long form of *bos* 'to be' is used with the virtual present participle consisting of the particle *ow* (*worth, orth* before possessive adjectives) and a verbal noun. Not infrequently this construction can be translated into English with the verb 'to be' and the present participle. Frequently, however, the sense is that of an unmarked present:

Bos + *ow* + verbal noun as a continuous present:

> *yma ov tegensywe hager gowes war ov feth* 'a nasty shower is threatening by my faith' OM 1079-80
> *ol y pobel ymons y orth y sywe pup huny* 'all his people, they are following him every one' OM 1687-88
> *ny glewaf yender thu'm trovs yth esaf ow clamdere* 'I feel no cold in my foot; I am losing sensation' PC 1223-34
> *nyns us peyn orth ow greffya* 'no pain is afflicting me' RD 454
> *nyns us tra orth ow greffya* 'nothing is affflicting me' RD 502
> *a nyns ese ynnon ny agan colon ow lesky a ihesu map maria pan wruk an bara terry* 'was our heart not burning within us concerning Jesus son of Mary when he broke the bread?' RD 1322-24
> *a thomas nynsyw goky yth esas ow muskegy yn mes a forth* 'O Thomas, it is not foolish; you are wandering away from the truth' RD 1465-67

---

13 This article has not appeared elsewhere.

namnag essof ow merwel orth agas gortos 'I am almost dying waiting for you' RD 2145-46

*dotho degogh lytherov del **ma** guelheven an pov **orth y exaltya** pur dek* 'take letters to him as the nobles of the country are very finely extolling him' BM 2796-98.

There are rare instances of the autonomous long forms of *bos* used with *ow* + verbal noun:

*arluth whek ny amount man an pyt a wrussyugh certan lemyn moy dysenour thys rag **ov keusel yth eder** aban ethe the'n teller bos clevyon dretho sawayys* 'sweet lord, what you did is of no avail indeed, but more dishonour to you, for people are saying since it went to the place that the sick are being healed by it' OM 2791-96.

Bos + *ow* + verbal noun as an unmarked present:

*Nyns **esos ov attendya** an laha del vya reys* 'You do not take notice of the law as should be done' BM 848-49

*in crist ihesu caradov **yth eseff** prest **ov cresy** y vos lel du* 'I indeed believe firmly in beloved Jesus Christ that he is true God' BM 833-35

*in crist **yma ov cresy*** 'he believes in Christ' BM 971

*yth eseff **orth y care** ny vanna y ankevy* 'I love him; I will not forget him' BM 4022-23

*yma an profet dauid **ow allegia** helma* 'the prophet David makes this claim' TH 1

*yma an lyver a skyantoleth **ow remembra** thyn may teffan ha tenna then dore an pryde vs ew raynya ynnan* 'the book of Wisdom reminds us that we should pull down the pride which reigns in us' TH 6a

*Arluth **esta ge ow jugia** mett the veras war onyn an par na* 'Lord, do you judge me worthy to look upon one of these?' TH 7

*yma du **ow tesquethas** pandra ony dre y profet Jheremy* 'God shows what we are through his prophet Jeremiah' TH 7a

*yma eff **worth agan dysky ny** in agan golahes the meneges agan honyn pehadorryan* 'he teaches us in our worship to confess ourselves sinners' TH 8a

*Rag **nyng esan ny ow cara** Du mar ver dell one ny kylmys the cara* 'For we do not love God as much as we are bound to love him' TH 9a

*Arluth theso ge **yma ow pertaynya** gwryoneth* 'Lord, to you belongs truth' TH 10

*ny a ra the well vnderstondia an mercy a thu, ha fatell **vgy** agan salvacion **ow tos** dre crist only* 'we will understand the mercy of God, and that our salvation comes only through Christ' TH 10 *hag in eff ha dretho eff* **yth esan ny ow kafas** *oll pub dadder theworth du an tas vs ow pertaynya kyffrys then corffe ha then ena* 'and in him and through him we all get every goodness from God our Father which pertains both to the body and the soul' TH 11

So whath te neb **vgy ow dysky** *re erall* **nyg esas ow dysky** *the honyn, te neb* **vgy ow progath** *warbyn avovter yth os advovtrar the honyn* 'But further you who teach others, do not teach yourself, you who preach against adultery, are an adulterer yourself' TH 14a

yma *ynweth S paull* **ow scriffa** *the timothe* **hay exortya** *eff ernyssly in study an scriptur* 'St Paul also writes to Timothy and exhorts him earnestly in the study of scripture' TH 18a

Hag in nese an ii commondment ma **yma** *oll an la han prophetys* **ow hangya** 'And upon these two commandments hang all the law and the prophets' TH 20a

Rag **yma** *crist y honyn* **ow leverell** *in awayll, Neb a garra y das po y vam, y vab po y virth, chy, trevyn po tyrryow, moy agesa ve, y myth crist, nyns ew worthy the vos dissipill na seruant thym* 'For Christ himself says in the gospel, Whoever loves his father or mother, his son or daughter, house, houses or lands more than me, says Christ, is not worthy to be a disciple or servant of mine' TH 21a

Hen ew the leverell, neb a rella golsowes worthow why, **yma ow golsowas** *wartha ve, ha neb a rella agys despisia why,* **yma worth ow despisia ve** 'That is to say, whoever listens to you, listens to me, and whoever despises you, despises me' TH 35a

neb a rella receva henna a rellan ve danvon, **yma worth ow receva ve** *ha neb a rella ow receva ve* **eff a vith ow receva** *neb a rug ow dynvon ve* 'whoever receives him whom I send, receives me, and whoever receives me, will receive him who sent me' TH 41a

An martyr benegas S Ciprian, in lyas tyller **yma ow affirmya** *hemma* 'The blessed martyr St Cyprian affirms this in many places' TH 45

Ith esaff ow supposya *na ve va heb cowse bras an ii the suffra in vn dith* 'I suppose that it was not without much talk that the two suffered on the one day' TH 47

rag eth ony megys gans an keth sam tra **vgy** *an elath* **ow gwelas ha ow trembla** 'for we are nurtured by the same thing that the angels see and tremble at' SA 59.

The function of *bos* + *ow* + verbal noun as an unmarked present is also readily apparent in the following:

nena eff a gowsys thotha an tryssa trevath **esta worth ow cara ve?** *pedyr a gemeras dewan, rag crist the leverell thotheff try torne,* **esta ge worth ow cara ve?** *pedyr whath an gorthebys haga leverys, Arluth, te a wore pub tra, ha te a wore fatell ra ve the cara* 'then he spoke to him the third time: Do you love me? Peter was saddened that Christ has said to him the third time, Do you love me? Peter answered him again and said: Lord, you know everything, and you know that I love you' TH 43.

In that quotation *fatell ra ve the cara* 'I love you' is the answer to *esta worth ow cara ve?* 'do you love me?' It seems therefore that *esta worth ow cara ve* is an unmarked present, not a continuous present. It means 'do you love me?' not '*are you loving me?'

In some later texts the particle *ow* is often to *o* or *a*.The expected provection of the initial consonant of the verbal noun is also often absent:

mas Christ, an mammeth nyy, **neg esa o gwell** *indella genan* 'but Christ, our nurse, does not do thus with us' SA 59a

Ima lowarth onyn o bostia *fatla vgy faith an tasow coth a vam egglys inansy* 'Many boast that the faith of the Fathers of the Church is in them' SA 59a

eth esa ve o disquethas *these vmma waren nore, ew worthy the vose an moygha honoris, kepare ha mytearne, o setha in dan queth a stat* 'I show you here upon the earth him who is worthy to be the most highly honoured, like a king sitting under a cloth of state' SA 60

Reaw' moas choy, ha **ma wreag vee a pobaz** *metten* 'Go into the house, and my wife is baking this morning' BF: 16

enna e uelaz an ôst an tshei; ha dên kôτ o ê, a guadn, **a trailia** *an bêr* 'there he saw the host of the house; and he was an old man and weak, turning the spit' AB: 252a

An lÿzûan bîan ʒen i'ar nedhez, **ez a tivi** *en an haloụ nei, ez kreiez Plêth Maria* 'The small plant with the twisted stalk [which] grows on our Hills, is called *Plêth Marîa*' AB: 245a.

In later texts the *ow* before the verbal noun is sometimes omitted entirely:

rag **neg eran cregy** *nanyle* **regardia** *gerryow dew* 'for we neither believe nor respect the words of God' SA 59

O mirkell, ha blonogath da a thew, disquethis theny, **vgy setha** *in gwlas neff* 'O miracle and good will of God demonstrated to us, who sits in the kingdom of heaven' SA 60

an kigg **yma causya** *an ena the vos Junys the dew an neff* 'the flesh causes the soul to be joined to the God of heaven' SA 60a

rag henna gere Christ **ema gwiell** *an keth Sacrament ma* 'therefore the word of Christ makes this same sacrament' SA 62

n'ara dean bewah dreath bara e honnen buz gen kenefra geer **eze toaze** *meaz a ganaw Deaw* 'man does not live by bread alone, but by every word that comes out of the mouth of God' ÉCII: 186

Tregya, vrt an gurroll **iggeva gweell** *gen askern skooth davas, &c.* 'Third, because of the ship which he makes with a sheep's shoulder bone, etc.' BF: 9

Theram ry *do why an bele ma do gware gen bonogath da* 'I give you this ball to play with good will' BF: 12

ev a dhelledzhas an termen maldha va prêv **erra** *e wrêg* **guitha** *kympez et i gever: erra po nag erra* 'he spun out the time that he might prove was his wife keeping faithful to him, yes or no' BF: 18

Buz **'th erama wheelaz** *e'n skreef ma (mar mere dr' ellama) tho gurra an geer na a treneuhan ra dismiggia 'gun Tavaz ny senges tho re 'rol* 'But I am trying in this text (as far as I can) to put that word aside which will show that our language is indebted to others' BF: 29

E wreeanath ol termen **ma seval** *kreaue* 'His truth always stands firm' BF: 39

ha kanifer tra kramia **es guaya** *var an aor* 'and every creeping thing which moves upon the earth' BF: 52

Mi 'rig guelaz an Karnou **idzha** *an gullez ha'n idhen môr aral kîl ỳ ʒe neitho* 'I saw the rocks [on which] the gulls and other sea birds make their nests' AB: 245a

ha **mouns screffa** *inna warbedden ni* 'and they are writing there against us' LAM: 238.

In Middle Cornish the particle *ow* may be omitted when the verbal noun precedes the inflected form of bos:

rag myghtern nep a ymwra erbyn cesar **cous yma** 'for who claims to be a king is speaking against Caesar' PC 2222-23

bewa yth esaf *pub eare in tomdar ha yender reaw sure nos ha dyth* 'I live always in heat and cold indeed night and day' CW 1667-69.

Though this is not obligatory:

ow **tybbry** *gynef* **yma** *a'm tallyovr yn keth vos ma neb rum guerthas sollabreys* 'eating with me from my dish on this same table is he who has already betrayed me' PC 744-46.

Omission of the particle *(w)orth* before possessive adjectives qualifying the verbal noun is common in the later texts:

ema ef agyn maga *gans e kegg e honyn, ha eweth insted a thewas emay vrth agen maga gans e woos* 'for he feeds us with his own flesh, and also instead of drink he feeds us with his blood' SA 59a.

tho ni an parah **ma eaue** *gon maga* 'we are the flock; he feeds us' BF: 39

Th era ve cara *why en colon* 'I love you in my heart' ACB: F f *verso*.

AUXILIARY VERBS IN CORNISH

Bos with the verbal adjective of transitive verbs

In the earliest Cornish passive meaning, particularly in the habitual present, is conveyed by autonomous forms of the verb. Such forms, however, are soon replaced by periphrasis with the parts of the verb *bos* 'to be' and the verbal adjective. In this context its is noteworthy that the opening lines of *Origo Mundi* (early fifteenth century) exhibit the present-future autonomous present of the verb *gelwel* 'to call':

> *En tas a nef y'm gylwyr, formyer pup tra a vyt gvrys* 'I am called the Father of heaven, creator of everything that is made' OM 1-2.

In contrast the opening lines of *Beunans Meriasek* (1504) show the same verb but with the periphrastic construction:

> *Me yw gylwys duk bryten ha seuys a goys ryel ha war an gwlascur cheften* 'I am called the Duke of Brittany, and am come from royal blood and am chieften over the kingdom' BM 1-3.

Compare also:

> *ennoc sur **yth of hynwys*** 'Enoch indeed I am named' RD 197
> ***Gelwys y3 of** conany mytern yn bryton vyan* 'I am called Conan, king in Brittany' BM 168-69
> *Meryasek **yth yv gelwys*** 'he is called Meryasek' BM 970
> ***Eff yv gelwys** meryasek den grassyes in y dethyov* 'He is called Meriasek, a gracious man in his days' BM 2225-26
> ***Ith off gelwys** costentyn in rome chyff cyte an beys emperour curunys certyn* 'I am called Constantine, in Rome, chief city of the world, a crowned emperor indeed' BM 2513-15
> ***Guelwys off** mytern massen alruth bolde in ov dethyov* 'I am called King Massen, a bold lord in my days' BM 3156-57
> *noy mabe lamec **gylwys ove*** 'I am called Noah son of Lamec' CW 2232.

On occasion the habitual present/future form of *bos* is used with the verbal adjective *gelwys*:

> *lader cleves thym yma **a veth gelwys** an seson* 'I have a treacherous disease which is called the ague' BM 679-80
> *Tevdar **me a veth gelwys*** 'I am called Teudar' BM 759
> *thym yma castel arel **a veth gelwys** tyndagyel* 'I have another castle which is called Tintagel' BM 2213-14
> *ha **me a vyth gylwys** Ke* 'and I am called Ke' BK 91.

The examples above with the habitual present-future, refer to a habitual present. There are occasional examples of the verbal adjective of other verbs used after the present of *bos* with habitual sense:

*gans pup ol **yth yv kerys*** 'he is loved by everybody' BM 2227.

Generally speaking, when the present of *bos* is used with the verbal adjective of a transitive verb, the sense is usually perfect. Here are a very few examples:

Del yw scrifys *prest yma adro ʒynny gans otry mara kyll ʒeworth an da ʒe weʒyll drok agan dry* 'As has been written, he is always around us with violent attack, if he can, bring us from the good to do evil' PA 21a

*dun alemma desempys bys yn meneth **yv ordnys** gans dev a ras* 'let us go hence to the mountain that has been ordained by God of grace' OM 1302-04

*gans nader **yth of guanheys** hag ol warbarth vynymmeys afyne trois the'n golon* 'I have been stung by a snake and all together poisoned completely foot to heart' OM 1756-58

shyndyys of *gans cronek dv ha **whethys** gans y venym* 'I have been injured by a black toad and swollen by its poison' OM 1778-79

*an sacryfys the thev **yv gurys** dun ny the dre* 'the sacrifice to God has been made; let us go home' OM 1391-92

*heyl ov arluth yn the thron **gurys yv** the temple hep son* 'hail, my lord, in your throne; your temple has been built without a sound' OM 2582-83

*go vy vyth pan yth thotho pan **of fythys** thyworto tergwyth hythew* 'alas that I went to him, since I have been defeated three times today' PC 145-47

*mab dev a tremyn a'n beys annotho del **yv scryfys** yn lyfryow yn lyes le* 'the Son of God will pass from the world, as has been written of him in many places in the scriptures' PC 747-49

dyspleytys yw *y uaner ha **kelmys** worth an grous pren* 'his banner has been unfurled and tied to the cross' PC 3044-45

confortys yv *ow colon pan clewys ow teryfas bones leghys the pascyon a fus tyn garow ha bras* 'My heart has been comforted, since I heard you saying that your suffering, bitter and harsh which you endured, has been lessened' RD 503-06

*lemmyn **yth of yaghys** a pup dyses* 'now I have been healed of all disease' RD 1741

*yma ree ov leferel heb ty vyth nag ovlya **delyfrys** der varia **fetel ywa** dyogel* 'some are saying without oath or shouting that he has been freed by Mary indeed' BM 3739-42 *an tecka parcel a'm tyr **ew kyllys**, re Syn Turpyn* 'the finest portion of my land has been lost, by Saint Turpyn' BK 1206-07

*Myghtern Arthur a'th tynnyrhys ha thys gena' pen Syr Lucy, war ow ena! rag degevy **ew danvenys*** 'King Arthur greets you, and to you by my hand the head of Sir Lucius, upon my soul has been sent to pay tribute!' BK 2856-63

*havall thotha **yth ew gwryes** oll y gorffe m[ar] pur sembly* 'like to him he has been made— all his body so seemly' CW 437-38

*gans dew **yth ew apoyntes** warden war oll paradys* 'by God his has been appointed warden over all paradise' CW 443-44

*gans pob **me ew ankevys*** 'I have been forgotten by everyone' CW 1498

*a false lader casadowe **squattys ew tha ampydnyan*** 'O false hateful brigand, your brains have been crushed' CW 1704-05.

Notice that the long form of *bos* followed *ow pos* 'being' can be used to express a continuous present passive:

*yth esaf **ow pose** gorthys ny won pylea* 'I am being put I know not where' CW 2125-26.

With the preterite of *bos* the verbal adjective of a transitive verb signifies a simple past passive:

*gans luas **y fons gwelys*** 'they were seen by many' PA 210c

*An peynys a wotheuys ny ve ragtho y honan lemmyn rag pobyll an bys **pan vons y kefys** mar wan* 'The pains he suffered were not for himself, but for the people of the world, when they were found to be so weak' PA 6ab

*lauar annes ov bos vy a'm bewnens, my th'y bysy a leuerel guryoneth thy'so a'n oyl a versy o dythywys thy'mmo vy gans an tas a'y dregereth **pan vef chacys** gans an el yn pur thefry* 'tell him that I am weary of my life, that I beg him to tell you the truth about the oil of mercy promised to me by the Father in his mercy when I was chased by the angel in very truth' OM 700-06

*my ha'm gvrek rag gul foly **helhys** warbarth **a fuen ny** in mes scon a paradys* 'I and my wife were pursued together quickly out of paradise for committing foly' OM 707-10

*ef yv an oyl a versy **a fue** the'th tas **dythywys*** 'he is the oil of mercy that was promised to your father' OM 815-16

*yn uvr ne ef dysmegys py gansse **y fue guyskys*** 'then let him guess by which of them he was struck' PC 1372-73

*ihesu **a fue anclethyys** hag yn beth a ven **gorrys** gans ioseph ha tus erel* 'Jesus was buried and put in a tomb of stone by Joseph and other men' RD 1-3 *a'n dour y fue drehevys ha dreys arte the'n tyr mur* 'he was lifted out of the water and brought to the mainland again' RD 2327-28

meryasek ganso lemen helhys vue in kerth heb fael 'Meriasek by him now was driven away without fail' BM 2248-49

fetel vusta delyfrys laver thymo me ath peys ov map kerra 'how you were delivered tell me, I beg you, my dearest son' BM 3764-66

Dre an spuris sans an scripturs benegas a ve kefys, gwrys ha skryffes 'By the Holy Spirit the holy scriptures were found, made and written' TH 6

ha Christ a commandias ha y a ve creatis 'and Christ commanded and they were created' SA 61a

Ha lagagow angie ve gerres ha angie oyah tel er angye en noath 'And their eyes were opened and they knew that they were naked' ÉCII: 177

Ha e ve enna terebah mernaz Herod malga boaz composez a ve cowsez gen Arleth neue der der an prophet 'And he was there until the death of Herod, that might be fulfilled what was spoken by the Lord through the prophet' ÉCII: 198-99.

The imperfect of *bos* and the verbal adjective are used to express pluperfect passive sense:

hen ev an oel a versy o dethywys dy'so sy theworth an tas dev a'n nef 'that is the oil of mercy which had been promised to you from the Father, God of heaven' OM 841-43.

The habitual present-future of *bos* can also be used with the verbal adjective to express a future passive:

Pylat arte a gowsas a Ihesus pyth a vyth guris 'Pilate spoke again: what will be done with Jesus?' PA 126c

ha ty a veth prysonys na wylly golow yn bys bys pen vlythen 'and you will be imprisoned so that you do not see any light in the world for a year' OM 70-2

arluth the voth a vyth gvrys 'Lord, your will shall be done' OM 431

my ny won leuerel prak gans pup na vethaf lethys 'I cannot say why I shall not be killed by everybody' OM 595-96

py hanow y fyth gylwys lauar thy'mmo er the feth 'what name shall he be called, tell me upon your faith' OM 676-77

yn nef agas enefow neffre a tryg hep ponow yn ioy na vyth dywythys 'in heaven you souls will dwell forever in joy that will not be ended' PC 7-9

scon y gallos a vyth lehys 'soon his power will be lessened' PC 21

hep tovl pur wyr me a grys drethos **y fythyn sylwys** *a vap dev thy's lowyne*
'without deceit indeed I believe we will be saved by you, O son of
God, greetings to you' PC 285-87

y fyth *agan enefow dre leuarow dev* **mygys** 'our souls will be nourished
by the words of God' PC 75-6

clewys vyth *agas desyr* **why a vyth aquyttys** *da rak an onor yn tor ma a
wrussough thy'mmo pur wyr* 'your desire will be heard; you will be
well recompensed for the honour in very truth you have done me
now' PC 309-12

dretho ef prynnys **vytheugh** *ol ow tus gour ha benen* 'by it you will be
redeemed, all my people, man and woman' PC 767-68

mar **ny fethe ef guythys** *gans y tus* **y fyth leddrys** *ha'n corf yn mes kymerys
ha gorrys ef the ken pow* 'if he is not guarded he will be stolen by his
men and the body taken out and moved to another country' RD
353-56

wharre an emscumunys yn trok horn **y fyth teulys** *yn tyber yn dour pur
dovn* 'straightway the accursed one will be thrown into the Tiber
into very deep water in an iron box' RD 2165-67

Rag covs geryov mar velen in cloghprennyer pur certen oma **y fetheth cregys**
'For speaking such wicked words on a gallows in very truth here
you will be hanged' BM 1240-42

Helma dis **a veth grontis** *poren del yv deserijs dre grath du ha tra nahen*
'This will be granted to you exactly as has been desired by the
grace of God and nothing else' BM 2080-82

na ra intra in jugement gans the servant rag nyns us den bew **a vith keffys**
iust in the sight ge, arluth 'do not enter into judgement with thy
servant, for there is no man alive who will be found just in thy
sight, O Lord' TH 10a

Scon **te a vyth gorthybys** *heb hyrwyge* 'You will soon be answered
without long delay' BK 152-53

Mara pethaf dywenhys, *me a'm bues gallos i'n bys ha'm yskerans a throkfar*
'If I am aggrieved, I have power in the world and my enemies will
fare badly' BK 1410-12

Mar **ny vethaf curunys,** *in tan por doun te a lysk* 'If I am not crowned,
you will burn in very deep fire' BK 3095-96

mar **pyth y frute hy tastys te a vyth dampnys** *ractha ha subiect ankowe
dretha te a vyth predar henna* 'if its fruit is tasted, you will be condemned for it and through it you will be subject to death; consider
that' CW 377-80 378

ha mar gwreta bargayne sure **ty a vith** *lower* **honorys** 'and if you make a
bargain, surely you will be amply honoured' CW 488-89

me **ne vethaf confethes** *om bos ynaff fallsurye* 'I shall not be found out,
that there is falsehood in me' CW 532-33

Benytha woza hebma in ybbern y fyth gwelys an gabmthavas in teffry 'Forever hereafter the rainbow will be seen in the sky indeed' CW 2499-51.

Occasionally one finds the past habitual (third person singular *betha*) used with the verbal adjective also:

> *ha yth ew redys inweth in scriptur fatell rug Judith, Hester, Job, Jheremye, gans mere moy tus benegas ha benenas in testament coth (a rug) vsia gwyska yscar ha canfas garow, an pith a vetha gwrys syehar anotha* 'and it is read also in scripture that Judith, Esther, Job, Jeremiah with many more holy men and women in the Old Testament used to wear sackcloth and rough canvas, that from which sacks used to be made' TH 6a
> *mas pub tra oll a rella pertaynya tha concernya an feithfull cristonnyan a vetha rulyys ha gouernys dre an abosteleth a crist, neb o nena an pen war an egglos* 'but everything pertaining to and concerning the faithful Christians, who were ruled and governed by the apostles of Christ, who were then the authority over the Church' TH 37a.

The verbal adjective is widely used with the present and past subjunctives of *bos*:

> *pyseygh toythda ol kescolon dev dreys pup tra evs a huhon theygh yn bys ma y grath danvon yn dyweth may feugh sylwys* 'pray straightway all of one accord above all things to God who is over us that he may send you his grace in this world, that you may be saved in the end' PC 2-5
> *lafurye a wra pupprys rak dry den the vos dampnys the ponow na fe sylwys* 'he works always to bring man to be damned to pains that he be not saved' PC 15-7
> *a mester whek gorthys re by* 'O sweet master, may you be revered' PC 35
> *peder ha iowan kerthuegh may fo va parys wharre* 'Peter and John go that it may be prepared straightway' PC 619-20
> *nebas lowre a vyt an gwayne pan vo genas cowle comptys* 'small enough will the gain be, when it has been reckoned completely' CW 793-94
> *gorthys re bo dew an tase* 'may God the Father be worshipped!' CW 1394
> *gorthis re bo dew an taes ow ry thym an nowethys* 'may God the Father be worshipped for giving me the news!' CW 1911-12.

The verbal adjective is also often used with the imperative of *bos*:

> *en box oll be3ens gwerthys* 'let all the box be sold' PA 36b

Maras ew ʒe voth ow ʒas gura ʒen payn ma ow gasa mes **beʒens guris** *ʒe vynnas* 'If it is your wish, my Father, let this pain leave me, but let your will be done' PA 55ab

y lauaraf nef ha tyr **bethens formyys** *orth ov brys* 'I say heaven and earth, let them be created according to my mind' OM 7-8

gans pek **bethens stanchvrys** *ha tryhans keuelyn da an lester a vyth a hys* 'let it be made waterproof with pitch and there will be a good three hundred cubits in the length of the ark' OM 954-56

kymer thy'mmo ve kunys gans louan **bethens strothys** *ha war the keyn doga ef* 'take for me firewood; let it be fastened with a rope and bear it upon your back' OM 1296-98

bethens *yn mes* **exilyys** *na theffo onan yn beys the tryge omma neffre* 'let them be exiled from the land that not one in the world come to dwell here ever' OM 1576-78

aspyeugh yn ov cossow pren the gyst hep tol na gyl **bethens gurys** *thyugh hep whethlow* 'seek in my forests a tree for a beam without deceit or guile; let it be done for you without senseless talk' OM 2558-60

bethens kyrhys *masons plente* 'let there be fetched masons aplenty' OM 2262

yn bason **bethens gorrys** *ha me a's goulgh dysempys may fons gulan a pup plos ol* 'let it be put into a bason and I will wash them straightway, that they may be clean of all dirt' PC 843-45

sav the voth thegy arluth **bethens gruys** *yn pup termyn* 'but your will, Lord, let it be done at all times' PC 1039-40

gorr e the'n mernans gorr e yn pren crous athysempis ha kelmys treys ha dule ynny hy **bethens taclyys** 'put him to death! put him on the cross immediately and with feet and hands bound let him be fixed to it' PC 2161-64

yn pren crous **bethens gorrys** *ha troys ha dyulef kelmys ha guenys dre an golon* 'let him be put upon the cross and foot and hands bound and pierced through the heart' PC 2374-76

y dreys ha'y dule yn ten gans kentrow worth an plynken **bethens tackys** 'let his feet and his hands stretched out be fastened to the timber with nails' PC 2516-18

myserough tol th'y thule ha tol th'y trys hep lettye **bythens** *scon* **gurys** 'measure a hole for his hands and a hole for his feet let it be made soon without delay' PC 2740-42

ha why dreheueugh y beyn may farwe an thew vylen quyk hep hokkye **bethens gurys** 'and you raise up the other that the two criminals may die; quick let it be done without hesitation' PC 2826-28

py ma tregys thym **leferys bethyns** *dyson* 'where does he live? Let it be told me immediately' BM 816-18

genogh why **bethens** *sesijs* 'let him be seized by you!' BM 972

131

han re na **bethens lethys** *hage goys pur ysawys tek a glan yn vn vecyl* 'let those be killed and their pure and clean blood saved in a vessel BM 1517-19

bethens eff consecratis *gans worschyp ha revvte* 'let him be consecrated with reverence and ceremony' BM 2984-85

goer sprusan in y anowe han thew arall kekeffrys **bethans gorrys** *in ye thywfridg* 'put a pip in his mouth and the other two let them be put in his nostrils' CW 1852-54

gans peyke **bethance stanche** *gwryes* 'let them be made waterproof with pitch' CW 2259

An Taz ny es yn nêf, **bethens** *thy hannow* **ughelles** 'Our Father, who is in heaven, let your name be exalted' ACB: E e 2 *verso.*

The verbal adjective of a transitive verb + *bos* with active sense

Rarely the verbal adjective of a transitive verb is used with active sense when there is no expressed object. I know of only one example:

> *peder me a leuer thy's* **kyns ys bos** *cullyek* **kenys** *te terguyth y wregh ov naghe* 'Peter, I tell you, before the cock has crowed you will deny me three times' PC 901-03.

Bos with the verbal adjective of intransitive verbs
When the verbal adjective that follows the present of *bos* is intransitive, the meaning cannot of course be passive. The sense is active and can be translated as perfect. Since examples of this kind are numerous, each verb will be dealt with individually below:

Present of *bos* + *cothys* 'fallen:

> *lowene the flour an beys* **yma** *cas bras wharfethys ha* **cothys** *war the pobel* 'greetings to the flower of the world; a great matter has happened and fallen upon your people' OM 1541-43
> *yth apyas thy'm gul foly trystya a wraf y'th vercy* **cothys of** *yn edrek bras* 'I happened to commit folly; I shall trust in your mercy; I have fallen into great regret' PC 1438-40
> *Ellas, ellas pendrama in ov fays* **cothys yma** *cleves vthyk num car den* 'Alas, alas, what shall I do? A dreadful sickness has fallen upon my face. No man loves me' BM 727-29
> *in neys rum caradevder* **yma cothys** *golovder dretho mayth off amuwys* 'by my goodness, near me has fallen a light, by which I am startled' BM 1309-11
> **yma** *ortheff lovrygyan* **cothys** *ha ny won fetla* 'leprosy has fallen upon me and I do not know how' BM 1356-57

nos tevle yth o namnygen ha lemen sur golvygyen adro thym **yma cothys** 'just now it was dark night and now indeed brilliance has fallen around me' BM 3680-82

So in mer ver dell ew an stat na kyllys, ha mabden dre an koll a henna **cothes** *in extreme miseri ha wretchednes* 'But in as much as that state has been lost and mankind has fallen by that loss into extreme misery and wretchedness' TH 3.

Present of *bos* + *dasserhys* 'risen again':

datherghys na wra doutye of a vernans ow melder 'I have risen again from death, my dearest, do not doubt it' RD 475-76

en trege deyth yv hythew corf cryst **dasserhys** *mars* **yw** *mos the vyras* 'today is the third day to go to see whether the body of Christ has risen again' RD 691-93

a na lauar yn della ihesu an arluth guella na yl syuel rak pur wyr **dasserghys** **yw** 'Oh, do not say thus that Jesus, the best of lords, cannot rise, for in very truth he has risen again' RD 1001-04

cryst a fue yn grous gorrys yn mes a'n beth **dasserghys** *certan* **yth yw** 'Christ who was put upon the cross, certainly has risen again from the tomb' RD 1234-35.

Present of *bos* + *devethys* 'come':

dyuythys yv *hag yma yn hy myyn branch olyf glas* 'she has come and in her beak a branch of green olive' OM 1121-22

tus venenes ha fleghys **ymons** *omma* **dyuythys** *ha'ga pyth degys ganse* 'men, women and children, they have come here and their possessions brought with them' OM 1611-13

dyuythys yv *ov thermyn a'm bevnans sur yn bys ma* 'my time has come of my life in this world' OM 1885-86

ol the'th voth ov arluth ker **dyuythys on** *hep danger bys dy's omma hep ardak* 'all at your wish, my dear lord, we have come without demur to you here without delay' PC 1868-70

Devethys off *in tereth ha squeth me yv ow kerthes* 'I have come to land and I am tired walking' BM 632-33

devethys on *bys in tyr lemen quik thagis desyr* 'we have come to land now quickly as you wished' BM 1091-92

devethys yth on *warbarth rag enour dis ha gorthyans* 'together we have come for your honour and worship' BM 1174-75

Heyl ov arluth costentyn kekefrys gal ha brentyn oma **yth on devethys** 'Hail, my lord Constantine, both common and noble we have come here' BM 1527-29

Costentyn **devethys** *dre* **me** **yv** *hag yma gene vi cans flogh inweth* 'Constantine, I have come home and I have with me six hundred children also' BM 1572-74

yma purguir meryasek **devethys** *oma then pov ryb pontelyne eredy* 'in very truth Meriasek has come to the district here by Ponteline' BM 1945-47

Meryasek lowene dys omma **yth on devethys** *rag pesy the cusel preyst* 'Meriasek, greetings to you, we have come here to ask your advice indeed' BM 2139-41

tus nobil in stallasconn deth gore **yv devethys** 'noble men have come to perform your installation' BM 3017-18

me ny won thum confortia pyv **us** *oma* **devethys** 'I do not know who has come here to comfort me' BM 4038-39

Devethys yth off *then plays dorsona thys a thremays* 'I have come to the place. God speed you, good man' BM 4148-49

Welcum pan **owgh devethys***!* 'Welcome, since you have come!' BK 2219

Christ **ew devethis***, not dir subtelnath bus openly the kenever a whelha ha vo o sevall rebta* 'Christ has come not by subtlety but openly to whoever seeks him and stands beside him' SA 60

devethis **yth of** *omma* 'I have come here' CW 1780

Lowena thewhy ow thas **devethis** *a paradice* **yth of** *lemyn tha thew gras* 'Joy to you, my father! I have come now from paradise, thanks be to God' CW 1880-82

ankaw **yth ew devethys** *ny vyn omma ow gasa tha vewa omma vdn spyes* 'Death has come; he will not let me live here a single moment' CW 1967-69

devethys *tha baradice me a wore gwyre* **yth oma** 'I know truly that I have come to paradise' CW 2129-30

noy mar lenwys ew an byes lemyn a sherewynsy mayth **ew** *dewathe* **devethys** *vnna a gyke pub huny* 'Noah, so full is the world of wickedness, that the end has come in it of the flesh of everyone' CW 2244-47

a das lemyn gwrewh parys an lyw nang **ew devethys** 'O father, now get ready; the flood has now come' CW 2419-20

tho ni devethez *tha gorthe thotha* 'we have come to worship him' ÉCII: 194.

Present of *bos* + *gyllys* 'gone, become':

del leuaraf arluth thy's **yma** *moyses pel* **gyllys** *yn mor del heuel thy'mmo arag dywhans ov kerthes* 'as I tell you, lord, Moses has gone far into the sea, as it seems to me straightway walking forward' OM 1681-84

gyllys of *yn pryderow mur yv ow fyenasow* 'I have gone into worry; great is my anxiety' RD 16-7 *yth oma gyllys* leper del leuer pup ol hager 'I have become a leper; as everybody says very ugly' BM 1359-60

an laddren pel mes an pov gyllys yns pur thyogeyll 'the robbers have gone far out of the country very certainly' BM 2186-87

ran in kerth re ruk feya ran ny won pyth ens gyllys 'some have fled off; some I don't know where they have gone' BM 2156-57

kynth os gyllys feynt ha guan wath ty a veth confortys 'though you have become faint and weak, you will be comforted' BM 3672-73

nyns es onyn ow sewya ha folya Du, yth yns oll gyllys mes a forth 'there is no one following and obeying God, they have all gone out of the way' TH 7a

chardges yth of indella [gans] ow thas omma thewhy ages bothe mars ew henna rag yth ew ef cothe gyllys 'I have been commanded thus by my father here to you, if that is your will, for he has become old' CW 1788-91

coth ha gwan yth of gyllys nym beas bewa na fella 'I have become old and weak; I cannot live any longer' CW 1965-66

pub beast oll ymma gyllys in lester thaga kynda dell yw ornys thymo ve 'every single animal has gone into the ark to its kind, as was commanded to me' CW 2433-35.

Present of *bos* + *sevys* 'arisen':

ihesu omma nyns ugy rak seuys yw 'Jesus is not here, for he has risen' RD 782-83

lemmyn ow abesteleth seueugh yn agas crygyans aban of seuys a'n beth gothfetheugh y's byth sylwans 'now my apostles, stand firm in your faith; since I have risen from the tomb, know that you will have salvation' RD 1571-74

Sevys oys a woys worthy 'You have risen from distinguished stock' BM 839

Trueth mur yv ahanas den yv sevys a lyne bras ty the vynnes mar sempel bones omma in ponvos 'It is a great pity of you: a man risen from a great line, that you should want so simply to be here in misery' BM 1992-95.

Present of *bos* + *tremenys* 'passed away, dead':

ro thy'm kummeas me a'th pys a kymeres corf ihesu yv yn pren crous tremenys may hallo bos anclethys yn beth men the voth mars yw 'give me permission, I beg you, to take the body of Jesus, who has died upon the cross, so that he may be buried in the tomb, if it is your wish' RD 3112-16 *meryasek an den worthy del glowa* **yv tremenis** 'Meriasek, the worthy man, as I hear has passed away' BM 4369-70

tremenys yv meryasek 'Meriasek has passed away' BM 4383

ser deyn leferugh thynny **yv meryasek tremenis** 'sir dean, tell us: has Meriasek passed away?' BM 4408-09

Arluth **eff yv tremenys** *y eneff gans an drensys creseff y voys* 'Lord, he has passed away; I believe his soul is with the Trinity' BM 4413-15.

Present of *bos* + *wharvethys* 'happened':

pan venyons **ev** *a'n re ma dre vn venen* **wharvethys** *govy pan welys eva* 'what vengeance are these things, that have happened through one woman! Alas that I saw Eve' OM 619-21

lowene the flour an beys **yma** *cas bras* **wharfethys** *ha cothys war the pobel* 'greetings to the flower of the world; a great matter has happened and fallen upon your people' OM 1541-43

ov arluth myghtern salmon **yma** *mur a varthogyon a'n keth gyst ma* **warvethys** 'my lord Solomon, many wonders of this same beam have happened' OM 2545-47

bos trest thywhy pendra wher ha ponfosyk agas cher mayth ough serrys nag ues ioy y ges colon lemyn dar nep marthegyon **vs wharfethys** 'what is the matter with you that you are sad and your mood afflicted so that you are aggrieved, and that there is no no joy in your hearts? What, have some wonders occurred?' RD 1255-60

Pyv an jovle **us warfethys** *lauer thymmo ty lorden* 'What the devil has happened? Tell me, you clown' BM 775-76.

Collocations of this kind are so common in the texts, that expressions like *cothys yw, devethys yw, gyllys yw,* etc. seem to be the default ways of saying 'has fallen', 'has come', 'has gone, has become,' etc., in Cornish.

The Cornish for 'to dwell, to reside'
The verbal adjective of *trega, tryga* 'to dwell' is also used with *bos* in all tenses, both short and long forms, to render the idea of 'dwelling, residing':

War lyrgh mab den ʒe begha reson prag y fe prynnys yw ihesus crist ʒe ordna **yn neff** *y* **vonas tregys** 'After mankind sinned the reason that he was redeemed is that Jesus Christ ordained that he should dwell in heaven' PA 7ab

ha lauar my th'y warnye vyth na wrella compressa ow tus **vs trygys** *ena* 'and tell him that I warn him that he should not oppress my people who dwell there' OM 1423-25

dev a'm danfonas thy'so the wofyn prak yv genes punscie y tus mar calas **vs trygys** *agy the'th wlas* 'God has sent me to you to ask why you are intent on punishing his people so harshly who live within your kingdom' OM 1480-82

*lauar thy'mmo kyns mones py tyller yma moyses ha py cost **yma trygys*** 'tell me before you go, whereabouts is Moses and in which region does he dwell' OM 1550-52

*guyn y vys a **vo trigys** yn the seruys ragh tristys nyn dygemmer vynytha* 'happy the man who dwells in your service, for sorrow will never take possession of him' PC 122-24

*en den ma war ow ene gans ihesu a nazare yn certan a **fue trygys*** 'that man upon my soul certainly dwelt with Jesus of Nazareth' PC 1277-79

*pan fy a'n bys tremenys gans cryst **y fythyth trygys** agy th'y clos* 'when you depart from the world, you will dwell with Christ within his close' PC 3232-34

***yma tregys** in cambron den ov cul merclys dyson* 'there lives in Camborne a man working miracles indeed' BM 687-88

*The ihesu re bo grasseys omma **yth ese tregys** avel hermyt in guelfos* 'Thanks be to Jesus, here I dwell in the wilderness as a hermit' BM 1962-64

*Ihesu eff re thendelas in gluas neff **bones treges*** 'Jesus he has deserved to dwell in the kingdom of heaven' BM 4337-38

*ny a yll bos sure fatell ra eff in tyrmyn ay vicitacyon agan humbrag ny in ban then wlas **vgy** y vab Jhesus crist inhy **tregys*** 'we can be sure that he will in the time of his visitation lead us above to the kingdom in which his son Jesus Christ dwells' TH 11a

***Yma tregys** in Kembra in Urbe Legionum* 'He lives in Wales in the City of the Legions' BK 1292-93

*ena **ty a vyth tregys** ha myns assentyas genas* 'there you shall dwell and as many as sided with you' CW 246-47

*En termen ez passiez **thera trigaz** en St. Levan dean ha bennen en tellar creiez Chei an Horr* 'In former times there lived in St Levan a man and a woman in a place called the House of the Ram' BF: 15.

This is an idiomatic use and is comparable with expression *tá sé ina chónaí* 'he lives, he dwells' in Irish. The expression *a dryg* on the other hand can only mean '... will dwell, ... will remain', as is clear from the following examples:

*abel ty **a dryg** nefre awos ol the wyr thege yn tewolgow bras hep ioy* 'Abel, you will remain forever, inspite of your true tithe, in great darkness without joy' OM 556-58

*lucyfer kelmys yv whath pur fast yn y golmennow hag ef **a dryk** heb fynweth yn yffarn yn tewolgow* 'Lucifer is still bound very fast in his bonds and he will remain without end in hell in darkness' PA 212cd

*ow spyrys **ny dryc** nefre yn corf map den vyth yn beys* 'my spirit will not remain forever in the body of any man in the world' OM 925-26

137

*mar kyf carynnyas certan warnethe **y tryg** pup preys* 'if it finds carcasses, it will remain on them always' OM 1103-04

*rof thy's ov thour hel ha chammbour bethaf the wour warbarth ny **a dryg** nefre* 'I will give you my tower, hall and chamber; I shall be your husband; together we shall live forever' OM 2110-12

*gans an eleth in golow yn nef agas enefow neffre **a tryg** hep ponow yn ioy na vyth dywythys* 'with the angels in light in heaven your souls will dwell without pain in the joy that will not end' PC 6-9

*ytho gyneugh me **a tryk** yges byth ioy na thyfyk theugh lauara* 'therefore I shall stay with you; you will have endless joy, I tell you' RD 1309-11

*lemmyn omma ty **a dryk** bys pan pottro ol the gyk iuggys may fey* 'now here you will remain until all your flesh rots, that you may be judged' RD 2021-23

*pendra dal an bohosek kyn fo brays y devethyans ef **a dryk** pennoth in hans nyn guel an rych galosek* 'what value is the poor man, even though his pedigree is great? He will remain bareheaded yonder; the rich powerful man does not see him' BM 438-41

*Gesowgh oll rancor, anger ha malice alemma rag the vos vtterly banysshys theworthan ny ha may hallan ny bewa ha trega in charite, ha nena ny **a dryg** in du ha gans du, ha du **a dryg** innan ny ha genan* 'Let all rancour, anger and malice to be completely banished from us and that we may live and dwell in charity, and then we shall dwell in God and with God, and God will dwell in us and with us' TH 30

*Rag heb dowt nyns es thyn trygva in crist, mas ny **a dryg** in vnyta ay Catholik egglos, kepar dell levar S Ciprian* 'For without doubt we have no dwelling place in Christ, unless we dwell in the unity of his catholic Church, as St Cyprian says' TH 39a

*y vabe cayne in paynes brase ef **a dryg** bys venytha yma ef barth awollas in pytt downe ow leskye* 'his son Cain, in great torments he will dwell forever; he is below burning in the deep pit' CW 2031-34

*rag henna bys venary eve **a dryg** ena deffry in paynes bras avel ky* 'therefore forever he will stay there in great torments indeed like a dog' CW 2052-54

*an sperys **ny drige** neffra in corf mabe dean vyth in byes* 'the spirit will not remain forever in the body of any human in the world' CW 2219-20.

In the texts the verbal adjective *ysethys* of *ysetha* 'to sit' can be used with *bos* in a way similar to *bos tregys*:

*huhel **yth os ysethys** ha dyantel ro'm laute* 'you are seated on high and unsafely upon my word' PC 93-4 *mygthern yethewon y'th se heil thy'so ha lowene gentyl* **yth os ysethys** 'king of the Jews in your seat, hail to you and greetings, nobly you are seated' PC 2835-37

pennagel ew na lavara nag ew lucyfer worthy omma thagan governa ha bos pedn in nef defry a lavar gowe yea ha worthy pub preyse **tha vos** *in trone* **ysethys** *avel dewe sure heb parowe* 'whoever it is who says that Lucifer is not worthy to govern us here and to be chief in heaven indeed, speaks falsehood, yes and worthy always to be seated on the throne like God indeed without equal' CW 179-86.

It should be noted, however, that *owth esetha* 'sitting' is also attested:

heyl syr epscop esos y'th cop **owth ysethe** 'hail, sir bishop, who are sitting in your cope' PC 931-32

woge hemma ty a wel map dev sur **owth esethe** *abart dyow thy lawe the'n tas dev arluth huhel* 'hereafter you will see the son of God indeed sitting on the right hand of the God the Father on high, may he be praised' PC 1327-30

woge hemma why a wel map dev sur **ov ysethe** *a barth dyov dyougel then tas dev yn lowene* 'hereafter you will see the Son of God surely sitting on the right hand indeed of God the father in joy' PC 14485-88

rak why a scon ahanan the pilat re synt malan rak yma **owth ysethe** 'for you will soon go hence to Pilate by St Malan, for he is seated' PC 2340-42

O mirkell, ha blonogath da a thew, disquethis theny, **vgy setha** *in gwlas neff* 'O miracle and good will of God demonstrated to us, who sits in the kingdom of heaven' SA 60.

Negative unreal conditions: the imperfect subjunctive of *bos*

There is further way in which the verb *bos* 'to be' can function as an auxiliary. In Cornish the past subjunctive can be used after the leniting particle *na* 'if not' to give a phrase *na ve* 'if ... were not, if ... had not been':

myl wel vye renav thas yn bys ma genys **na ve** 'by my father, it would be a thousand times better if he had not been born in this world' PC 751-52

lues oma deworijs gans an dragon ongrassijs **na ve** *eff sur a vya* 'many here would surely have been devoured by the graceless dragon, had it not been for him' BM 4178-80

maria **na ve** *the rays gon guyr y fyen dyswreys* 'Mary, had it not been for your grace, I know well I should have been destroyed' BM 3703-04

ha **na ve** *agan savyowre crist intendys the ry the pedyr specyall auctorite, a vgh aga hensa, pan a othom vea cowse hemma* 'and had not our Saviour

Christ been determined to give Peter special authority above his
companions, what need would there have been to say this?' TH 44a
Na ve ow mayster, heb dowt me a thothya solabrys 'Had it not been for my
master, without doubt I should have come a while ago' BK 380-81
Owt! Ny vith vas, me a grys, na ny vyan dyelhis, na ve both Du a'n gwelha
'Woe! It will not be well, I believe, nor would we suffer vengeance,
were it not the will of God for the best' BK 3271-73.

The collocation *na ve* when followed by a verbal noun can function as an
auxiliary to express unreal negative conditions:

na ve bos fals an den ma nyn drossen ny bys deso 'if this man were not
false, we would not have brought him to you' PA 99b

gallos warnaf ny fyes na fe y vos grantys thy's dyworth uhella arloth 'you
would have no power over me had it not been granted you by a
higher lord' PC 2187-89

na ve y vose guir sans mar lues merkyl dyblans byth ny russe 'if he were
not a true saint, he certainly would not do as many miracles' BM
2051-53

na ve creya warnogh why kellys ol y fyen ny yowynk ha loys 'had it not
been for calling on you, we all should have been lost, young and
old' BM 2169-71

*Surely, ny vynsan cresy an aweyll, na ve an Catholyk egglos the ry thym
experiens* 'Surely I should not believe the gospel, if the catholic
Church were not to give me the experience' TH 37a

*An kyth office ma ny vynsa pedyr kemeras na ve crist the ry thotha an
auctorite* 'This same office Peter would not have accepted, if Christ
had not given him the authority' TH 44a.

*Me a thothya gans an ger, na ve ow maw thu'm lettya, drog-chawns th'y
ben!* 'I would have come at the word, were it not that my servant
hindered me, bad luck on his head!' BK 469-71.

In Later Cornish in unreal conditions generally the past subjunctive in the
protasis is replaced by the conditional. Examples are not common:

*Mar kressa an dean deskez feer na gwellaz hemma [ev] a venga kavaz fraga
e ouna en skreefa-composter* 'If that learned wise man were to see this, he
would find reason to emend it in orthography' BF: 27.

Here the conditional *kressa < qurussa* has replaced the past subjunctive *qurella*
< gwrella. The same replacement of the past subjunctive by the conditional is
also apparent in the use of *na vea* (i.e. *na vya*) for *na ve*:

na vea me theth cara ny vynsan theth cossyllya tha vos bargayne mar vras gwryes 'were I not to love you, I would not advise you that such a great bargain be made' CW 669-71

na vea me theth cara ny vynsan awos neb tra yn ban tha vos exaltys 'were I not to love you, I would not for anything wish for you to be high exalted' CW 699-701

Sendzhyz ôn nei ∂v huei: **Na vîa** *ragoh huei nei a vîa tîz oll dizurêyz* 'We are beholden to you; Had it not been for you we should all have been dead men' AB: 252a.

3. *CARA* 'TO LOVE, TO LIKE'

Cara as full verb means 'to love'. Here are some examples:

ow arluth nep a'm **care** *y'n naghen ef a'm guarnyas* 'my lord who loved me, warned me that I should deny him' PC 1419-20

pynyl o mogha sengys an keth den ma the **care** 'who was the most obliged to love this man?' PC 510-11

neb may fe moghya geffys a **gar** *moghye yn pup le* 'to whom is most forgiven, loves most everywhere' PC 513-14

lauar an guyr thy'm peder del y'th **caraf** *mur pup prys* 'tell me the truth, Peter, as I love you greatly always' PC 709-10

me a'n **caruyth** *alemma bys gorfen beys* 'I will love him from henceforth till the end of the world' PC 1703-04

mur me a'n **car** 'I love him greatly' RD 1801

ny **gara** *sevel in creys* 'I do not love standing at peace' BM 1271

te a ra **cara** *theth kyscristyan kepar ha te the honyn* 'you shall love your fellow Christian as yourself' TH 20a

Neb a **garra** *y das po y vam, y vab po y virth, chy, trevyn po tyrryow, moy agesa ve, y myth crist, nyns ew worthy the vos dissipill na seruant thym* 'Whoever loves his father or his mother, his son or his daughter, houses or lands, more than me, says Christ, is not worthyt to be a disciple or servant of mine' TH 21a.

Because the present of *mynnes* when used with a verbal noun tended to lose its volitional force (see **10.** *MYNNES* below), it appears that the conditional of *cara* 'to love' was used to express the idea of wishing or wanting to do something in the immediate future:

ov thas ev coth ha squytheys **ny garse** *pelle bewe* 'my father is old and exhausted; he does not wish to live any longer' OM 737-38

er y byn mennaf mones me **a garse** *y weles ef yw dev luen a pite* 'I will go to meet him; I want to see him; he is God full of pity' PC 232-34 *a garsesta bynene mar mynnyth war ow ene me a gergh onan dek thy's* 'do you want to consort with a woman? If you do upon my soul I will get you a nice one' PC 2838-40

dun alemma cowethe y weles me ***a garse*** *owth astel ymthreheuel* 'let us go hence, companions; I want to see him failing to rise' RD 393-95

y weles me ***a garse*** *ha cous orth ow map ihesu* 'I want to see him and speak to my son Jesus' RD 435-36

guelas ow map ***y carsen*** *a tas dre the luen weres* 'I want to see my son, O Father, by your full help' RD 442-44

y carsen *guelas an fou anotho y voth mar pe* 'I should like to see the sight of him, were it his will' RD 469-70

cous ganso ***me a garse*** *y volungeth mar a pe yn par deffry* 'I should like to speak to him if it were his will in very truth' RD 744-46

mars yv gans du plygadow ***y karsen*** *y exaltya may fo perhennek gwlasow* 'if it is pleasing to God, I want to exalt him, so that he may be the owner of kingdoms' BM 14-16

gans golyas ha gans pynys me ***a garsa*** *crist ʒe plesya a newyth hag a henys* 'with watching and with fasting I wish to please Christ in youth and in old age' BM 164-67

bones sacris marrek du an order mar [leg. *mur*] *thym a plek benitha hedre ven byv me* ***a garse*** *lowenek* 'I want to be consecrated a knight of Christ of the order that greatly pleases me forever I wish gladly as long as I live' BM 350-53

pronter boys ***me a garse*** *corff ihesu thy venystra mar myn ov descans servya* 'I want to be a priest to administer the body of Christ, if my learning is found sufficient' BM 522-24

the kernov mars egh defry mones genogh ***y carsen*** 'if you are going to Cornwall, I should like to go with you' BM 588-89

grua ov gedya vy bys dy rag mur ***y carsen*** *defry guthel thymmo oratry in herwyth chy maria* 'guide me thither for I greatly wish indeed to build an oratory for myself close by the church of Mary' BM 637-40

byth ***ny garsen*** *gul da certen na y predery dyogel* 'never do I want to do good nor consider it indeed' BM 2341-43

yma drok turant in pov ***ny garsen*** *orto metya* 'there is an evil tyrant in the land; I do not want to meet him' BM 3206-07

confort thum cervons dyson boys ***y carsen*** 'I want to be a comfort to my servants indeed' BM 3651-52

me ***a garsa*** *in norvys ma pup vr socra bohogogyon* 'I want always in this world to succour poor people'

Me ***a garsa*** *thotha ef dusquethas unwyth pew of* 'I wish to show him once who I am' BK 2067-68

Me ***a garsa*** *in tefry cafas gorthyb in certan* 'I want indeed to get answer certainly' BK 2100-01

*rag drys pub tra us war an bys me **a garsa** gul both the vrys, ow arluth ker*
'for above everything in the world I want to do the will of your
mind, my beloved lord' BK 2849-53.

4. *COTHA* 'TO FALL, TO BE INCUMBENT'

Although *cotha* literally means 'to fall, to become', as an impersonal verb it can
also mean 'to fall to, to be incumbent upon.' In this sense is also not
infrequently found as a personal verb also. As an impersonal and a personal
verb it is attested at all periods and in various tenses.

Present indicative of *cotha*:

*ʒe thu **ny goth** thys temptye yn neb ehan a seruys* 'you ought not tempt
your God in any kind of service' PA 15a

*Ihesus crist a leueris y vos scryfys yn lyffrow yn pub gwythres **y coth** thys
gorʒye ʒe ʒu hay hanow* 'Jesus Christ said that it was written in the
scriptures: in all doing you should worship God and his name' PA
17ab

*Bos segh ha tek an awel the dev **y coth** thy's grasse* 'You should thank God
that the weather is dry and fair' OM 1147-48

*ytho worthyf **ny goth** thy's govyn yn nos dyougel* 'therefore indeed you
ought not ask me by night indeed' PC 1263-4

***ny goth** aga bos gorrys yn arghov rak bos prennys ganse mernans den
bryntyn* 'they ought not be put into the treasury because the death
of a fine man was bought with them' PC 1540-42

*mara mennough yndella leuerough dre py laha **y coth** thotho bos lethys* 'if
you wish thus, say by which law he ought to be killed' PC 2377-79

*ytho dre pup reson da **ny goth** thotho bos crousys* 'therefore for every good
reason he ought not be crucified' PC 2389-90

*syr doctor lauaraf thy's ef **a goth** thotho merwel* 'sir doctor, I tell you: he
ought to die' PC 2407-08

*Indelma yma an scriptur playnly ow declaria fatell ew an egglos catholik the
vos aswonys ha fatell **goth** theth hy bos aswonys* 'Thus scripture
declares how the catholic Church is to be recognized and how she
ought to be recognized' TH 32.

Present subjunctive of *cotha*:

*my ny gafaf ynno ken **may cothfo** thy'm y lathe* 'I find no cause in him that
I should kill him' PC 1797-98

*me a's guarn yowynk ha hen my ny gafaf ynno ken **may cothfo** thy'm y
dampne* 'I warn you young and old: I find no reason in him that I
should condemn him' PC 2031-33.

Past subjunctive of *cotha*:

> *dre guyrvrus sur y **cothe** dotho gothaf bos lethys yn pur defry* 'by true judgement surely it would be right for him to be suffer to be killed in very truth' OM 2237-39
>
> *pup pystryor **y cothe** dre reson da y leysky* 'every wizard should by good reason be burnt' PC 1766-67
>
> *rag henna ny **a gottha** thyn bois inflammyes the voy the gara ha the servia du agan gwrer ha creator kerngeek* 'therefore we should be inflamed the more to love and to serve God our maker and loving creator' TH 3
>
> *han lesson na **a gotha** agen gwarnya ny oll the consydra a behane one ny ha pan a dra one ny* 'and that lesson should warn us all to consider of what kind we are and what we are' TH 6
>
> *nyg esan ny ow dowtya du mar ver dell **gottha** thyn* 'we do not fear God as much as we should' TH 9
>
> *mar mynnyn ny judgia compis, hag inta, ny **a gottha** thyn leverall a vgh pub tra oll ew da the vos dyskys thyn cristonnyon nynses tra vith moy neces-sary the vos gylwys warnotha ha kowsys anotha dayly moy ys charite* 'if we are to judge correctly, we should say above everything that it is good to be taught to Christians, there is nothing more necessary to be invoked and spoken of daily more than charity' TH 21
>
> *ny **a gottha** thyn omry agan honyn the wetha ha the colynwall y commond-ment eff* 'we should devote ourselves to keeping and to fulfilling his commandment' TH 21a
>
> *Han kythsam kerensa na **a gottha** thyn ny kafus in agan myske agan honyn peb oll the gela* 'And that same love we should find in our midst ourselves each man to his fellow' TH 21a.

The conditional of *cotha*:

> *ny gafaf ken th'y lathe na blam uyth ol ynno ef rak henna my **a gosse** alemma y thylyffrye* 'I find no reason to kill him nor any blame in him; therefore I should deliver him hence' PC 2214-17
>
> *Ha po 'rŷg an ðzhei ðvz ðv'n tshei lebma **gôτ fīa** an dzhei ostia; ameð Dzhûan me dal ʒuellaz an ôst an tshei* 'And when they came to the house where they should lodge, Jowan said, I must see the host of the house' AB: 252a.

5. *DOS* 'TO COME'

The verb *dos* 'to come' is widely used with the sense 'to happen to, to chance to' as an auxiliary preceding a verbal noun. The verbal noun is usually, but not invariably, introduced by *ha* 'and'. The commonest usages are in real conditions; in unreal conditions and in final clauses. There are also a few examples of *dos* as an auxiliary in indefinite relative clauses and in temporal clauses after *pan* 'when.' Less certain is the use of *reffo / reffa* < *?re dheffo / ?re dheffa* in third person singular jussives.

Dos in real conditions:

mar te venions **ha cothe** *war agan flehys yn fras ha warnan be3ans neffre* 'if vengeance fall upon our children and upon us, let it be so forever' PA 149cd

myrugh **mar te drehevell** *ay beynys 3y delyffre* 'look if he arises to deliver him from his torments' PA 203c

mar tue nep guas **ha laddre** *en gueel theworthyn pryve meth vyth ol d'agen ehen* 'if some fellow steals the rods from us surreptitiously, it will be a disgrace for all our kind' OM 2064-66

mar tufe **ha datherghy** *mur a tus a wra crygy ynno y vos dev a nef* 'if he rises from the dead, many men will believe in him, that he is God of heaven' RD 7-9

hythew yv an trege deyth mones the vyras deffry **mara tueth ha dasserhy** *del leuerys thy'm perfyth* 'today is the third day to go to observe indeed whether he has risen as he told me perfectly' RD 681-84

mara tuen **ha debatya** *mas an nyyl party omma ov teberth purguir ny warth* 'if we debate, only one party here will laugh on departure' BM 3476-7

An tryssa, the le inclynacion an geffa den the begh, the voy **ha the vrassa** *ew y begh* **mar te ha gull** *an dra* 'The third, the less inclination a man would have to sin, the more and the greater is his sin if he does the thing' TH 4a

An peswora, **mar te den ha receva** *royow bras theworth y gothman po y soveran,* **mar te** *in byanby* **ha tyrry** *blonogath y soveran hay displesya, an fowt han disobediens dretho ew gwrys the vrassa* 'The fourth, if a man receives great boons from his friend or his sovereign, if shortly he violates his sovereign's will and displeases him, the fault and the disobedience is by it made the greater' TH 4a

Mar ten ny **ha leverell** *nag ony pehadoryan, yth esan ow desyvya agan honyn han gweroneth nys ugy genyn* 'If we say we are not sinners, we deceive ourselves and the truth is not in us' TH 8

mar ten **ha menegas** *agan pehosow du ew lene a vercy, just ha fethfull the gava thyn agan pehosow ha thegan glanhe a bup filth* 'if we confess our sins, God is full of mercy, just and faithful to forgive us our sins and to cleanse us of all filth' TH 8

ha **mar tene leverall** *na russyn peha, ny a ra eff gowak hay er nyns ugy innan ny* 'and if we sawy we have not sinned, we make him a liar and his word is not in us' TH 8 *ha henna* **mar tene** *ny consyddra hag vnderstondia in ta, ny a ra the well vnderstondia an mercy a thu* 'and if we consider and understand that well, we will better understand the mercy of God' TH 10

mar ten ny *indelma* **submyttya** *agan honyn in sight a thu ny a yll bos sure fatell ra eff in tyrmyn ay vicitacyon agan humbrag ny in ban then wlas vgy y vab Jhesus crist inhy tregys* 'if we thus submit ourselves in the sight of God, we can be sure that he in the time of his visitation will lead us above to the kingdom where his son Jesus Christ dwells' TH 11a

ha the rena **mar ten ha kemeras** *with in ta, kepar ha the wolow a rella shynya in tyllar tewlle, why a ra da bys may teffa an Jeth hag egery, han vurluan agery in agys colonow* 'and to those if we pay attention well, as though to light that shines in a dark place, you will do well until the day opens and the morning star opens in your hearts' TH 18

Rag **mar tewgh why ha cara** *an re vsy worth agys cara why pana rewarde a vethow why?* 'For if you love those who love you, what reward will you have?' TH 22

mar tewgh why ha cowse *da only an re na neb ew agys brederath ha cothmans, pan a vattar bras ew henna?* 'if you speak well only of those who are your brothers and friends, what great matter is that?' TH 22

ha henna ny a vith sure anotha, y myth crist, **mar ten ny ha cara** *pub den heb exception. So* **mar ten ha gull ken,** *y myth crist, nyg esan ow kull bithwell agys an pharises, publicans, han hethens* 'And that we will be sure of, says Christ, if we love everybody without exception. But if we do otherwise, says Christ, we do no better than the Pharisees, publicans and the heathens' TH 22a

Ha **mar ten ny ha consyddra** *henna neb a rug agan offendia ny nyg usy ow deservya the gafus gyvyans theworthan, gesow ny the consydra fatell essan ny ow deservia le gyvyans theworth du* 'And if we consider that he who offended us does not deserve to obtain forgiveness from us, let us consider that we deserve less forgiveness from God' TH 24a

mar te cherite requyria *the predyry, the cowsse da, ha the wull da the bub den, da ha bad, fatell yll an rewlysy a'n wlas executia justis war drog pobill gans charite?* 'if charity enjoins thinking, speaking and doing good to everyone, good and bad, how can the rulers of the country execute justice upon evil people with charity?' TH 24a

ken nyns ugens y ow regardya du nan re vsy in dan aga governans, **mar towns y ha suffra** *du the vos offendys rag lak a correccion, han re vsy in aga gouernans the vos perisshys* 'otherwise they do not regard God nor those under their rule, if they suffer God to be offended for lack of correction, and those under their rule to be corrupted' TH 25

*Ha **mar ten ny** in delma dyrectya agan bewnans dre kerensa ha lell charite,
nena yma crist ow promysya ha ow assurya thyn, fatell vsy eff worth agan
cara ny* 'And if we so direct our life by love and true charity, then
Christ promises and assures us that he loves us' TH 26

*lymmyn **mar te** cristonyan ha concevya anger in aga colonow, ha na
rellans by an by suppressia an kythsam anger na, mas procedia pella inna,
ha tyrry charite, henna ew the vttra aga anger dre sygne ha tokyn, nena
an kythsame fawt ma ew brassa ys y gela* 'now if Christians conceive
anger in their hearts, and do not soon suppress that same anger,
but proceed further in it and rupture charity, then this same fault is
greater than the other' TH 28a

***Mar te** the brother **ha gull** trespas war the byn, ke in kerth ha lavar thotha y
fowt intre te hag eff only* 'If your brother trespass against you, go off
and tell him his fault between you and him only' TH 31a

***mar te** ran ahanow why **dowtya** an vnderstonding an scriptur ma, omma
why a glew fatell ma S Austyn ow scriffa anotha* 'if some of you dowt
the understanding of this passage of scripture, here you will hear
how St Augustine writes about it' TH 32

*An dra ma, tus vas, why a yll inta vnderstondia y bosa lell, **mar tewgh why
gylwall** thegys remembrans, pew ew an guyde han gouernar an egglos*
'This matter, good people, you will understand to be true, if you
call to your remembrance who is the guide and governor of the
Church' TH 36

*So **mar tewhy ha chauncya** the naha agys mam egglos catholik ha govyn
cusullyow worthow agys honyn, po theworth an re na vsy ow swarvya
theworth an Catholyk egglos, nena in mar ver nag ew an spuris sans agys
gyde, why a ra cotha mes a ignarans the error* 'But if you chance to
deny your mother, the catholic Church, and ask for advice from
yourselves or from those who deviate from the catholic Church,
then in as much as the Holy Spirit is not your guide, you will fall
from ignorance into error' TH 38

***Mar teugh why ha gurtas** inno ve, ha ow gyrryow ve inno why, govynnogh
an pith a vennogh hag eff a vith res the why* 'If you remain in me and
my words in you, ask what you will and it will be given to you'
TH 39a

*Dre hemma ny ew sure, **mar ten ny ha gurtas** in Catholik egglos, ha
imbrasya ha strotha an feith han discans an egglos, nena crist y honyn dre
grace a ra trega innan ny ha inweth agan pesadow a vith clowys*
'Through this we are sure, if we remain in the catholic Church and
embrace and clasp the faith and the teaching of the Church, then
Christ himself by grace will dwell in us and also our prayers will
be heard' TH 39a.

*fynally **mar ten ny ha contynewa** fleghys obedyent, in ascra agan mam Sans
egglos, ny a vith megys gans an bos a lell feith ha bewek* 'finally if we

continue obedient children in the bosom of our mother, holy Church, we will be nurtured by the food of true and lively faith' TH 41

may ra an tryssa han peswora aes ahanan ny y glowas, ea, ha smyrtya ragtha, **mar te an bys ha durya** *mar bell* 'so that the third and fourth age of us will feel it, yes, and smart because of it, if the world endure so long' TH 50a

Mar tene ny comparia *an gyrryow cowsys gans crist pan rug eff gul an promes a vois, the vos dretha eff thynny res, gans an gyrryow ma erall, a rug eff vttra ow ry an dra na, ny res thynny dowtya an pith a rug eff ry* 'If we compare the words spoken by Christ when he made the promise of food, which would be given us by him, with these other words, which he uttered giving that, it is not necessary for us to doubt what he did give' TH 52

pandre vynnough leverall **mar tema disquethas** *theugh certyn tacclow arall mere moy agis helma* 'what will you say, if I show you certain further things much greater than this?' SA 60

Mar tewhy demandea *praga a ruke an egglos dewys mar galys vnderstandyng an keth Artickell ma girryow an scripture a yll bos easiy vnderstandis* 'If you ask why the Church chose such a hard interpretation of this article, the words of scripture can easily be understood' SA 64

Mar tue *Teuder Ke* **latha,** *ef a'n kef war e forth hyr* 'If Teudar kills Ke, he will pay for it in the long run' BK 584 (stage direction)

Mara tof ha trewelas, *ny vyth mab den ou gwelas rag arsevnans ha terrur* 'If I rage, no human being will dare look at me for ?persecution and terror' BK 1402-04

Bethans pur glor, rag **mar tema ha rowtya ha ferneuwhy ha stowtya,** *ny vith mab den na'm dowtya* 'Let them be very quiet, for if I dominere and rage and swagger, there will be no human being who will not fear me' BK 1638-41

Glaze Neave tha enna ni veath a heaze **mar ta ni gweel** *da war an Beaze* 'The goodly kingdom of heaven we will have at length if we do good upon the earth' LAM: 228.

Dos in unreal conditions:

ha leuerell yredy **mar teffa tus ha gweȝe** *bos ȝe ȝu ȝe wull gynsy* 'and say indeed, if men were to prevent them, that God had need of her' PA 27cd

Rag **mar teffa** *crist* **ha dos** *in dallath an bys whare whosa mabden the beha ha the vos kyllys, tus a russa supposia* **mar teffa** *du aga* **suffra** *the vsya aga naturall powers y a vynsa optaynya salvacion in ta lovr heb gweras vith arell in party du* 'For if Christ had come at the beginning of the world, shortly after mankind had sinned and been lost, men would have supposed, if God has allowed them to use their natural powers, they would have obtained salvation well enough without any further remedy on God's part' TH 13a

fattla **mar teffa** *ha contradicion ha varians* **chansya** *the vos drehevys war questyon bean?* 'what if a small contradiction and disagreement had chanced to be raised upon a minor question?' TH 19

Mar teffa *den vith* **ha pregoth** *thyn kythsame barbarus nacions ma in aga eyth y aga honyn an vencions ma a heritickys in by an by y a vynsa stoppya aga scovurnow* 'If anyone were to preach to these same barbarous peoples in their own language these inventions of heretics, they would soon enough stop up their ears' TH 19

Mar teffa *an epscobow han brontyryan in tyrmyn passis inweth an dus leg* **dysky ha practysya** *aga duty haga vocacyons, dre an exampill ma surly ny russa an egglos a crist dos then dishonor han disordyr a wylsyn ny* 'If the bishops and the priests in the past, the laity also, had taught and practised their duty and their vocations, by this example, surely the Church of Christ would not have come to the dishonour and to the disorder which we have seen' TH 39

mar teffa *an holl brodereth* **obeya** *according then commondmentys a thu, ny vynsa den vith styrrya na gwaya warbyn an colleges po company a prontyrryan* 'if all the brotherhood had obeyed according to the commandments of God, no one would have stirred or moved against the colleges or the company of priests' TH 42a.

The subjunctive of *dos* in final clauses:

me an felge adrus then pen **may teffo** *y ompynnen* **ha skynnya** *avel mottis* 'I will split him across the head that his brains may fall in little bits' BM 1273-75

I wysce ath face te a thebbyr the vara bys **may tyffy** *arta* **ha trelya** *the thore ha pry* 'In the sweat of your face you will eat your bread until you again turn to earth and clay' TH 6

yma an lyver a skyantoleth ow remembra thyn **may teffan ha tenna** *then dore an pryde vs ew raynya ynnan* 'the book of Wisdom reminds us that we should cast down the pride which reigns in us' TH 6a

Rag henna the gemeras oll excuses an parna the ves, ha **may teffan** *pleynly vnderstondia awosa ny vnwith the skynnya in pegh* 'therefore, to take away all excuses of that kind, and that we may plainly understand after we have once fallen into sin' TH 13a

why a ra da bys **may teffa** *an jeth* **hag egery**, *han vurluan agery in agys colonow* 'you will do well until the day breaks and the morning star opens in your hearts' TH 18

149

*Indelma an lell charite [a] crist an discas **may teffa** pub den ha benyn **cara du drys pub tra*** 'Thus the true charity of Christ taught us, that every man and woman should love God above all things' TH 22a

*ha eff a assas ensampill thynny **may teffen hay folya** eff* 'and he left us an example that we might follow it' TH 24

*rag crist a rug deservya theworthan ny **may teffan ha gava** the bub den an trespas gwrys er aga pyn, rag y gerensa eff* 'for Christ deserved from us that we should for his sake forgive everybody the trespas committed against us' TH 24a

*martesyn y a yll skynnya in myschew an par na **may teffans ha tenna** re erell dre aga teball examplis ha gwrythyans* 'perhaps they may fall into crime of that kind so that they draw others by their evil examples and behaviour' TH 25a

*Rag henna pan vsy agan Savyowre ow requyrya theworthan ny **may teffan ny ha passia** an scribes han pharises in gwryoneth ha iustice* 'Therefore when our Saviour requires of us that we should excel the scribes and pharisees in truth and justice' TH 26a

*inweth tytus eff an gasas in Creta, **may teffa eff inna hag ordenya** prontiran in pub cita* 'also he left Titus in Crete, that there he might ordain priests in every city' TH 33a

*hag eff a ros thethy power war teball spurugian, **may teffens y haga thowllell** in mes* 'and he gave them power over evil spirits, that they might cast them out' TH 35a

*yth ew openly gothvethis in mar ver dell rug crist promysya an conforter, vt maneat vobiscum in eternum, **may teffa ha gurtas** genowgh rag neffra* 'it is well known, in as much as Christ promised the Comforter, That he may remain with you forever' TH 36a

*the wull an obereth a mynystra rag edyfya an corfe a crist, bys **may teffan ny** oll **ha dos** warbarth in vn vnyte a crisgians ha feith* 'to perform the works of ministering to build up the body of Christ, untill we all might come together in one unity of belief and faith' TH 42

*Ith ew scryffys in viii-as chapter in actys an appostolis fatell rug Symon magus offra the ry mona the pedyr mar mynna pedyr ry power thotheff, penagull person a rella eff ha gora y thewleff warnotha **may teffans ha receva** an spurissans* 'It is written in the eighth chapter in the Acts of the Apostles that Simon Magus offered money to Peter, if Peter would give him power, whoever he might lay his hands upon, that they would receive the Holy Spirit' TH 46a

*A ra tus vsya offra bois ha dewas the re rag purpos vith arall, mas **may teffans dybry** hag eva anotha?* 'Do men usually offer food and drink to people for any other purpose than that they may eat and drink of them?' TH 52a

*ha in oll an processe ma nyg us matter vith rag agan discans ny, mas **may teffan ha cresy** anotha y bos ynna an very corfe ha gois agan Savyour*

Jhesu crist 'and in all this business there is no matter for our learning but that we should believe of it that in it is the very body and blood of our Saviour Jesus Christ' TH 53a

pan ruga in della y ordeyna **may teffa** *pub naturall mam* **ha maga** *y flehes gans an substans ay corfe y honyn* 'when he ordained that every natural mother should nurture her children with the substance of her own body' TH 54a

dew a ornas contrary **na thesan** [leg. **thefan**] *tastya henna* 'on the contrary God ordained that we should not taste that' CW 630-31.

Dos in indefinite relative clauses:

neg ew ef compti[s ve]l e heare nep **ne theffa regardya** *an keth gyrryow ma* 'he is not considered as his heir who doe not respect these same words' SA 59

An bara **a theffan ry**, *ew ow kigg ve* 'The bread which I give, is my flesh' SA 66

ha mar petha indella me a vidn ye requyrya a thewla an kethe dean na y woose **a theffa scullya** 'and if it be so, I will require it from the hands of that same man who sheds his blood' CW 2519-22.

A further example of the present subjunctive of *dos* used as an auxiliary in an indefinite relative clausemay possibly be seen at *Jowan Chy an Hordh* §32. Lhuyd's text reads: *Piu a 'ryg an bad-ober? medh Dzhûan; mar nyz medra dheffa previ peu a 'ryg an bad-ober; mî a vedn krêg ragta*. This I would emend slightly to *Piu a 'ryʒ an bad-ober? með Dzhûan; mar nyz medra* **ðeffa previ** *peu a 'rŷʒ an bad-ober; mî a vedn krêʒ raʒta* (AB: 252a). Here *dheffa* is the present/past subjunctive of *dos* 'to come' used after an indefinite subject and with the following verbal noun *previ* 'to prove'. I assume that the definite article has been lost before *dra*, although the initial lenition survives. I translate my emended text as: 'Who committed the crime? said Jowan; 'if I have not the thing which would prove who committed the crime, I will hang for it.'

Dos in temporal clauses:

a'n beth **pan thueth ha lamme** *y fyys yn vn vramme ovn kemerys* 'when he jumped out of the tomb, I fled farting; I was afraid' RD 2093-95

rag **pan deffen ha moys** *fol an iovle a thue mes ay dol kyns es ov ruthy purguir* 'for when I become frenzied the devil will come out of his hole before I repent indeed' BM 906-08

rag **pan deffa** *an welsan* **ha dalleth** *seeha an flowre a ra clamdera ha cotha the ves* 'for when the grass begins to wither the flower fades and falls away' TH 7

Nyng vs [den]vyth ow tybbry an kigg na arrne theffa [ha e worthia] 'No one eats this flesh until he worships it] SA 64a-65.

There are also a number of instances in the verses of John Tonkin of *reffa* + verbal noun expressing a jussive. It might be that *reffa* is for earlier **re theffo*, **re theffa*, where the verb is the third person present subjunctive of *dos*:

> *Dew reffa e sowia tre ha leaze ha gweel a vownans mear a heaze* 'May God save him at home and abroad and render his life great in extent' LAM: 226
> *Dew reffa sowia an Egles ni ha an prounterian da eze et angy* 'May God save our Church and the good priests who are in them' LAM: 226
> *Lebben Dewe reffa gun sowia ul, nenna na geath denneth tha gul* 'Now may God save us all; then no man has been lost' LAM: 228.

With *reffa* in those examples compare *reffo why* in:

> *Contrevak Nicholas Pentreath, Pa reffo why doaz war an dreath Gen puscas, komero why 'wyth Tha geil compez* 'Neighbour Nicholas Pentreath, when you come to the shore with fish, be careful to act honestly' LAM: 244 .

6. *GALLOS* 'TO BE ABLE'
Gallos 'to be able' is essentially an auxiliary verb. It is found in four indicative tenses, i.e. the present-future, the imperfect; the preterite and the conditional. *Gallos* is also very common indeed after *may* 'so that'. It is also common in the present and past subjunctive.

The present-future of *gallos*:

> *Colon den a yll crakye a vynha prest predery an paynys bras an geve* 'A man's heart can crack who would continually consider the great torments he endured' PA 139ab
> *a das dew ker beneges, ny yllyr re the worthe* 'O dear blessed Father, it is not possible to worship you too much' OM 1851-52
> *lauar cowyth da del os fatel yllyn aswonvos en harlot yn mysk y tus* 'say, good companion as you are, how can we recognize the scoundrel in the midst of his men?' PC 965-67
> *ol an doctors yn bys ma byth ny yllons y sawye* 'all the doctors in this world can never save him' PC 2429-30
> *ha galwy dre a pup sorn an thewolow mara keller y wythe achy na alla yntre the'n darasow* 'and call them home from every corner, the devils, if he can be prevented from entering through the doors' PC 3056-60

*me a whyth gans mur a grys kynyuer dyaul vs yn beys certan yn ta may clewfo rak **mara kylle** entre agy the'n yet ru'm leute ef a wra thy'nny drok tro* 'I will blow with great vigour, so that every devil that is in the world can hear it, for if he can enter in the gate, by my loyalty he will do us an evil turn' PC 3061-66

*yth orden agan lathe rak **na yl** agan fethe dre lauarow* 'he will order us to be killed, since he cannot conquer us by words' RD 253-55

*rag esow galsof ysel **na allaf** kerthes yn fas* 'for hunger I have become weak so that I cannot walk properly' OM 373-74

*ha me ynweth a'n guelas ha ganso ef company bras orth y sywe lyes guas **ny yllons** bos nyfyrys* 'I also saw him and with him a great company following him, many fellows; they cannot be numbered' RD 555-58

ny a yl bos lowenek guelas ihesu galosek arluth a ras 'we can be joyful to have seen might Jesus, gracious lord' RD 1333-35

*ken teffo yges golok thotho **ny yllough** gul drok sur me a grys* 'though he come into your presence you will not be able to do harm to him, I believe' RD 1861-63

*pyv **a ylta** gy bones pan yw mar ruth the thylles* 'who can you be, when your clothes are so red' RD 2511-12

*gothe mernans dyn a reys byth **ny yller** y sconya* 'we must suffer death; it cannot be avoided for ever' BM 1753-54.

The form *ylta* in the penultimate example is *gylta* with lenited initial < **gyllyth* + *ta*. A later and analogical form *gyllys* seems to occur in *Panna weal 'lesta geeal meth an teeack* 'What kind of work can you do? said the farmer' BF: 15. Notice that a distinctive future form of *gallos* is also attested: *Ef ew pen an vethogyan hag **a ylwyth** the sawya* 'He is chief of physicians and he will be able to heal you' BK 795-96.

Imperfect of *gallos*:

*Goȝaff paynys pan vynnas neb **na ylly** gull peghes* 'When he intended to suffer torment, he who could not commit sin' PA 3d

*Gans gloteny ef pan welas cam **na ylly** y dolla, an tebell el a vynnas yn ken maner y demptya* 'When he saw that he could not deceive him with gluttony, the devil wished to tempt him in another way' PA 13ab

*ef e wre oll y vynnas y **ny yllens** y weȝe* 'he did all his will; they were not able to prevent him' PA 243d

*ha **na yllens** y gwyȝe y voth na vo colenwys* 'and they were not able to prevent that his will be not fulfilled' PA 248d

*me a vynse y wythe ha **ny yllyn** cammen vyth* 'I wished to preserve him but I could not in any way at all' PC 3125-26.

The preterite of *gallos*:

Eneff iudas **ny allas** *dos yn mes war y anow rag y anow a ammas 3e ihesu leun a rasow* 'The soul of Judas could not come out by his mouth, for his mouth kissed Jesus, full of grace' PA 106ab

whet **ny ellys** *yn nep tu gothfos ganso fatel fe* 'still I could not on any side learn how it was with him' RD 467-68

lowene thy's syr pilat awos bos ny peswar smat guythe an beth ny **ylsyn** 'hail to you, Sir Pilate! Although we are four smart lads, we could not guard the tomb' RD 601-03

ov envy in kerth galsons ov metya byth **ny alsons** *du a vynnas indella* 'my enemies have gone away; they were not able to meet me ever; God wished thus' BM 1069-71.

The conditional of *gallos*:

tekke alter yn neppow **ny alse** *den aspye es del vs genen hep wow dres an mount calvarye* 'a finer altar no man could espy in any country than that I have indeed over Mount Calvary' OM 1177-80

ef a galse *bos guyrthys a try cans dyner ha moy ha re na* **galser** *the rey the voghesegyon yn beys* 'it could have been sold for 300 pence and more and those could have been given to the poor in the world' PC 535-38

a peue den drok y gnas **ny alse** *yn nep maner pur wyr cafus mar mur ras rak sawye tus dre vn ger* 'if he were an man of evil nature, he would not in truth be able in any way to find such great grace as to heal men by a single word' PC 2969-72

gorthya du ty **alse** *sur kyn fy reoute an beys* 'you could indeed worship God even though you possessed the splendour of the world' BM 2017-18

An kyth cyrcomstans ma **a alse** *bos geses in part du an tas rag eff* **a alsa** *creatya ha gull mab den hebtha* 'This same circumstance could have been ignored by God, for he could have created and an made mankind without it' TH 1

pendra **alsan** *ny predery fatell ylly du gull moy ragan in agen creacion dell ruga gull* 'what could we think that God could have done more for us in our creation than he did?' TH 2a

Owt, galsof gwan a'm skyans! **Ny alsa** *moy dyswryans wharvos neffra er ow fyn* 'Oh, I have become weak in my head! No greater destruction could ever happen against me' BK 3137b-39b

Drog-chauns war an kynwelas, **na alsan** *ny teulal dyal* 'Evil fate upon the encounter, that I could not take vengeance' BK 3278-79

*yn er na re sent deffry **yth halsan** rowtya pur gay ha bos stately ʒom deuyse* 'Then by St Verily I could rule very nobly and be as stately as I wished' CW 606-08.

Some of the persons of the preterite are indistinguishable from the conditional and this seems to have led to the confusion of the two tenses. Moreover and probably more importantly, the English 'could' i.e. 'was able', is identical with 'could' i.e. 'would be able' and this identity of the English conditional with the English past tense appears to have affected later Cornish At all events, the later language the only past tense is identical in form with the conditional. It is noteworthy, however, that the distinctive feature of this past/conditional is that the consonant group *-ls-* is invariably *-lj-* (usually spelt ‹lg›):

*ma ko them pe nag oma buz dro tho wheeath bloah coth, **na olga ma** e clappia na skant e guthvaz* 'I remember when I was only about six years old that I could not speak it nor hardly understand it' BF: 27

*radden **olga** bose parrez tho leverol dr' erama gweel nebbaz aga a Curnoack* 'some could be prepared to say that I am making little there of Cornish' BF: 31

*Ha whaeh an Sousen metessen **olga** gawaz maga nebbaz skeeanz vel an Brittez it'ge clappia 'ge for* 'And yet the English perhaps could find as little sense as the Britons in speaking it in their way' BF: 31

*Mattern James rig quachas e stoppia bus e **na allja**, eth eath tha gloppia* 'King James expected to stop him, but he couldn't; he went limping' LAM: 224

*Rag **na algia** ea clappia na screffa Curnoack precarra why. Thera moy Gembrack peath rig ea gweele* 'For he could not speak or write Cornish like you. What he did was more Welsh' LAM: 238.

The subjunctive of *gallos* after *may* to introduce final clauses

By far the commonest use of *gallos* in Cornish involves the relevant person, or the autonomous form, of the present or past subjunctive after the conjunction *may* 'so that'. The collocation *may hallo, may halla*, etc., is used in Cornish of all periods as a way of introducing final clauses. Though it should be noted that in the later language the conditional sometimes replaces the subjunctive. Here are a few examples:

*yn meʒens y forth nyng es **may hallo bos** deflam guris* 'they said: There is no way that she may be made blameless' PA 32d

*golyough ha pesough ow ʒas **may hallough mos** ʒy aseth* 'watch and pray to my Father that you may go to his seat' PA 52c

*ha me a ra the crist amme **may hallough y asswonvos*** 'and I will kiss Christ that you may recognize him' PA 63d *yndella ef a vynne* **may halle** *dre baynys bras* **merwel** *rag 3e gerense* 'thus he wished that he might die by great torments for your sake' PA 70cd

Stop an wethen trogha'n dor **may hyllyf** *aga* **hethes** 'Bend the tree down so that I may reach them' OM 201-02

growet yn guely ahys **may hyllyf** *genes coske* 'lie at length in the bed that I may sleep with you' OM 2127-28

ha kyrghough the dre an guas **may hallo cane** *ellas nefre yn tewolgow tew* 'and fetch the fellow home that he may sing alas! forever in thick darkness' OM 514-16

my re gyrhas thy's the dre mab adam a fals huder **may hallo** *genen* **trege** 'I have fetched home to you the false enchanter Adam, that he may dwell with us' OM 564-66

guask gynsy dywyth an men hag y res gover fenten marth erhyth thotho hep fal **may hallo** *tus ha bestes ha myns a vynno* **eve** 'with it twice strike the rock and a well stream will run, if you bid it, so that men and beasts and as many as wish may drink' OM 1844-48

eugh growetheugh ov arlut **may haller agas cuthe** *gans dylles rych del deguth the vyghtern a dynyte* 'go, lie down, my lord, that you may be covered with rich cloths, as is fitting for a king of dignity' OM 1923-26

my a's gor adro thotho **may haller govos** *the wyr ha gueles yn blethen hyr py gymmys hys may teffo* 'I will put them around it, so that one may know truly and see in a full year how far it will grow' OM 2101-04

guyskys lemmyn nep cowyth **may hallo ef dysmygy** *mars yv map dev a vercy pyv a'n guyskys an barth kleth* 'let some colleague strike him now that he may guess, if he is the son of God of mercy, who struck him on the left' PC 1377-80

drou e thy'mmo the tackye a vgh y pen gans mur greys **may hallo** *pup y* **redye** *gour ha benen kekyffrys* 'bring it to me to fix above his head with great speed that every one may read it, man and woman also' PC 2807-10

arluth yma dour tommys lour **may hallons bos** *golhys aga trys yn kettep pol* 'lord, enough water has been warmed that they may be washed, the feet of everyone' PC 839-41

en prysners bras ha byan drewhy thy'm kettep onan **may haller aga iugge** 'the prisoners great and small bring them to me every one that they may be judged' PC 2250-52

ro thy'm kummeas me a'th pys a kymeres corf ihesu yv yn pren crous tremenys **may hallo bos** *anclethys yn beth men the voth mars yw* 'give me permission, I beg you, to take the body of Jesus, who is dead upon the cross, that he may be buried in a tomb, if it is your wish' PC 3112-3116 *eugh tenneugh athysempys y goyl yn ban **may hallo mos** gans an guyns* 'go, pull its sail up straightway that it may go with the wind' RD 2290-92

*3e scole lemmyn y worra me a vyn heb falladow **dysky** dader **may halla** 'I will now send him to school without fail so that he may learn goodness' BM 11-3

*Me a vyn moys then guylfoys ena ermet purguir boys **may hallen gorthya** ov du* 'I will go to the wilderness and be a hermit there, that I may worship my God' BM 1132-34

*an turant a vyn cowel gul sakyrfeys **may hallo guthel** moy drok* 'the tyrant will make full sacrifice that he may do more evil' BM 3383-85

*pybugh menstrels colonnek **may hyllyn donsia** dyson* 'pipe, minstrels, heartily that we may straightway dance' BM 2511-12

*lymmyn rag **may hallogh vnderstondia** an mater ma the well ha the pleynnya, why a ra vnderstondia nag o an heveleb a then havall the thu in bodily symblans* 'now, so that you may understand this matter better and more plainly, you will understand that the likeness of man to God was not in bodily appearance' TH 1

*Du a wrappyas pub nacion in discregyans **may halla eff** kafus mercy war oll* 'God wrapped every nation in unbelief that he might have mercy on all' TH 7a

*rag innan agan honyn na drethan agan honyn ny geffyn travith vas, dretha **may hallan bos** delyuerys theworth an miserabill stat ha captiuite a veny ynna towlys dre agan mortall yskar an teball ell* 'for in ourselves, nor through ourselves we found nothing good, by which we might be delivered from the miserable state and captivity into which we had been cast by our mortal enemy the devil' TH 10

*ha rag **may halla** an raunson ma **bois** perfect eff a suffras lyas kynde ha sorte a kammynsoth ha paynys intollerabill ha turmontys yn y pur ha innocent corffe* 'and in order that this ransom might be perfect, he suffered many kinds and sorts of wrong and intolerable pains in his pure and innocent body' TH 15a

*Rag henna **may hallogh why gothvas** in pub poynt oll pandra vsy an catholyk egglos ow menya haw cresy, eff a vith particularly disquethis ha settys in mes theugh wosa hemma* 'Therefore so that you may know in every detail what the catholic Church means and believes, it will be particularly demonstrated and set out for you hereafter' TH 20

*pesough rag an re na esy worth agys vexia hagys persecutia, **may hallow why bos** flehes agys tas vsy in neff* 'pray for those who vex and persecute you, that you may be children of your Father who is in heaven' TH 22

*yth ew gwris da aga rebukya **may hallans bos** methek ha kemeras sham aga fawtys* 'it is well done to rebuke them that they may be embarrassed and be ashamed of their faults' TH 29a

*I pesy eff pub yr **may hallan ny bos** an esely a crist agan savyowre ha agan mam sans egglos catholik omma in nore* 'To beseech him at all times that we may be the members of Christ our saviour and of our mother, holy catholic Church here on earth' TH 35

*gwren confessia agan transgressyon ha humbly desyre **may hallan bos** recevys gans crist in y chy, henna ew, an egglos* 'let us confess our sins and humbly desire that we may be received by Christ in his house, that is, the Church' TH 41

*an kigg ew anoyntis, **may halla** an nenaf **bos** consecratis; an kigg ew selis, **may halla** an nenaf **bos** defendis; an kigg ew touchis gans dowla, rag **malla** an nenaf **bos** golowis gans an spirissans* 'the flesh is anointed that the soul may be consecrated; the flesh is sealed, that the soul may be defended; the flesh is touched by hands, that the soul may be illuminated by the Holy Spirit' SA 60a

*A wylta kyrwas enos del vynnas Du whar ha dof orth an ewyow devethys gansa **may hallan gonys?*** 'Do you see stags yonder, as God wished, having come gentle and tame to the yoke that I might plough with them?' BK 847-50

*In rag degough ou banar, **may halla bos** dyglynnys, hag ef ha'y bobyl keffrys, kepar del ew an vanar* 'Carry my banner in front, so that he may be terrified, both he and his people, as is the custom' BK 2796-99

*Ow amor, denvenough why etho warlerth arlythy **may hallowgh bos** curunys* 'My love, do you send therefore for lords that you may be crowned' BK 3012-14

*lead ve quycke besyn thotha **may hallan ve attendya** pan vanar lon yth ewa* 'lead me quickly up to him that I may consider what kind of beast he is' CW 1567-69

*me a wra ge dean a bry havall thagan face whare hag a wheth in [th]y body sperys **may hallas bewa*** 'I make you, O man, of clay swiftly like to our face, and blow into your body spirit that you may live' CW 345-48

*mynstrels growgh theny peba **may hallan** warbarthe **downssya** del ew an vaner han geys* 'minstrels, do you pipe for us that we may dance together, as is the manner and custom' CW 2546-48

*Ha po ɖo ev ӡilliz ɖort an Vartshants ev a dhelledzhas an termen **mal ɖa va prêv** erra e urêg guiɔa kÿmpez et i ӡever, erra po nag erra* 'And when he had gone from the merchants, he delayed the time so that he could prove whether his wife was remaining faithful to him, was she or was she not' AB: 253a

*dro geer tha ve arta **mala ve moaze** ha gortha thotha aweeth* 'bring me word again that I may go and worship him also' ÉCII: 196

*Grua worry de taz ha de vam, **mol de dethyo boz** pel en tereath neb a regue de Arlith Due ry dez* 'Honour thy father and thy mother, that thy days may be long in the land which thy Lord God gave you' BF: 42

Te ra dege colon debour trog thy taz, ha thy mam **mollough** *thy dythyow* **boz** *hyr yn tyr, es reys thys ganz an Arluth thy Dew* 'Thou shalt bear a ?humble heart towards thy father and thy mother, that thy days may be long in the land which has been given to you by the Lord your God' ACB: E e 2 *verso*

Dibre tabm da hag eva badna, **Mal** *nagwunnen* **moaz** *gwadn trea* 'To eat a bite and drink a dram so that no one may go home weak' ACB: F f 4.

In Late Cornish the conditional is used in this construction, instead of the present or past subjunctive:

Ha e ve enna terebah mernaz Herod **malga boaz** *composez a ve cowsez gen Arleth neue der an prophet, o laule a vez a Egyp me vedn crya a mâb* 'And he was there until the death of Herod, that ththe word spoken by the Lord of heaven by the prophet might be fulfilled, saying, out of Egypt I will call my son' ÉCII: 198-99

Ha garah Nazareth, eth eath ha tregaz en Capernahum, lebah ywa trea vore, en pow Zebalon ha Nepthaly **malga e boaz** *composez ave cowsez gen dean Deew Izias* 'And leaving Nazareth, he went and stayed in Capernaum, which is a town by the sea in the land of Zebulon and Napthali, that what was spoken by Isaiah the man of God might be fulfilled' ÉCII: 189

Gwra mere da zeerah ha da dama, **malga** *da deethow* **booze** *heer en powe reg an Taaze da Deew ry theeze* 'Make much of your father and your mother, that your days may be long in the land which the Father, your God, gave you' ECa: 8

The negative equivalent of *may hallo, may halla* is *na allo, na alla,* etc.

kelmeugh warbarth y thywvreg **na allo dyank** *dre wal* 'tie together his two arms that he doesn't escape by mistake' PC 1199-80

ha galwy dre a pup sorn an thewolow mara keller y wythe achy **na alla yntre** *the'n darasow* 'and call them home from every corner, the devils, if he can be prevented from entering through the doors' PC 3056-60.

7. *GASA* 'TO LET, TO ALLOW'

The verb *gasa* means 'to let, to allow', but *gasa* can be used either in the second singular imperative with the suffixed pronouns *vy* 'me' or *ny* 'us' followed by *the* 'to' and a verbal noun to express an imperative in the first person singular or plural respectively:

Gas 'let!' (singular):

> *war **gas vy the thehesy** gans morben bom trewysy the'n vyl hora war an taal* 'watch out! let me give a nasty blow with a mallet to the vile whore on her forehead!' OM 2703-05

> ***gas vy** lemmyn th'y hure yn queth kyns ys y vayle gans aloes mer keffrys* 'let me anoint him now before wrapping him in a cloth with aloes and myrrh as well' PC 3196-98

> ***Gas ny the wull** den thegan heveleb ny agan honyn* 'Let us make man in our own likeness ourselves' TH 1a

> *ha in henna an drynsys tas a leverys, **gas ny the wull** den* 'and in that the Trinity, the Father, said Let us make man' TH 1

> *henna ew the leverall, **gas ve the remembra** fatla ra ve inta tha honora* 'that is to say, let me remember how I honour you well' SA 59

> ***gas ve tha entra** agye rag ty ny vethys dowtyes drefan y bosta mar deke* 'let me enter in, for you will not be feared, since you will be so fair' CW 522-25

> *des nes **gas ve thy wellas** maras ewa avall da* 'come here; let me see whether it is a good apple' CW 741-42

> *gorta **gas vy the dava** drefan gwelas mar nebas* 'wait, let me touch because I can see so little' CW 1591-92

> ***gas ny tha vos** alemma rag nang ew hy pryes yn tean math ew res in ker vaggya* 'let us go hence for it is now fully time that we must journey away' CW 1333-35.

Gas is rarely followed by a prepositional pronoun with *the*:

> *Tav **gays thym the ombrene*** 'Silence, let me redeem myself' BM 1253.

Occasionally the object of *gas* is a substantive rather than a pronoun:

> *bys may fons ov teharas **the gerthes gays an guelan*** 'until they are apologizing let the rod proceed!' BM 3344-45

> *Mar kylla bos possibly, **gas an haneth** ma a virnans the vos thewortha ve* 'If it can possibly be, let this cup of death pass from me' TH 22a

> ***gas an mynd confessia** da achy, an pith a whrella an ganow cows, **gas an golan percyvia** da an geer a vo soundis* 'let the mind confess well internally what the mouth speaks, let the heart perceive well the word that is uttered' SA 61a.

Notice that in the third sentence above *the* 'to' before the verbal noun is omitted.

AUXILIARY VERBS IN CORNISH

More commonly in imperative constructions of this kind *gasa* appears in the second person plural imperative, i.e. *gesowgh* 'let!' and the sense is either first person imperative or third person imperative, either singular or plural:

*hedre vyyn ov predery yn glassygyon **gesough y** aga thyr the **wrowethe*** 'while we are considering, let them all three rest upon the grass' OM 2035-37

*ytho mar qureugh ov wylas **gesough ov thus** vs gene the ves quyt the **tremene*** 'therefore if you seek me, let my men who are with me depart completely' PC 1121-23

*a syre iustis mercy **geseugh vy the worthyby** kyns ry brues the vos dyswrys* 'Oh, sir justice, mercy! Let me answer before passing my death sentence' PC 2492-94

***geseugh y the thysplevyas** ha heilyough an myghtern bras athysempys* 'let them spread out and say hail to the great king without delay' PC 2832-34

gesough hy** abart malan yn morter skuat the **gothe 'in the name of the devil let it fall bang into the socket' PC 2815-16

*dreugh thy'm ow map cuf colon ha **gesough vy th'y handle*** 'bring me my son, dear heart, and let me touch him' PC 3164-65

*arluth **gesugh vy the govs*** 'lord, let me speak' BM 3310

***Gesow ny the wull** den thegan similitud ha hevelep ny* 'Let us make man to our own likeness and image' TH 1a

*Rag an vnderstonding a henna **gesowgh ny the gafus** recourse then tryssa chapter a genesis* 'For the understanding of that let us have recourse to the third chapter of Genesis' TH 3

***gesow ny the aswon** agan oberow agan honyn fatell engy vnperfect* 'let us acknowledge our works, that they were imperfect' TH 9a

*whath **gesow ny the remembra** pana displesure a russyn ny gull warbyn du, pesqueth a russyn ny y offendya* 'still let us remember what displeasure we did against God, as often as we offended him' TH 4

*Rag henna in hanow crist **gesogh ny the lamentya** oll warbarth ha bos eddryggys rag agan mos war straye* 'Therefore in the name of Christ let us all lament together and regret our having gone astray' TH 40a.

The form *gesowgh* can also be used in the negative:

***na esow ny the vos** methek the confessia an stat agan vnperfectnes* 'let us not be ashamed to confess the state of our imperfection' TH 9a

*Ha **na esow ny the vos** methek the confessia nag ony mar perfect dell vea res thyn* 'And let us not be ashamed to confess that we are not as perfect as we should be' TH 9a *na esow ny the vos methek the confessia agan foly* 'let us not be ashamed to confess our folly' TH 9a.

On occasion the first person plurals *gesyn* 'let us' and *na esyn* 'let us not' are found rather than the second persons *gas* or *gesowgh*:

> **Gesyn ny the consyddra** *an circumstans an dra, ha nena ny a ra whare persevya nag o offence bean mas very grevaws ha poos* 'Let us consider the circumstances of the matter and then we will soon perceive that it was not a slight offence but very grievous and serious' TH 4
>
> **Na esyn vsya** *argumentys, mas vsya exampels Christ ha e negegath* 'Let us not use arguments, but use the examples of Christ and his birth' SA 61a
>
> **Na esyn** [*n*]*y miras wor an bara han dewas ew sittys deragen mas derevall agen mynd ha colan da* 'Let us not look upon the bread and drink that is set before us, but lift up our mind and good will' SA 65a.

Notice that in those two last negative examples *the* 'to' is omitted before the verbal noun.

8. *GOTHVOS* 'TO KNOW'
The verb *gothvos* 'to know' can be used to mean 'to be able', particularly when intellectual ability is involved. Here are some examples:

> *lemyn dyfreth of ha gvak pur wyr dres ol tus an beys my* **ny won leuerel** *prak gans pup na vethaf lethys* 'now I am weak and hungry above all men of the world; I cannot say why I will not be killed by everybody' OM 593-96
>
> **y threheuel mara kor** *y coth thy'n ol y worthye kefrys yn tyr hag* [*yn*] *mor* 'if he can build it, we all should worship him both on land and at sea' PC 390-92
>
> *worthyf na wovyn lemyn worth nep a glewas govyn rak* **y a wor leuerel** *kemmys thethe re gevsys* 'do not ask of me but of those who heard me, for they can say as much as I spoke to them' PC 1259-62
>
> *mara cofynnaf trauyth* **ny wothough ow gorthyby** 'if I ask anything, you cannot answer me' PC 1483-84
>
> *me a'n conclud yredy* **ma na wothfo gorthyby** *vn reson thu'm argument* 'I will silence him indeed, so that we will not be able to answer any reason against my argument' PC 1659-61
>
> *ty* **a wor guel** *bremmyn bras dyllo menough mes ath tyn* 'better can you often let fly from your arse great farts' PC 2104-05
>
> *Maseger athesempys kergh thym an epscop omma han doctour brays kekefrys yv gelwys flour an bys ma sur in clergy* **mar cothens** *dym* **leferel** *boys neb gueres dyogel orth an cleves ambus vy* 'Messenger, immediately

fetch the bishop to me here and the great doctor also, who are called the flower of this world indeed among the clergy, to see whether they can tell me is there indeed any remedy for the disease which I have' BM 1379-85

*ov cleves prest wy a weyl nyns yv grefons in dan geyl **a wothogh gul** dym guereys* 'You see my sickness openly; it is not a hidden complaint; can you assist me?' BM 1437-39

*ny grese vy mas pystry **y wore gul** eredy thagen tolla pur certen* 'I do not believe that he can do anything but sorcery indeed to deceive us certainly' BM 4077-79

*Rag in dede neb a rella predery an creacyon a vabden ha pondra in ta in y remembrans a behan o agan dallath **ny wore gull** ken ys ry honor, lawde ha preysse the du neb o y gwrer ha creator* 'For indeed whoever thinks of the creation of mankind and ponders well in his mind of what sort was our beginning, he cannot do otherwise than give honour, laud and praise to God who was his maker and creator' TH 1

*yma S paul worth agan payntia ny in mes in colors in leas tellar in scriptur, orth agan gylwall ny an flehes a thesplesians hag a angras du, rag **ny wothyn predery** vn preder da ahanan agan honyn, na bith moy cows da na gul da thyn agan honyn* 'St Paul depicts us in colours in many places in scripture, calling us the children of displeasure and those who angered God, for we cannot think any good thought of ourselves, nor for that matter speak well or do good by ourselves' TH 7a-8

*Rag henna **ny wothya du** dre gwryoneth ha iustus **receva** mabden arta thy favowre* 'therefore God was not able in truth and justice accept mankind back into his favour' TH 12

*rag henna yth esans y heb excusse dre reson pan **wothyans aswon du**, ny rens y honora* 'therefore they were without excuse, since when they were able to recognize God, they did not honour him' TH 14

*Rag theworth an daynger an teball ell ha pegh **ny wothya** mabden **bos** ryddys ha delyuerys mas dre an cruell ha paynfull mernans a vab du* 'For mankind could not be rid and delivered from the dominion of the devil and of sin except by the cruel and painful death of the Son of God' TH 15a

*pana dra **a wothyn ny vny** mar tha ragan ys an tas a neff thegan reputya hagan kemeras ny rag y flehes?* 'what can we desire so good for us as that the Father of heaven acknowledge us and take us for his children?' TH 22a

*ha pan **na wothia eff aga amyndya** whath eff a pegis the das a neff ragtha* 'and when he was unable to correct them, still he prayed the Father of heaven for them' TH 22a

*So keneuer **a wothfa redya ha vnderstondia** a yll gwellas fatell ra ran y vsya gloriusly* 'But whoever can read and understand, can see that some use it gloriously' TH 32a

*sera eve a gowsys 3ym mar deake **ny wothyan** tabm y naha* 'sir, he spoke so nicely to me, I could not in any way deny him' CW 774-75

*sera ken foma cregys y flattering o mur gloryes **ny wothyan guthell** nahean ram lowta* 'sir, though I be hanged, his pleasant words were so glorious, that I could not do otherwise, upon my loyalty' CW 1022-25

*sera **ny won convethas** ages dewan in neb for* 'sir, I cannot understand your anguish in any way' CW 1232-33

*cayne whath kenth ota ow hendas **tha aswon me ny wothyan*** 'Cain, though you are my grandfather, I could not recognize you' CW 1660-61

***Hye oare gwile** padn da gen hye glân; Hag et eye ollaz hye dalveath gowas tane* 'She can make good cloth with her wool; and on her hearth she should have fire' ACB F f 3

*rag radden el bose keevez na el skant clappia na guthvaz Curnooack, buz skant den veeth buz **ore guthvaz ha clappia** Sousenack* 'for some can be found who can hardly talk or understand Cornish, but hardly anybody who does not understand and speak English' BF: 25.

9. GUL 'TO DO'

Apart from *bos* 'to be' *gul* 'to make, to do' is the most important of the auxiliary verbs in Cornish. *Gul* can be found in all tenses.

The present-future of *gul*:

*drove thy'mmo dysempys ha **my a ra y dybry*** 'bring it to me immediately and I will eat it' OM 247-48

*Aban golste worty hy ha gruthyl dres ov defen **mylyge a wraf defry** an nor y'th whythres hogen* 'Since you listened to her and did contrary to my prohibition, I will curse the earth indeed in you labour henceforth' OM 269-72

*Omma **ny wreugh why tryge*** 'Here you shall not dwell' OM 317

*ov holan ol the dymmyn rag moreth **a wra terry*** 'my heart all to pieces will break for sorrow' OM 357-58

*mar tue moy nys tevyth man rag nown **y wrons clamdere*** 'if more come they will have nothing; they will faint from hunger' OM 399-400

*Rag **the verkye my a gura** yn bys den vyth na'th latho* 'For I shall mark you so that no man in the world may kill you' OM 602-03

*A bub eghen a kunda gorow ha benow ynweth **aga gore ty a wra** yn the worhel aberveth* 'Of every kind male and female also, you shall put them into your ship' OM 989-92

0

*kynyuer den vs yn wlas na tra yn bys ov pewe sav vnsol ty ha'th flehas gans lyf y **wraf the lathe** 'every man who is in the land and everything living in the world, except you only and your children, with a flood I will kill' OM 1029-32

my a wra hy delyfre whare a das caradow ha hy a wra aspye mars us dor segh yn nep pow 'I will let her out straightway, dear father, and she will see if there is dry land in any region' OM 1113-16

seuel war tyr beneges a **wreth** del lauaraf thy's 'you stand upon blessed ground as I tell you' OM 1407-08

ellas govy buthys on ny **ny wren scapye** 'alas, woe is me! We are drowned. We will not escape' OM 1705-06

pyv ytho a's hembronk th'y mar **ny wraf vy** nag aron **aga ledya** benary 'who therefore will lead them thither, if I do not nor Aaron?' OM 1874-76

yn enour bras d'agan dev mur an guel a ras thyworth an lur **guraf the drehy** 'in great honour to our great God I will cut the rods of grace from the ground' OM 1986-88

gonys a wreugh pur vysy thy'm del hevel 'it seems to me you work very diligently' OM 2448-49

kergh thy's ov ene gans el **pan wraf** a'n beys **tremene** 'bring my soul to yourself with an angel when I pass from the world' PC 429-30

the rewardye my a wra rak the servys 'I will reward you for your service' PC 612-13

dyth brues **y wregh ysethe** ol an bys ma rak iugge pup ol herwyth y ober 'on the day of judgement you will sit to judge all this world, everyone according to his work' PC 814-16

a gothman da prak **y wreta** thy'mmo **amme** 'O good friend, why do you kiss me?' PC 1104-06

tra vyth **ny wreth gorthyby** er byn dustenyow lel yth heuel bos falsury gynes pan wreta tewel 'you answer nothing against true witnesses; you seem to be guilty of falsehood when you remain silent' PC 1317-20

ha my caugeon lawethan **merwel a wren** ow cul tan yn dan an chek 'Ha, my changeling Leviathan, we will die making a fire under the cauldron' RD 137-39

rak henna **mos a wren** th'y del yv leuerys thy'nny 'therefore we are going thither as has been told to us' RD 1270-71

gans dour **y raff the golhy** 'with water I wash you' BM 744

pra na **wreta predery** y festa formys devery der y wreans eve omma 'why do you not consider that you were made indeed by his activity here?' CW 207-09

why na ra seere **merwall** 'you shall surely not die' ÉCII: 175

En wheeze tha godna talle **che ra debre** tha vara 'In the sweat of your brow you shall eat your bread' ÉCII: 182.

The autonomous form of the present-future of *gul*:

> *ha mar **ny wrer y wythe** y thyskyblon yn pryve a'n lader yn mes a'n beyth* 'and if he is not guarded, his disciples privately will steal him out of the tomb' RD 341-43
>
> *menogh **y rer y pesy** gans agen kerens nessa* 'he is often besought by our closest relatives' BM 3439-40.

The imperfect/potential of *gul*:

> *Ihesu crist in pow adro pub er oll **pregoth a wre*** 'Jesus Christ in the country round about preached continually' PA 23a
>
> *me a'n glewas dyougel lyes guyth ov leuerel an temple **y wre terry** hag arte y threheuel yn try dyth na vye guel* 'I heard him indeed saying many times that he would break down the temple and build it up again in three days that it had never been better' PC 1307-11
>
> *y'n naghen ef a'm guarnyas rak henna me a sorras hag a tos **na wren** neffre* 'he warned me that I would deny him; therefore I became angry and swore I never would' PC 1420-22
>
> *y leverys ef yn weth **datherghy** an tressa deth **y wre** pur wyr hep fyllel* 'he said also that he would rise again on the third day very truly without fail' RD 4-6
>
> ***mos a wren** ny the'n castel emavs gylwys dyougel leuaraf thy's ha war forth ny a gafas ihesu yv arluth a ras* 'we were going to the village called Emmaus indeed, I tell you, and upon the way we met Jesus, who is lord of grace' RD 1471-75
>
> *hag **y a re dehesy** dowst ha lusew drys aga pennow ha war aga pennow pan rellens remembra ha lamentya aga pehosow haga drog bewnans esans ow ledya* 'and they did throw dust and ashes over their heads and on their heads when they remembered and lamented their sins and their evil life which they were leading' TH 6a
>
> *Eff a promysyas fatell vetha onyn genys mes an stok han has a Eva **a re overcommya** agan agan eskar ny an teball ell* 'He promised that one would be born of the stock and seed of Eve, who would overcome our enemy the devil' TH 13
>
> *Eff a promysyas the viterne Dauid fatell **re** haes inweth **dos** anotheff* 'He promised to king David that see would come also from him' TH 13a.

The preterite/perfect of *gul*:

> *lauar thy'mmo ty venen an frut ple **russys tyrry*** 'tell me, woman, where did you pluck the apple?' OM 209-10

ef a wruk ow husullye frut annethy may torren 'he advised me that I should pluck fruit from it' OM 217-18

pythneth re rug ov syndye 'avarice ruined me' OM 288

Ellas gveles an termyn ov arluth pan wruk serry pan ruk drys y worhenmyn ov ertech gruk the gylly 'Alas to see the time when I angered my Lord; when I trangressed his command I lost my inheritance' OM 351-54

govy pan wruge pehe 'woe is me that I sinned' OM 2250

the fay re wruk the sawye ke yn cres lauaraf thy's 'your faith has healed you; I bid you go in peace' PC 531-32

pan dyskys yn eglusyow ny wrug den fyth ow sensy 'when I taught in the churches no man seized me' PC 1175-76

as wrussough camtremene 'how you transgressed!' RD 40

bewe pel a wruk yn beys yn lafur hag yn anken 'I lived long in the world in labour and sorrow' RD 210-11

ny a fyn leuerel ol yn pow sur the pub den ol fatel wrussyn ny keusel orth an arluth ker ihesu 'we will all tell in the country inded to everybody that we spoke to the beloved lord Jesus' RD 1339-42

Drefen na russys scollia goys then ynocens oma crist dys agen danvonas 'Because you did not spill the blood of the innocents here, Christ has sent us to you' BM 1707-09.

The present and past subjunctive of *gul*:

Neb a'm gruk vy ha'm gorty ef a ruk agan dyfen aual na wrellen dybbry na mos oges the'n wethen 'He who made me and my husband, he forbade us that we should not eat an apple nor go near the tree' OM 181-84

rag neb a'n gruk ny a bry a ros thy'n defennadow frut na wrellen the thybry a'n wethen hep falladow 'for he who made us of clay gave us a prohibition, that we should not without fail eat of the tree' OM 237-40

ha pan wryllyf tremene a'n bys ru'm gorre th'y wlas 'and when I depart from the world, may he take me to his kingdom' OM 531-32

penag a wryllyf amme henna yv ef ru'm laute 'whomever I kiss, it is he by my faith' PC 1084-85

Saw vn kynda a frut an tas du a chargias mab den na rella myllya na tuchia worta war bayne merwall a vernans 'But one kind of fruit the Father ordered man that he should not interfere with or touch on pain of dying the death' TH 2

helma a vith rag agys exortia why na rellogh fillall pub dith ha pub owre the ry grace the du golosek rag y thaddar thynny disquethis war agan creatya 'this will be to exhort you that you should not fail every day and at every hour to give thanks to mighty God for his goodness shown towards us in our creation' TH 5

*Kemerogh why an spuris sans, pana behosow **a rellogh gava**, y a vith gevys thetha, han pehosogh **a relogh retaynya**, y a vith retaynys* 'Receive the Holy Spirit, what sins you forgive, they will be forgiven, and the sins you retain, they will be retained' TH 38a.

The conditional of *gul*:

*kepar yn beys ha dves the'n nef **grusses yskynne*** 'like a goddess in the world you would ascend to heaven' OM 155-56

*awos tra vyth **ny wrussen venytha the gvhuthas*** 'not for anything would I denounce you' OM 163-64

*lauar thy'm awos tra uyth mara cruste leuerel ken fe an temple dyswrys kyn pen try dyth **y wrussys** guel ys kyns **y threheuel*** 'tell me in spite of anything if you said, though the temple be destroyed, in three days you would raise it up better than before' PC 1757-61.

The imperative of *gul*:

*dyson hep whethe the gorn dysempys **gvra y thybry*** 'immediately without making a fuss eat it' OM 207-08

*agan corfow noth gallas gans deyl agan **cuthe gvren*** 'our bodies have become naked; let us cover ourselves with leaves' OM 253-54

*ty dyowl **gvra ov gorthyby** prag y tolste sy hep ken* 'you devil, answer me: why did you deceive her without cause?' OM 301-02

*an lyf woth **gurens ymdenne*** 'let the flood-stream withdraw' OM 1093

*an golom glas hy lagas yn mes **gura hy delyfre*** 'let out the dove with the blue eye' OM 1109-10

*yn hanow an tas vhel an gorhel **gvren dyscuthe*** 'in the name of the Father on high let us uncover the ship' OM 1145-46

***gureugh why trestye** in y gras* 'trust in his grace' OM 1659

*ha mara leuer den vyth er agas pyn why tra vyth ware **guregh y gorthyby** the'n arluth ethom yma the wruthyl gans an re na* 'and if any man says anything against you, straightway answer him: the lord needs to do with those' PC 179-83

*neb na whytho **grens fannye** gans y lappa worth an eth* 'whoever does not blow, let him fan with his lappet at the hearth' PC 1243-44

*ytho why kemereugh e ha herwyth agas laha ha concyans **guregh y iuggye*** 'so take him and according to your law and conscience judge him' PC 1977-79

***guregh y cronkye** tor ha keyn* 'beat him belly and back' PC 2057

*ha mar ny fyn dynaghe y gow ha mercy crye hag amendye y treyson gans spern **guregh y curene*** 'and if he does not deny his falsehood and cry for mercy and amend his treason, crown him with thorns' PC 2061-64

yntre dev **guren y trehy** 'let us cut it in two' PC 2561

lemmyn **gurens y thyllyffrye** *mar myn a throk* 'now let him save him, if he wishes, from evil' PC 2886-87

ymcusylle gureny *ny pyth yv guella the bos gurys* 'let us consult together what is the best thing to be done' RD 561-62

ha wheth **greugh y thry** *omma arte thywhy ha dyscow y theworto* 'and yet bring him here to you again and take it off him' RD1868-70

greugh y tenne *mes a'n dour* 'pull him out of the water' RD 2232

pup ay du **gruens aspya** *ov quandra mars us treytour* 'let everyman look out on his side to see whether a traitor is wandering about' BM 1202-03

whath kynth usy pub den ow contya y honyn y bosa in charite na rens whath **na rens ef examnya** *den vith arell, mas y golan y honyn, y vewnans, y conversacion* 'though still everybody considers that he himself is in charity, let him not examine any other man, but his own heart, his life, his behaviour' TH 23-23a

rag henna **gwren ny kemeras** *with hay avoydia* 'therefore let us take care and avoid him' TH 5a

Rag henna, ow flehys, gesow ny the vos war a re an parna ha **gwryn avoydya** *hypocrisy, vaynglory, ha na ren iustyfia agan honyn* 'Therefore, my children, let us beware of people of that sort, and let us avoid hypocrisy, vainglory, and let us not justify ourselves' TH 9

Rag henna **gwregh drehevall** *in ban agas colonow hag egerogh y a leis* 'Therefore lift up your hearts and open them wide' TH 16

gwregh *awosa hemma* **avoydya** *pub kynd a pehosow, ha* **gwregh** *incessantly* **omlath** *warbyn agys yskar an teball ell* 'hereafter avoid every kind of sin, and fight incessantly against your enemy the devil' TH 16

Gwregh why lowsya *an tempill ha in iii dith me a ra y wull arta* 'Demolish the temple and in three days I will build it again' TH 53

gwregh ymbracya *ha sewya ha* **gwreugh glena** *agys honyn then catholyk egglos* 'embrace and follow and adhere to the catholic Church' TH 58

gwren *in kerthe* **helly yef** *tha effarn tha dewolgowe* 'let us pursue him away to hell, to darkness' CW 321-22

ha then tas **gwren** *oll* **pegy** *na skydnya an keth vengeans in neb termyn warnan ny nagen flehys* 'and let us all pray to the Father that the same vengeance never fall upon us nor our children' CW 2207-10

rag henna **gwrewh ow gorthya** *ha warbarth trustyowh vnnaf* 'therefore worship me and together trust in me' CW 221-22.

Gul as an auxiliary with *gul*.

The verb *gul* is sometimes used as an auxiliary with itself:

> *gul ges ahanaf a **wreth*** 'you are making fun of me' RD 1390
> *hag eff ew agan gwrer ny, rag ny ny **russyn gull** agan honyn* 'and he is our Creator, for we did not make ourselves' TH 1
> *omma **ny a ra gull** den* 'here we will make man' TH 1
> *pan **ruga gull** y pesadow ernestly rag Sodome ha Gamorre* 'when he made his supplication earnestly for Sodom and Gomorrah' TH 6a
> *sow **ny rug y wull** a pry kepar dell ruga gull an corf a Adam* 'but he did not make him from clay as he did with the body of Adam' TH 12a
> *An re ma ew contrary an neyll thy gela indella **na rellow gull** an pith a vynnow* 'These are contrary to each other, so that you may not do what you wish' TH 16a
> *na ny yll kantyll bos annowys ha gorys in dan busshell, mas war coltrebyn bo chandeler, ha nena **hy a ra gull** golow an kymmys a vo in chy* 'nor can a candle be lit and put under a basket, but upon a candlestick or chandelier and then it will make light for everybody in the house' TH 17a
> *Rag Du a rug declarya in kythsam parabill ma dre y profet pandra **ruga gull** rag an chy a Israell fugur an egglos a crist* 'For God declared in this same parable by his prophet what he did for the house of Israel, a figure of the Church of Christ' TH 40
> *y a cowse gwell dell **ronsy gull*** 'they speak better as they do' TH 48a
> *Lebben an hager-breeve o moy foulze avell onen veth ell an bestaz an gweale **a reege** an arleth Deew **geele*** 'Now the evil serpent was more treacherous than any other of the beasts of the field which the Lord God made' ÉCII: 174.

Gul as an auxiliary with *bos* 'to be'

In earlier Middle Cornish *gul* is not found governing *bos* 'to be', but by the later sixteenth century examples are forthcoming both in the future; in the preterite and in the third singular and plural imperative:

The future of *gul* with *bos*:

> *n'ena agoz lagagow **ra bos** geres; ha why ra boaze pocara Deew a cothaz da ha droag* 'then your eyes will be opened; and you will be like God knowing good and evil' ÉCII: 176
> *ha tha dezerio **ra boaze** tha goore, ha e ra tha rowlia* 'and your desire swill be for your husband and he shall rule you' ÉCII: 181
> ***Why ra boz** e seera, sarra wheag* 'You will be his father, sweet sir' ACB: F f 4 *verso*.

Forms like those above are not common, for their function is more usually performed by *beth, byth* 'will be' or *a vyn bos* 'will be' (for the latter see *mynnes* below).

The preterite of *gul* + *bos*:

*indella wosa henna eff a rug y perfumya, Evyn an dewetha nois **a rug eff bos** in company gans y aposteleth the rag y virnans* 'thus after that he performed it, even on the last night he was in the company of his apostles before his death' TH 51a-52.

Imperative of *gul* + *bos*:

*ha **gwrens gi bos** rag signezou, rag termen, ha rag dethiou ha blethaniou* 'and let them be for signs, for time, and for days and years' BF: 52
*Ha Deu laveraz **gwrens boz** golou, ha thera golou* 'And God said: Let there be light, and there was light' BF: 51-3
*Ha Deu laveraz, **gwrens boz** ebron en kreis an dour, ha gwrens a debarra an dour vrt an dour* 'And God said: Let there be a heaven in the middle of the water, and let it separate the water from the water' BF: 51-3.

Gul as a causative verb

As with 'to make' in English *gul* 'to do, to make' can be used in Cornish with causative sense. There are four possible constructions.

Causative *gul* + *dhe* + noun + *may* + subjunctive:

*hag inweth **gvra the'th worty may tebro** ef annotho* 'and also make your husband eat of it' OM 199-200

Causative *gul dhe* + noun/pronoun + verbal noun:

*y **wreg 3e re ane3e mos** 3en dre ha degylmy an asen ha dry ganse* 'he made some of them go to the town and untie the ass and bring it with them' PA 27bc
*ty re gam wruk eredy ha re'n dros the vur anken pan **russys thotho dybry ha tastye** frut a'n wethen* 'you did wrong indeed and have brought him to great misery when you made him eat and taste the fruit of the tree' OM 281-84
*leuereugh thy'mmo whare pandra vynnogh thy'm the ry ha **me a wra thygh spedye** ow cafus crist yredy* 'tell me straightway what you will give me and I will make you succeed in finding Christ indeed' PC 585-88

ny grysaf thy's ty a fyl **gul thy'm crygy** 'I do not believe you; you will fail to make me believe' RD 1056-57

tus dal eff a ra sawya ha tus vother mageta inweth **gul dethe cloweys** 'blind men he will heal and deaf men also make them hear as well' BM 804-06

omma duthen theth vereys hag inweth theth confortia ha **gul dyso aswonfos** *the nessevyn in ponfos ymons ragos in bys ma* 'we have come here to visit you and to comfort you and to make you realize that your relatives are anxious for you' BM 1981-85

laddron mur us in pov ma lues den ov tustruya **grua then re na avodya** *par del yv mur the galloys* 'there are many robbers in this country destroying many men; make those depart, as your power is great' BM 2059-62

Pegh o an pith **a rug then tas a neff humbrak** *mabden in mes a baradise, pegh o an pith* **a rug then kyge stryvya** *gans an spuris han spuris warbyn an kyge* 'Sin was that which made the Father of heaven drive mankind out of paradise, sin was that which made the flesh strive with the spirit and the spirit against the flesh' TH 3

eff ny rug cessia dre crefte ha dre questonow adro the eva neb o an gwanha in power han medalha vessell bys **may rug gull thethy terry** *commandment an tas* 'he did not cease by craft and by questions around Eve, who was the weaker in power and the softer vessel, until he made her break the Father's commandment' TH 4

dre reson y bosans y ow pretendya an gyrryow a thu ha gans henna ow dalhe lagasow an bobyll neb ew sempill, hag **y a ra thetha cresy** *fatell ew kepar dell vsans y ow cowse* 'because they lay claim to the words of God and thus blind the eyes of the people who are simple and they make them believe as they speak' TH 19a

Rag **eff a ra then howle drehevell ha shynya** *kyffrys war an da han drog* 'For he makes the sun rise and shine both upon the good and the evil' TH 22

an tryssa dyth **me a wra than gwyth sevall** *yn ban ha doen dellyow teke ha da ha flowres wheag in serten* 'on the third day I will make the trees stand up and bear fair and good leaves and sweet flowers certainly' CW 92-5.

Causative *gul dhe* + noun/pronoun + *dhe* + verbal noun:

Pegh o an cawse **a rug the oll an vssew a Adam ha Eva the vos** *genys in state a thampnacion* 'Sin was the cause that made all the issue of Adam and Eve to be born in a state of damnation' TH 3

Causative *gul* + pronoun + *dhe* + verbal noun:

Gu̠reu̠h vî dhv u̠elaz 'Shew me [i.e. make me see]' AB: 250b.

10. *MYNNES* 'TO WISH'

Mynnes can function as a full verb meaning 'to wish, to desire':

Del yrghys ihesus ʒeʒe y a rug aʒesympys ol y voth ef del vynne 'As Jesus bade them, they did immediately all his desire, as he wished' PA 28a

In meth pylat why a vyn drys pub tra me ʒy laʒe 'Said Pilate, You wish that above all things I should kill him' PA 148a

yn pympes dyth me a vyn may fo formyys dre ov nel bestes puskes hag ethyn tyr ha mor the goullenwel 'on the fifth day I wish that by my power be created beast, fish and birds to fill the land and the sea' OM 41-44

Aban vyn an tas a'n nef res yv sywe y voth ef pepenag vo 'Since the Father of heaven wishes, it is necessary to follow his will, whatever it may be' OM 660-62

yn vhelder my a vyn dek warn ugans y vos gures 'I want it to be made thirty [cubits] in height' OM 959-60

ny vyn dev ker th'y lawe na fella my the vewe 'dear God, praised be he! does not wish that I should live any longer' OM 2359-60

ol del vynny arluth ker my a wra yn pup tyller hedre veyn bev yn bus ma 'entirely as you wish, dear lord, I will do in every place, while I am alive in this world' PC 113-15

ol th'y voth a's kymerens aban vynne yndella 'let him take them entirely to his desire, since he wishes thus' PC 210

anotho grens del vyn pan glevfo y lauarow 'let him do with him what he wants, when he hears his words' PC 371-72

the days ha me ny a yl statya an tyr dyogeyl mar mynen the den areyl na thefo dis benytha 'your father and I, we can bequeath the land indeed, if we wish, to another man, so that it will never come to you' BM 412-15

eva gent[i]ll na vyth serrys me a ra oll del vynny 'gentle Eve, do not be angry; I will do entirely as you wish' CW 842-43.

Notice also how Cornish renders 'whether you want to or not' in the following:

mynny gy kyn na vynny te a in kerth genen ny hag oma gays the cummyys 'whether you want to or not you will come away with us and take your leave of here' BM 2967-69.

Frequently, however, *mynnes* is used as an auxiliary with another verb which appears as a verbal noun. In many cases such use of *mynnes* clearly involves volition.

The present-future of *mynnes* 'to wish, to want, to be willing':

*ov bolungeth **mar mynnyth** y **collenwel** hep let vyth the vap ysac a geryth y offrynne reys yv thy's* 'if you wish to fulfill my will without hesitation, it is necessary for you to offer your son Isaac, whom you love' OM 1277-80

***aban vynnyth** yndella **y resseve** my a wra yn gorthyans the'n tas a'n nef* 'since you wish it thus, I will accept it in worship to the Father of heaven' OM 2617-19

***mar mynnyth hy dystrewy** orden the'th tus hy knoukye gans meyn* 'if you want to kill her, order your men to strike her with stones' OM 2675-76

*my **ny vennaf cafus** le yn guyryoneth* 'I am not willing to accept less in truth' PC 594-95

*re iovyn drok yv gyne **na venta** kammen **tryle** yn maner tek* 'by Jove I regret that you don't want to turn at all in a pleasant way' PC 1292-94

*as yv an den na goky **mar myn** er agan pyn ny **cous** reson vyth uerement* 'how foolish is that man, if he will utter any argument against us in very truth' PC 1662-64

*bysy vye thy's gothuos yn certan mur a scryptours **mara mynnyth gorthyby** hytheu concludys na vy mar kevs thy'so an doctours* 'it would be necessary for you to know much of the scriptures if you wish to answer today so as not to be silenced, if the learned men speak to you' PC 1671-76

*ny fyn an guas **gelwel** tru na pygy cafus merci* 'the fellow will not cry "alas!" nor beg to obtain mercy' PC 2089-90

*rag **y fynner** mara kyller gans paynys mer **ow dyswul** glan* 'for one wishes, if one can, to ruin me utterly with torments' PC 2600-02

*ny **fynnaf leuerel** gow awos dout bones marow* 'I will not tell a lie in spite of fearing death' RD 585-86

*So **mar ny vyn golsowas** this, whath kemer genas onyn bo dew, ha mar na vyn nena clowas, lavar then egglos* 'But if he is not willing to listen to you, then take with you one or two, and if he will not then listen, tell the Church' TH 31a

The imperfect of *mynnes* 'to wish, to want':

*Y vos kellys **ny vynna*** 'He did not wish that he be lost' PA 7c.

AUXILIARY VERBS IN CORNISH

The present subjunctive of *mynnes* 'to wish, to want':

> *Suel a vynno bos sylwys golsowens ow lauarow a ihesu del ve helheys war an bys avel carow* 'whoever wishes to be save, let him listen to my words about Jesus, as he was pursued in the world like a stag' PA 2ab
>
> *dre worʒyp crist yn vr na lemmyn ny a yll gwelas lauar du maga del wra* **neb a vynno y glewas** 'by Christ's answer then now we can see that the word of God nourishes him who wishes to hear it' PA 12cd
>
> **kyn fynnyf** *war an bys ma* **tevlel** *vyngeanns na dyal my a vyr scon orth honna hag a'n acord a vyth cof* 'though I should wish to cast vengeance or revenge upon this world, I will soon look at that and there will be remembrance of the accord' OM 1249-52
>
> *dog manerlich ov baner* **del vynny bos** *rewardyys* 'carry my banner valiantly as you wish to be rewarded' OM 2200-01
>
> *Crist indelma a leuer* **ov sywa** *neb a* **vynna** *forsakyans byen ha muer teryov trefov an bys ma y days hay vam* 'Christ says thus: whoever wishes to follow me, let him forsake great and small, lands, dwellings of this world, his father and his mother' BM 382-85.

The past subjunctive of *mynnes* 'to wish, to want':

> *ny a vya lowenek* **a mynnes** *oma trega* 'we should be joyful, if you wished to remain here' BM 582-83
>
> **mara mynne** *amendye guel vye y thylyfrye hep drocoloeth thyworthy'n* 'if he were to emend, it would be better to deliver him unharmed from us' PC 1862-64.

The preterite of *mynnes* 'to wish, to want':

> *gans aga garm hag olua ihesus crist a ve mevijs* **may fynnas dijskynna** *yn gwerhas ha bos genys* 'by their cry and weeping Jesus Christ was moved, so that he wished to descend in a virgin and be born' PA 4bc
>
> *Gans gloteny ef pan welas cam na ylly y dolla en tebell el a* **vynnas** *yn ken maner y* **demptye** 'When he saw that he could not in any way seduce him with gluttony, the evil angel wanted to tempt him in another way' PA 13ab
>
> *seth pandra yv the nygys mar hyr forth* **dos may fynsys** 'Seth, what is your errand, that you wished to come such a long way?' OM 733-34
>
> *pendra yv henna thy'nny* **aban vynsys** *y* **werthe** 'what is that to us, since you wished to betray him?' PC 1509-10
>
> *rag prenna adam hay hays* **doys y fynnas** *then bys ma* 'to redeem Adam and his seed he desired to come to this world' BM 868-69

maria wath **ny vynsys** *thymo vy* **gul** *confort vyth* 'Mary, still you have not wished to give me any comfort' BM 3617-18

oma atte guythys clos y **aperia ny vynnys** *maria lowene dis maria dyso mur grays ov map dym* **dry pan vynsys** 'here he is closely guarded; I did not want to hurt him; Mary hail to thee, Mary, much thanks to thee, since you wished to bring me my son' BM 3792-96.

Mynnes with reduced volitional sense

Perhaps the commonest use of *mynnes* as an auxiliary is in the present with a following verbal noun to render a periphrastic future. There are many examples, however, where *mynnes* clearly does not carry any sense of volition. Such futures with *mynnes* but without volition can be grouped into four categories: 1. where the subject of the verb is inanimate and thus cannot be understood to wish or desire anything; 2. where the context renders volition highly unlikely; 3. where *mynnes* is used with the verbal *desyrya* 'to desire.' In these cases any volition is in the verbal noun and *mynnes* expresses future sense only; 4. where *mynnes* is used as an auxiliary in translating a Latin future.

1. The subject of *myn* is inanimate:

rag **an lahys** *ʒynny es* **a vyn** *y* **dampnye** *porres yn meʒens y forth nyn ges may hallo bos deflam guris* 'for the laws which we have will condemn her of necessity, they said. There is no way that she can be made blameless' PA 32cd

ancombrynsy yv hemma then the'n myghtern the thysta **a'n gyst na vyn dos** *the squyr* 'this is an annoyance for us have to testify to the king about the beam that will not come to the right measurement' OM 2542-44

pronter boys me a garse corff ihesu thy venystra **mar myn ov descans servya** *genogh pan ven apposijs* 'I should like to be a priest, to administer the body of Christ, if my learning is found sufficient, when I am examined by you' BM 522-25.

2. The required sense of *mynnes* excludes the possibility of volition:

gans ov clethe sur **the lathe** *scon* **me a vyn** 'with my sword soon surely I will kill you' OM 1362-63

Ny vedn *e nevra* **dvz** *vêz a ʒŷndan* 'He will never get out of debt' AB: 230c.

In the first example Abraham is about to kill his beloved son, Isaac. He does not want to kill him, but believes he has no choice, since God has ordered him to do so. In the second example from *Archæologia Britannica* (1707) the subject clearly wants to clear his debts, since otherwise he faces the prospect of a debtor's prison. He is not going to get out of debt, although he wants to.

3. The present-future of *mynnes* used with *desyryra* 'to desire':

> *whath me a vyn agys desyrya why the vynnas dylygently merkya, notya, ha done in kerth genowgh, vn rulle, ha honna ny ra agys desevia* 'yet I will desire you to be prepared diligently to mark, to note and carry away with you a single rule and that will not deceive you' TH 34a
>
> *me a vyn agys desyrrya why oll an lell cristonyyan, why the vynnas resortya thegys mam egglos catholik, in pub dowt oll, in pub opynyon ha contravercyte* 'I will desire you, all faithful Christians, that you will be prepared to resort to your mother, the catholic Church, in all doubt, in all opinions and controversies' TH 38.

4. The present-future of *mynnes* + verbal noun to translate a Latin future:

> *Jam non dicam vos seruos, etc., hen ew the leuerell Lymmyn ny vanna ve na moy agys gylwell why servantes, mas cothmans* 'Jam non dicam vos seruos sed amicos, etc., that is to say Now I will not anymore call you servants, but friends' TH 35a
>
> *Auferam sepem eius et erit in direptionem, etc. y myth eff, me a vyn kemeras the veis an ke aw vyne yard, may halla peryssya* 'Auferam sepem eius et erit in direptionem, etc., he says: I will take away the hedge of the vinyard, that it may perish' TH 40.

It seems that the gradual loss of the sense of volition from *mynnes* as an auxiliary when forming the future, had an important result in the verbal system of Cornish. Since, for example, *me a vyn mos* and *me a vyn gul* came to mean 'I will go' and 'I will do' respectively, with little or no sense of wishing or desiring to go or to do, another way had to be found to express the idea 'I want to go' and 'I want to do', respectively. The verb *cara* 'to love' in the conditional tense appears to have been adopted for this purpose. See above.

Mynnes is also commonly found in the conditional (*mynsen, mensen*, later *menjen*) as an auxiliary to form a periphrastic conditional of another verb. It will be seen from the following examples that volition is present in some, but in others there is little if any sense of wishing:

> *vrry ov marrek guella my a vynsa the pysy gor ost genes yrvys da the omlath del y'm kerry* 'Uriah, my best knight, I would ask you: take a host well armed with you to fight, as you love me' OM 2139-42
>
> *ef a vynse gul deray hag a ros strokosow tyn saw vn marrek a'n lathas* 'he wished to rout the enemy and he gave severe blows, but a horseman killed him' OM 2224-26

me a vynse y wythe ha ny yllyn cammen vyth 'I would have saved him, and I could not at all' PC 3125-26

ow map whek **me a vynse** a luen golon **the pygy** a thos thy'm ha fystyne del thethyvsys thy'mmo vy 'my sweet son, I would from the bottom of my heart pray you to come to me and to hasten as you promised me' RD 447-50

the pesy me a vynsa hag in ov gallus mar seff the aquyttya mar mynnes gul dym guelas 'I would beseech you and would repay you, if it is in my power, were you to make me see' BM 2556-59

rag meryasek den worthy epscop in venetensy **y cafus** prest **y fensyn** 'for Meriasek, a worthy man, as bishop of Vannes, we would wish indeed to get' BM 2726-28

tus a russa supposia mar teffa du aga suffra the vsya aga naturall powers **y a vynsa optaynya** salvacion in ta lovr heb gweras vith arell in party du 'men would suppose, if God had allowed them to use their natural powers, they would have obtained salvation well enough without further assistance on the part of God' TH 13a

Hag in myske company an par na may halla an gwyr bos pregowthis ha gothvethis openly, bo ken crist **ny vensa leverell**, kepar dell ew scriffys in v. chapter a mathew 'And among company of that kind that the truth might be preached and acknowledged openly, otherwise Christ would not have said, as is written in the fifth chapter of Matthew' TH 17a

Mar teffa den vith ha pregoth thyn kythsame barbarus nacions ma in aga eyth y aga honyn an vencions ma a heritickys in by an by **y a vynsa stoppya** aga scovurnow 'If anyone were to preach to these same barbarous peoples in their own language these inventions of the heretics, they would soon enough stop up their ears' TH 19

Eff a attendias fatell vynna oll an heretikys gylwall thetha an auctorite an aposteleth, han prophettys, ha fatell **vynsans y wrestia** aga screffa 'He noticed that all the heretics would invoke for themselves the authority of the apostles and prophets, and that they would twist their writing' TH 33

ha rag an cawse ma an auncyent dasow a ve kyns lymmyn, kyn fonsy vith mar tha diskys, **ny vensans y presumya** war aga judgement aga honyn 'and for this cause the ancient fathers who lived before now, though they be never so well educated, they would not have presumed upon their own judgement' TH 36a

Surely **ny vynsan cresy** an aweyll, na ve an Catholyk egglos the ry thym experiens 'Surely I would not believe the gospel, if the catholic Church did not give me the experience' TH 37a

na vea me theth cara **ny vynsan theth cossyllya** tha vos bargayne mar vras gwryes 'if I did not love you, I would not advise you that such a great bargain be made' CW 669-71

*En Rama a ve clowez olva, whola ha garma, Rachal wholo rag e flehaz ha **na venga hye boaze** comfortyes, rag tho an gye lathez* 'In Rama was heard weeping, lamenting and crying, Rachel weeping for her children and she would not be comforted, for they have been killed' ÉCII: 200

*Rag **me a venja** cowas napeath della na veea denneth tha weath* 'For I would have something thus so that no man might be the worse' LAM: 224

*Bus gen nebas lavirians **Eye venjah dendle** go booz ha dillaz* 'But with a little labour they would earn their food and clothes' ACB: F f 3

*Lebmen Dzhûan **e na vendzha servia** na velha, bʊz **e vendzha mʊs** teua ꝺa e urêg* 'Now John would not serve any further, but he would go to his wife' AB: 251a

*Ha po 'rŷʒ e dʊz ꝺʊn darraz, **eʊ a vendzha klouaz** ꝺên aral en ʒuili* 'And when he came to the door, he would hear another man in the bed' AB: 253a

*Mar kressa an dean deskez feer na gwellaz hemma [e] **a venya kavaz** fraga e ouna en skreefa-composter* 'If that learned wise man were to see this, he would find reason to correct it in orthography' BF: 27.

11. *RES* 'MUST'

Res is a substantive meaning 'necessity'. It is also a defective impersonal verb 'it is necessary' where the logical agent is introduced by the preposition *the* 'to, for.' Here are some examples of the latter:

*Cafes moy **thy's aban res** try heys the bal kemery* 'Since it is necessary for you to have more, three lengths of your spade, take them' OM 391-92

*serry orthyf **ny res thy's** lemyn sur yth yʊ evnhys* 'there is no need to be angry with me; now indeed it is has been repaired' OM 2524-25

*saʊ y wothaf **thy'm a reys** 'but I must suffer it' PC 1071

*me a wor lemen in ta **gothe** mernans **dyn a reys** 'I now know well that we must endure death' BM 1752-53

Ny res theugh bos duwenyk awos lavarow drog-den 'You do not need to be miserable because of the statement of an evil man' BK 2659-60.

Occasionally *res* behaves like an inflected verb and takes a personal subject. There is also an imperfect form *resa*:

*guyryoneth **a reys bos** dreys aberueth yn mater ma* 'truth must be brought into this matter' PC 2447-78

*Rag **why a res vnderstondia** ha cresy fatell ew an dewses spuris ha not substans a corffe* 'For you must understand and believe that the Godhead is spirit and not substance of body' TH 1a *in kepar maner **ny a res thy casa** an teball ell hay power* 'in the same way we must hate the devil and his power' TH 3a

*The thu rag henna **ny a res mos** hay gemeras rag agan socure, pokene benytha ny ny gefyn cresse* 'To God therefore we must goe and take him for our succour, otherwise never will we find peace' TH 10

*Henna ew, **crist a res** in pub poynt oll **bos** havall thy bredereth, may halla eff bos lene a vercy the procuria mercy rag pehosow an bobyll* 'That is: Christ must in every point be similar to his brethren, that he might be full of mercy to procure mercy for the sins of the people' TH 13a

*ha pan ruga colynwell pub tra according then scriptur han prophetes, an pith **a resa bos** colynwys anotheff therag y pascion, nena eff a suffras myrnans colonnek, henn o myrnans in crowsse* 'and when he had fulfilled everything according to the scripture and the prophets, that which had to be fulfilled by him before his passion, then he suffered a courageous death, that is death upon the cross' TH 15

*Rag **why a res gothfas hemma**, fatell rug du requiria innan ny certan taclennow the vos colynwys keffrys dre lell blonogeth ha conscent* 'For you must understand this, that God required in us certain things to be fulfilled also by full desire and consent' TH 16

*An kythsame catholyk egglos ma **a res bos** guthvethis in pub ois oll a vabden* 'This very same catholic Church must be known in every age of mankind' TH 17a

*rag henna an re na **ny a res avoydya**, han discans vgy an egglos ow dysky ny a res thyn y gara* 'therefore those we must avoid, and the teaching which the Church teaches we must love' TH 19.

There are also a few examples of a mixed construction:

*rag henna an re na ny a res avoydya, han discans vgy an egglos ow dysky **ny a res thyn y gara*** 'therefore those we must avoid, and the teaching which the Church teaches we must love it' TH 19

***ny a res thin consyddra** cara agan cothmans nyn sew mas kepar dell ra an laddron, advltrers, denlath, hag oll an drog pobill erell* 'we must consider that loving our friends is only what thieves, adulterers, murderers and all other evil people do' TH 24

*warbyn oll an kithsam reasons ma **ny a res thyn kemeras** wyth* 'against all these same reasons we must be on our guard' TH 24-5

*Rag an kythsame ii cawse ma **ny cristonyan a res thyn supposia** an yocke a crist the vois wheg* 'For these same two reasons we Christians must consider the yoke of Christ to be sweet' TH 28.

12. *TYLLY* 'TO PAY, TO BE WORTH'

The verb *tylly* means 'to pay, to recompense' or 'to be worth'. These senses can be seen from the following examples:

yn y golen fast regeth mur a gerense wor3ys hag ef a **dalvyth** *3is wheth y honore del wrussys* 'in his heart has entered much love for you, and he will recompense you yet for honouring him as you did' PA 115cd

ol th'y voth a's kymerens aban vynne yndella me a vynse a **talfens** *myl pvns thotho a our da* 'let him take them according to his desire, since he wishes it thus; I should wish that they were worth a thousand pounds of pure gold for him' PC 209-12

vn deyth a thue yredy **ma'n taluethaf** *ol thywhy kemmys enor thy'm yv gurys* 'a day is coming indeed when I will repay you all as much honour as has been shown to me' PC 268-270

an nyl thotho a **delle** *pymp cans dyner monyys ha hanter cans y gyle* 'one of them owed him five hundred of minted pence, and the other fifty' PC 504-06

ol agan maystry me a grys **ny daluyth** *bram* 'all our power will not be worth a fart, I believe' PC 3095-97

y thadder yw **droktylys** *pan y'n lathsons dybyte* 'his goodness has been poorly requited, when they killed him pitilessly' PC 3097-98

rag henna whela neb jyn po an vyadg **ny dale** *oye* 'therefore look for some subterfuge, or the enterprise isn't worth an egg' CW 983-84

Me a aore hemma urt e hoer, an Curnoack, dr' uava **talvez** *buz nebbaz tho bose gurrez warbarrha gen an Sousenack* 'I know this from its sister, the Cornish, that it is valued but a little to be compared with English' BF: 31.

From the sense 'to be worth' comes the use of *tylly* as an auxiliary verb meaning 'is worthwhile, is incumbent upon; should':

ny dal *thy's kauanscuse dre the wrek y vos terrys rag orty ty the gole myl vap mam a veyth damneys* 'you should not seek an excuse that it was plucked by your wife, for since you listened to her, a thousand mothers' sons will be condemned' OM 311-14

I fe leveris a tyrmyn coth, **ny dall** *this latha* 'It was said of olden times: thou shalt not kill' TH 27

whath pella agys henna, **ny dallvea** *thotheff mar ver predery a throg thy kentrevak* 'yet further than than that that he should not as much as meditate evil for his neighbour' TH 29

ny dalvea *thetha bos refusyys gans particular person vith* 'they ought not be rejected by any particular person' TH 38

inweth **ny dale** *3ym bos gwelys ow honyn in keth shape ma* 'also I myself ought not to be seen in this same form' CW 475-76

Ny dalle deez perna kinnis war an sawe, Na moaz cuntle an drize dro dan keaw 'You ought not buy firewood by the load, nor go to gather brambles about the hedges' ACB: F f 2

Hag et eye ollaz hye dalveath gowas tane 'And on her hearth she ought to have fire' ACB: F f 2

Why a dalveya gowas an brossa mine 'You must have the biggest stones' ACB: F f 2.

13. *USYA* 'TO BE ACCUSTOMED'

In Tregear's Homilies the verb *usya* 'to use' is employed with a verbal noun to mean 'to wont to, to be accustomed to'. It seems that the usage is in imitation of the English 'to use' with a habitual sense, i.e. 'I used not understand', etc. Notice that in the two extant example *usya* itself follows *gul* as an auxiliary.

tus benegas ha benenas in testament coth a rug vsia gwyska yscar ha canfas garow, an pith a vetha gwrys syehar anotha 'holy men and women in the Old Testament used to wear sackcloth and rough canvas, that from which sacks used to be made' TH 6a

A ra tus vsya offra bois ha dewas the re rag purpos vith arall, mas may teffans dybry hag eva anotha? 'Are men accustomed to offer food and drink to people for any other purpose than that they should eat and drink of them?' TH 52a

14. *Y'M BUS* 'I HAVE'

The Cornish verb *y'm bus* means 'I have', but is also used with the extended sense 'I can, I am able':

ow thermyn a the yn scon genough me nvm byth trege 'my time will soon come; I will not be able to remain with you' PA 37b

na thegovgh sor yn colon worth neb a wra ow vre rak ow thorment a the scon genogh na'm byve tryge 'do not be angry with her who will anoint me, for my torment will happen soon, so that I cannot remain with you' PC 539-42

ny'm bus bywe na fella an dour re wruk thy'm henna yn pur deffry 'I cannot live any longer; the water has done this to me in very truth' RD 2208-10

the pesy me a vynsa hag in ov gallus mar seff the aquyttya mar mynnes gul dym guelas fout syght numbus ommeras 'I would beg you and recompense you, if it is in my power, if you would cause me to see; without sight I cannot look after myself' BM 2556-60

me yv vexijs anhethek gans tebel speris oma num bus bewa 'I am constantly afflicted here by an evil spirit; I cannot live' BM 2630-32

Hy rum lathes gans hy gvyns re vahum wek pen an sens alemma num bus gvaya 'She has killed me with her breath; by sweet Mahound, chief of the saints, I cannot shift from here' BM 4096-98
num bus kerthes mas sklynkya 'I cannot walk but crawl' BM 4214
owt aylas me yw marowe nymbes bewa na fella 'Oh, alas! I am dead; I cannot live any longer' CW 1570-71.

Notice that *ny'm bus bewa* 'I cannot live, I must die' occurs in three separate texts. It appears therefore to be a set phrase in the traditional language.

The verb *y'm bus* with the verbal adjective

In Breton *em eus*, the sister verb to Cornish *y'm bus* 'I have,' has been used since the Middle Breton period with the verbal adjective to express a perfect, e.g. *discaret he deues an edeficc* 'she has pulled down the edifice', *c'hui oc'heus graet* 'you have made', *me-m eus desquet* 'I have learned' (see HMSB §155). There is some evidence in Cornish for a similar usage:

me am beth goys the colon scollys omma war an ton kyns hy bos nos 'I will have spilt your blood here on the meadow before it be night' BM 3494-96
ty a vyth mabe denethys a the corf sure na wra dowtya 'you will have a son born from your body; do not doubt' CW 1323-24
flehys am bef denethys a Eva ow freas mear 'I have begotten children of Eve, my great spouse' CW 1979-80.

15. CONCLUSIONS

The uses in traditional Cornish of the various auxiliary verbs in the language outlined above have implications for the revived language. In particular we might cite the following eight points:

1. Although the long forms of *bos* + ow + verbal nouns can literally be translated as continuous presents, frequently in the traditional language their sense is a simple unmarked present. Thus *yth esof ow screfa* means 'I write' rather than 'I am writing'. In this syntactic feature Cornish resembles both Welsh and Scottish Gaelic.
2. If one wants to say 'He lives in Wales', for example, one says: *Yma va tregys in Kembra* or *ev yw tregys in Kembra*. *Ev a drig in Kembra* can only mean 'He will remain in Wales'.
3. The verbal adjective of an instransitive verb after the present of the verb *bos* is perfect in sense, e.g. *yth ov devedhys* 'I have come' and *me yw gyllys* 'I have gone', Indeed such forms should perhaps be taught to learners in preference to *dufef*, etc., *galsof*, etc. or even *me re dheuth, me res êth*.

183

4. The phrase *na ve* provides a simple and authentic way in the revived language for expressing unreal conditions, e.g. *na ve ev, ny a via ledhys* 'had it not been for him, we would have been killed', and *na ve why dhe ry an mona dhybm, ny alsen mos* 'if you hadn't given me the money, I should not have been able to go.'

5. It is clear that *dos* 'to come' is frequently used as an auxiliary in conditional sentences and in final clauses. This means that revivalists can use such authentic expressions as *mar teu va ha dysqwedhes* 'if he shows', *mar teffa ev ha dysqwedhes* 'if he were to show, if he had shown', and *may teffo ev ha dysqwedhes* 'so that he may show'. *Dos* is also used in temporal clause of the sort *pàn dheuth ev ha dysqwedhes* 'when he showed'.

6. The verb *gallos* in the present or past subjunctive after *may* is the default construction in traditional Cornish in final clauses, e.g. *pibowgh whare may hallen dauncya* 'pipe straightway that we may dance'.

7. In traditional Cornish *mynnes* as an auxiliary is losing much of its volitional sense. Thus *me a vyn mos alemma* means 'I will go hence' rather than 'I wish to go hence'. Similarly *ef a vyn y wul* means 'he will do it', not 'he wants to do it'. Revivalists should perhaps imitate this usage, and employ *mynnes* simply as an auxiliary to express future sense.

8. In traditional Cornish the loss of volition from *mynnes* as an auxiliary, has led to the use of the conditional of *cara* 'to love' to express wishing to do something. *Me a garsa dos genes* rather than *me a vydn dos genes* is the unambiguous way of saying 'I want to come with you'. Revivalists should perhaps be encouragaged to imitate this syntax.

A final general point should perhaps be made. Since Nance's time it has been customary in handbooks of Cornish for revivalists to list all the forms of many verbs. Often in such paradigms, however, the inflected forms are conjectural, not being attested in the traditional texts. In traditional Cornish the majority of verbs are attested only a handful of forms at most, in particular, the third singular of the present-future and of the preterite, in the verbal noun and the verbal adjective. This is because most attested verbs in Cornish are attested only in conjunction with one or other of the auxiliary verbs. As a result, revivalist handbooks that cite a host of conjectural verbal forms, give a wholly misleading impression of the verbal system of the traditional language.